AUGUSTUS HOPKINS STRONG AND
THE STRUGGLE TO RECONCILE CHRISTIAN
THEOLOGY WITH MODERN THOUGHT

Augustus Hopkins Strong and the Struggle to Reconcile Christian Theology with Modern Thought

John Aloisi

UNIVERSITY OF ROCHESTER PRESS

First published 2021

University of Rochester Press
668 Mt. Hope Avenue, Rochester, NY 14620, USA
www.urpress.com
and Boydell & Brewer Limited
PO Box 9, Woodbridge, Suffolk IP12 3DF, UK
www.boydellandbrewer.com

ISBN-13: 978-1-64825-022-4 (paperback)
ISBN-13: 978-1-80010-267-5 (ePUB)
ISBN-13: 978-1-80010-266-8 (ePDF)

Library of Congress Cataloging-in-Publication Data
Names: Aloisi, John, author.
Title: Augustus Hopkins Strong and the struggle to reconcile Christian theology
    with modern thought / John Aloisi.
Description: Rochester, NY, USA . University of Rochester Press, 2021. |
    Includes bibliographical references and index.
Identifiers: LCCN 2020056159 | ISBN 9781648250224 (paperback)
Subjects: LCSH: Strong, Augustus Hopkins, 1836–1921. | Baptists—Doctrines—
    History. | Philosophy and religion. | Theology. | Monism.
Classification: LCC BX6495.S7985 A75 2021 | DDC 230/.6092—dc23
LC record available at https://lccn.loc.gov/2020056159

S | H   **The Sustainable History Monograph Pilot**
M | P   Opening up the Past, Publishing for the Future

We are eager to learn more about how you discovered this
title and how you are using it. We hope you will spend a few
minutes answering a couple of questions at this url:
https://www.longleafservices.org/shmp-survey/

More information about the Sustainable History Monograph
Pilot can be found at https://www.longleafservices.org.

CONTENTS

ACKNOWLEDGMENTS

Unlike financial debts, one's academic and familial debts can never be fully repaid. Nevertheless, I wish to express my thankfulness to a number of people who have supported and encouraged me in various ways while I completed this book.

When I began my doctoral studies in 2006, my wife, Marcia, and I moved to Louisville, Kentucky, with two children in tow. As I came to the end of the doctoral program, our family had grown to include six children. Somewhat coincidentally, like Augustus and Harriet Strong, at that point we had been blessed with four girls and two boys. As this book has come to completion, we now have eight. Thankfully, I have a very patient and supportive wife! Thank you, Marcia, for consistently encouraging me to keep moving forward, and thank you for reading countless papers and even this longer work with genuine interest and helpful insight.

Many others have also provided support along the way. David Doran and the board of Detroit Baptist Theological Seminary have generously ensured that I had the necessary time and resources to complete this project. My colleagues at DBTS have encouraged me at many points over the past several years. Mark Snoeberger, especially, took time out of his busy schedule to read an earlier version of the manuscript and provided many helpful comments. Matt Gass, Andrea Miller Studdard, and Ryan Meyer of DBTS, along with the interlibrary loan staff of James P. Boyce Library at Southern Baptist Theological Seminary, have tracked down scores of articles and books for me and have done so with cheerfulness and efficiency.

Tom Nettles was one of the early readers of the manuscript, and over the years he has been a joy to work with. His graciousness has been an example to me, and I consider his scholarship a model to follow. I could not have asked for a better mentor.

John Aloisi
Allen Park, Michigan

Introduction

N INETEENTH-CENTURY LIBERALISM was characterized by a distinctive emphasis on the doctrine of divine immanence, as observed by numerous writers at the end of the century and the beginning of the next. For example, reflecting on the theology of the nineteenth century, Arthur Cushman McGiffert identified divine immanence as the characteristic doctrine of the age.[1] Standing just inside the doorstep of the twentieth century, Francis J. McConnell noted that the concept of divine immanence was the most absorbing theme in contemporary theology.[2] Writing just a few years later in 1914, Hugh Ross Mackintosh remarked, "No conception has seized the modern mind more powerfully than that of divine immanence."[3] Clearly, the doctrine of divine immanence was a topic that captivated the minds of many theologians at the turn of the century.

At the close of the nineteenth and beginning of the twentieth century, American theological liberals were busy carving out a "third way" between rationalistic atheism and orthodox Christianity by positing a new theology based largely on the twin ideas that divine authority is not tied to an inerrant book and that God should not be viewed as completely distinct from the material world. When put in positive terms, this latter concept was often expressed by the phrase *divine immanence*. Numerous books were written around the turn of the century arguing that the pressing theological need was to move toward a new understanding of God as immanent in the world and working in and through the physical universe in a way quite different from that taught by orthodox theology.[4] Many conservatives firmly denounced liberal assertions about God's immanence as heterodox and destructive to true religion.[5] However, at least one conservative theologian, Augustus Hopkins Strong (1836–1921), attempted to wed orthodox theology to a new understanding of divine immanence. The result was something that Strong called *ethical monism*.

The Riddle of Augustus Hopkins Strong

Strong was in many ways a puzzling figure.[6] As president and professor of biblical theology at Rochester Theological Seminary for four decades (1872–1912),

Strong shaped a generation of seminary students.[7] As a leader among Northern
Baptists, he played a significant role in the denomination during the years leading up to the fundamentalist-modernist controversy. As the author of numerous
books, including a major systematic theology, Strong influenced the thinking of
countless theologians and pastors.[8] He was by any measure an important figure
in American theology at the beginning of the twentieth century, yet Strong has
persistently baffled historians.[9]

Grant Wacker noted that Strong's interpreters have generally placed him
in one of four categories: (a) an early fundamentalist who was both irenic and
open-minded, (b) a conservative theologian struggling to preserve Reformed
orthodoxy in a modern world, (c) a mediator between liberalism and orthodox
theology,[10] or (d) "a closet liberal hiding behind the garments of apparent orthodoxy."[11] Wacker himself never indicated which of these categories he thought
best described Strong. Instead, he argued that "Strong is best understood as
a tragic figure, forced to choose between incompatible yet, in his judgment,
equally cogent conceptual worlds."[12]

Part of the difficulty in interpreting Strong lies in some of his own enigmatic
statements and actions. Near the end of his life Strong wrote, "I am an evolutionist, but evolutionist of a peculiar sort. . . . I am a higher critic, but of a
certain sort. . . . I am both a premillennialist and a postmillennialist, strange as
this may seem to some."[13] If these self-appellations appeared somewhat less than
consistent, so did a number of his decisions during his presidency at Rochester Theological Seminary. For example, in the 1880s Strong, along with several
other faculty members at Rochester, expressed serious concern about the orthodoxy of their promising young student Walter Rauschenbusch (1861–1918).
Strong once told Rauschenbusch that his essay on Horace Bushnell's theory of
the atonement, although of very high quality, was "subversive of scripture."[14] In
fact, the theological errors Strong detected in this essay prompted him to offer
several "corrective lectures" to the entire class.[15] This was not the only time Rauschenbusch expressed his affinity for unorthodox views during his student days.
Shortly before graduation, Rauschenbusch preached a chapel sermon in which
he described personal conversion in terms of liberal presuppositions.[16] Although
Strong had significant reservations about his student's doctrinal fidelity, about
a decade later Strong hired Rauschenbusch to teach at Rochester, even though
the younger man had only continued the departure from orthodoxy since graduation.[17] If Rauschenbusch were the only modernist Strong added to the Rochester faculty, one might regard it as an isolated lapse of judgment, but he was
not: during his forty-year tenure Strong also hired other liberal scholars, such

as William Arnold Stevens (1877), Walter R. Betteridge (1891), J. W. A. Stewart (1903), Cornelius Woelfkin (1905), and Conrad Henry Moehlman (1907).[18]

Another factor contributing to the dilemma of interpreting Strong stems from the fact that his own theology evolved considerably during his career at Rochester.[19] The most significant change in his theology occurred in the early to mid-1890s, when he developed ethical monism.[20]

Strong's explanation of ethical monism did not change substantially over the years. In the final edition of his *Systematic Theology*, Strong defined ethical monism as a "method of thought which holds to a single substance, ground, or principle of being, namely, God, but which also holds to the ethical facts of God's transcendence as well as his immanence, and of God's personality as distinct from, and as guaranteeing, the personality of man."[21] In other words, he held to an ontological monism coupled with a personal pluralism. Strong believed that all that exists is ultimately one, but he recognized the existence of multiple personalities within this one thing. Strong viewed his doctrine of ethical monism as striking the proper and difficult balance between the truth of God's transcendence and the reality of his immanence in the world. He saw ethical monism as giving unity to all existence while preserving personal responsibility. He eventually came to regard this ethical monism as the "key to theology."[22]

Questions to Be Answered

The primary purpose of this book is to examine the role ethical monism played in Strong's theology and ministry. I also explore several related questions: What factors in Strong's own life and cultural milieu may have prompted him to embrace ethical monism? What relationship did Strong's ethical monism have to the philosophical idealism of his forbears? What tendencies in Strong's earlier theology may have led him to develop ethical monism as a distinct theological concept? What impact did ethical monism have on Strong's larger theological system? Answering these questions provides greater insight into both Strong's thought and his significance.

In this book, I argue that ethical monism was Strong's attempt to reconcile Christian theology and modern thought while solving tensions within his own theology. Strong hoped to bring together modernists and conservatives around the theological common ground of ethical monism. In the end, he was unable to persuade modernists to embrace ethical monism or to convince conservatives that ethical monism was a legitimate theological option. Strong's attempt at a theological synthesis failed largely because of the contradictions ethical monism produced within both Christian theology and philosophical monism. Yet his attempt sheds light on the philosophical and theological commitments of both conservatives and liberals around the beginning of the twentieth century.

Importance of the Study

Because Strong viewed ethical monism as the "key to theology," properly understanding this concept and its relationship to his theological system is foundational to correctly understanding his overall theology and his unique contributions to theology. As an influential figure within the Northern Baptist Convention, Strong hoped to bring together both liberals and conservatives around the idea of ethical monism. Although Strong failed in this ecumenical effort, his attempt to do so is highly instructive, and an examination of ethical monism may help explain his ecumenical ambitions.

Strong's forty-year presidency at the Rochester Theological Seminary showcased his desire to bring together conservatives and liberals. Under his leadership, theological liberals took the school much further left than Strong's personal theology would have suggested, establishing theological liberalism at the seminary. This change had a significant impact on the theological direction of many of the seminary's graduates and the churches they pastored.

No full-length biography of Strong has ever been written. Various reference works and survey texts give short sketches of his life, but most overlook the role ethical monism played in his life and thought, which affected how Strong viewed the entire world. For Strong, ethical monism was a major part of his contribution to the theological world. Chapter 1 helps explain how Strong's biography and theology were more closely related than often acknowledged.

CHAPTER I

The Making and Ministry of a Theologian

IN JANUARY 1913, students and alumni of Rochester Theological Seminary gathered for the unveiling of a bronze bust of Augustus Hopkins Strong that alumni presented in honor of Strong's forty years of service to the institution.[1] After the presentation, Strong addressed those who had gathered for the event. In his talk, titled "Theology and Experience,"[2] Strong engaged in a fair bit of autobiographical musing, for a purpose: he believed that one cannot understand his theological journey and development without knowing something of his life. As Strong confessed to his audience, "My views of evangelical doctrine have been necessarily determined by the circumstances of my individual history. . . . My religious history is so interwoven with my secular history, that it will be impossible to relate the one without also relating the other."[3] Taking Strong at his word, this chapter relates something of Strong's personal history to help explain some historical factors that may have affected his theological development.

Sources of information about Strong's life and ministry are plentiful, if somewhat hard to come by. When Strong sat down on his sixtieth birthday to write his life story, he followed in his father's footsteps: both men wrote autobiographies ostensibly for their children and grandchildren.[4] Much of the biographical material that follows is drawn from these two autobiographies and informed by numerous works related to the history of Rochester.[5]

Strong's Heritage

Emerson once asked, "How shall a man escape from his ancestors?" and Strong playfully replied, "Men of genius should select their ancestors with care."[6] Augustus Strong enjoyed a rich heritage, with roots that intertwined with Rochester's early days. Like many people bearing the name Strong in nineteenth-century America, Augustus could trace this family line back to Elder John Strong (c. 1605–99), who along with numerous Puritans sailed from England to the New

World in the 1630s.[7] During the seventeenth and eighteenth centuries, the descendants of John Strong were remarkably prolific. As Augustus put it,

> [John Strong] had no fewer than eighteen children, and it is scarcely a hyperbole to say that all of these eighteen had eighteen apiece. As a matter of sober fact, I find that the next in line of descent from Elder John Strong to me had fifteen children; the third in line had eight; but, as his excuse for having so few, it is said that he was killed by the Indians at the early age of forty-two, or he would doubtless have had many more. The fourth in the line had twelve children and the fifth, fifteen.[8]

The prolific Strongs soon spread throughout the northeast region of what would become the United States.

Augustus Strong's grandfather, Ezra Strong (1777–1846), was a physician who was born and raised in Warren, Connecticut.[9] Of the fifteen children who grew up on the family farm in Warren, only Ezra pursued a professional career. After completing a course of medical studies, Ezra settled in Scipio, New York, where he became the town's first physician. After a few years of medical practice, Ezra ventured into the mercantile trade and opened the town's first store in 1808. His business endeavors were prosperous during the War of 1812. He invested heavily in cattle and other supplies needed by the American army and managed to turn a significant profit for several years. However, during the deflationary period that followed, his business investments lost much of their value, and Ezra lost both his store and his house and was for a time subject to debtor's imprisonment in the village of Auburn, the county seat at the time.[10]

In 1821 Ezra moved to Rochester, New York, just a few years before the opening of the Erie Canal brought a flood of new residents to the town and the greater Genesee Valley area.[11] In this new environment, he revived his medical practice and lived out his remaining years, as his son put it, "without material incident."[12] Ezra Strong died in his rented home on Exchange Street in Rochester in September 1846. Some fifty years later, Augustus noted that he had but "slight recollection" of his paternal grandfather, but he deemed that his grandfather's ordeal with debtor's prison cast a pall on all his children and caused them to be "less sanguine and more cautious in business." This tendency extended to Augustus as well, for as he noted, "I am sure that my own eagerness to discharge all my pecuniary obligations and my success in preventing even my extravagance from going beyond the limit of my means in hand has been partly due to the story of my grandfather's misfortunes."[13] Despite his earlier financial troubles, Ezra developed a solid reputation as a hardworking physician in the early days of Rochester's history. As an early and respected citizen of the budding town of Rochester, Ezra left his descendants with a good name to uphold, but his earlier troubles with debt caused many of them to approach life and especially financial matters with a sober mindset and a conservative bent.

Augustus's father, Alvah Strong, was born in Scipio, New York, in 1809. He attended a small country school but had little other formal education, yet he had a strong desire to acquire knowledge in less formal settings. Many years later Augustus recalled, "Father was open-minded, courteous, inquiring, conciliatory, and he drank in information continually. . . . He liked to have interesting people at his house that he might hear them talk. If he had had his own way and my mother had permitted, he would have had a constant succession of guests." After working as a runner boy for various newspapers, Alvah secured a job as a journeyman printer in the summer of 1830. Augustus wrote, "He loved knowledge, and the printing office, in which he went through all the grades from roller boy to proprietor, served for his university."[14] In the early years, Alvah worked for Erastus Shepard, a printer in Palmyra, not far from Rochester. Alvah credited Shepard and his wife as important influences on his developing religious ideas.[15]

During the fall and winter of 1830 and 1831, the famed evangelist Charles G. Finney held revival meetings in Rochester. Alvah's friend and future brother-in-law, Augustus Hopkins, was converted under the preaching of Finney, and he soon wrote to Alvah encouraging him to come to Rochester to hear Finney and to get "the dirty water of your mind stirred up from the very depths."[16] Alvah initially resisted this pleading, but his own sense of conviction and the tugging of his conscience finally led him to return to Rochester, where he was converted in late 1830.

Augustus, no doubt having heard the story of his father's conversion many times, recounted what took place when his father sought out Finney in his room at the Eagle Hotel. Upon opening the hotel room door, the evangelist motioned for Alvah to sit by the stove while he finished a letter. A few minutes later, Finney approached the young man and asked why he had come. Alvah explained that he had been thinking about the subject of religion and thought he should become a Christian but that he had no feeling. Finney grabbed an iron poker that lay near the stove and waved it menacingly in Alvah's face. The young man stood up and moved to avoid the makeshift weapon. Finney retorted, "Ah, you feel *now*, don't you?" and then, laying aside the iron poker, he immediately returned to his correspondence. Alvah went away initially disappointed and somewhat offended, but on further reflection, he realized Finney had employed an object lesson: if he was afraid of an iron poker, he ought to fear hell much more. Alvah's mind was soon settled regarding his conversion.[17]

In September 1831, Alvah Strong was baptized and received into membership at the First Baptist Church of Rochester, where he would remain in fellowship for the next fifty-five years, serving for much of that time as a deacon.[18] In the early 1830s, Erastus Shepard moved to Rochester and invited Alvah to become his partner in publishing the *Anti-Masonic Inquirer*, a paper Shepard had recently acquired.[19] Alvah accepted the job. He would remain both a Baptist and a newspaperman for the rest of his life.

In December 1834, Alvah married Catherine Hopkins. Catherine was quiet and retiring. Unlike her husband, she had no desire to see an endless stream of guests through their home. In fact, Augustus once described her as "almost morbidly seclusive," a trait she shared with her brother, for whom Augustus was named.[20] A hard-working woman, she placed a high value on education. Orphaned as a youth, Catherine came to Rochester to work in the millinery business. From her meager earnings, she purchased a few choice books, and she passed her love of books and reading on to her children, not least to Augustus.

Strong's Early Life

The oldest son of Alvah and Catherine Strong, Augustus Hopkins Strong, was born in Rochester on August 3, 1836, in a little frame house on Troup Street.[21] Upon marrying, Alvah and Catherine had prayed that God would enable them to raise children who would be both useful in the world and "living instruments to His praise."[22] They also followed up this prayer with intentional action: the Strongs were faithful in attending the First Baptist Church in Rochester, and they worked hard to inculcate this habit in their children from an early age. Augustus recounted a day when he was only three or four years old when the front gate of their yard on Troup Street was left open and he wandered into town on his own. When his distraught parents finally found him half a mile from home and asked him where he was going, he replied that he was going to hear Mr. Church preach.[23]

Augustus also told of a time when he was about ten and woke to find the ground outside covered with a deep blanket of snow. It was a Sunday morning, and he assumed this meant the family would be staying home from church. He ran downstairs happily announcing, "Father, we can't go to church today!" His father asked, "Why so, my son?" The youth replied, "There won't be anybody there!" His father queried, "Won't be anybody there? Well, if there isn't anybody else there, it will be very important that *we* should be there!" So father and son plodded through the drifts to church that morning. As young Augustus had predicted, only about half a dozen people had made the snowy trek, but as he later noted, "*We* were there, and I had learned a lesson never to be forgotten."[24] Many years later, Augustus wrote, "Never since that time have I been able to be quite comfortable away from church on a Sunday morning."[25]

Although both parents were committed to teaching their children such lessons about the importance of church, Alvah Strong was a busy man who had relatively little time to spend with his children. By Augustus's account, with the exception of mealtimes and Sundays, his father worked at the printing office from sunrise until late at night.[26] Occasionally, Augustus would spend time at the offices of the *Rochester Daily Democrat*,[27] which could prove a schoolroom of sorts. One day when his father had left the key in a counting room drawer, Augustus stole five dollars and proceeded to hire a two-horse coach to give himself and a few schoolmates a ride home. Upon arriving home, Augustus was soon filled with fear. He hid the remaining money and waited to see what would happen. News soon reached his father that young Augustus had been seen sailing through town in a coach, and his father put two and two together. As Augustus summarized, "There was an investigation, a trial, a confession, a bringing forth of the stolen money from its hiding-place, and a most memorable application of the rod by way of punishment." More important, as the young Strong recalled, "My own remorse and shame before discovery, my positive gladness when at last my sin had found me out, my father's combined affection and severity, the justice and solemnity with which he pleaded with me and then chastised me gave me a permanent and valuable understanding of the folly and misery of sin, and of the mercy as well as the righteousness of God."[28] Through such events and the ill-advised witnessing of a hanging, Augustus was beginning to realize the awfulness of sin and guilt and the unchanging holiness of God, two themes that would later figure prominently in his theology.

After studying at several different schools that Augustus later described as "inferior," he transferred to the Collegiate Institute in Rochester. Here, at the age of fourteen, he studied Latin and Greek under the tutelage of principal N. W. Benedict. Augustus later praised Benedict as a "genuine pedagogue . . . a lover of classics, a man of learning, and entirely devoted to his calling."[29] Benedict had a significant influence on Augustus during his high school days.

It was not Benedict, however, who prompted Augustus to read beyond his peers in the Latin classics, thus setting him on a trajectory for academic excellence, but Chester Heywood, an older student and part-time janitor who encouraged Augustus to push himself and to study while others were taking time off.[30] Heywood challenged Augustus to spend the spring break studying Latin so he could move to a more advanced class. Augustus, taking Heywood's advice, for three weeks rose every morning at five o'clock and, with few intervals, studied Latin until late at night. When the new term began, Benedict found that Augustus had improved his Latin significantly and promoted him to an older class, where the boys were translating Cicero. These events had a lasting impact on Augustus's academic efforts: "I learned that, where there was a will, there was also a way. I became ambitious, and perhaps a trifle conceited. . . . Those three weeks of vacation work changed the whole current of my life and encouraged me to act independently of my teachers."[31]

Augustus's high school experience both aroused and confirmed the academic inclinations his parents had recognized early on. His father once noted, "Augustus' early taste ran for books, intellectual work and highest education."[32] Augustus's parents encouraged him to read widely and to acquire a solid education through a variety of means. His father, especially, thought travel was important for a good education, so Augustus visited places such as Albany, Buffalo, Niagara Falls, New York City, and various locales in Canada. Often his father accompanied him, but by the time he was twelve he was occasionally making such trips alone or with a friend. Augustus recalled that as a young teenager he went to see the wonders of the Astor House in New York City accompanied by a young companion. The experience was no doubt an education, and looking back he wrote, "I know of no harm that came from the trip."[33] It was all part of getting a broad and thorough education in the Strong household.

By age fifteen, Strong had completed his formal preparation for college, but his father thought he was still too young to begin college, so in 1852–53 Strong spent a year and a half in his father's newspaper office learning the business.[34] Strong became familiar with the telegraph, bookkeeping, writing, typesetting, and proofreading. The work also included a number of perquisites, including ready access to an abundance of good literature. Various booksellers would send their latest volumes to the paper hoping for a favorable review. Strong's father allowed him to take home any review copies he liked, and he devoured not only many dime novels but also a number of substantial works, including essays by Francis Bacon and Thomas Macaulay and poems by John Milton and Longfellow.[35] Strong later noted that this period greatly increased his stock of general information, which served him well in college essay writing and debate. Strong also believed that his administrative experiences in the newspaper counting room prepared him to interact skillfully with trustees at the seminary.[36] Interestingly, during this time Strong's father was treasurer of the newly founded Rochester Theological Seminary, so all the seminary funds passed through the paper's office and were recorded by Augustus in ledger books.[37] No one knew that the young man keeping track of the seminary finances would become the seminary president two decades later.

Strong's College Days

Having completed his eighteen-month stint in the newspaper office, Strong headed off to New Haven, Connecticut, where he soon passed his entrance exams and matriculated at Yale College in 1853. Although his father had helped found the University of Rochester just a few years earlier,[38] Strong chose to attend Yale rather than the nearby school, for at least two reasons. First, Theodore Whittlesey, one of his friends at the preparatory school in Rochester, praised the glories of Yale so frequently that Strong decided he could attend nowhere else. Second, in keeping with Alvah's understanding of the role of travel and new acquaintances in a well-rounded education, both Strong and his father thought the experience in a larger school and a new environment would be good for him.[39]

Strong went to Yale convinced that he would outpace his peers in every area of study, but he quickly discovered this was not the case. As he put it, "I was full of pride and full of ambition, but my pride and my ambition collapsed like a bubble at the first recitation in Homer's Iliad."[40] During this eye-opening session under Professor James Hadley, another student was called upon to demonstrate his mastery of the assigned text. Over the next several minutes the professor asked the young man scores of questions about the first four lines of Homer's *Iliad*. The student, an Andover man, was well prepared for the interrogation. Strong, on the other hand, found that he did not even understand the meaning of many of the questions. In that brief session, Strong realized that his preparation, while generally solid, was far from superior to that of his fellow students, so unwisely, he later confessed, he chose to pursue extracurricular activities with a fervor while letting his regular studies slide.[41] Throughout his college years, Strong devoted much of his time and energy to writing and speaking. He engaged in various competitions and debates, winning many of them and developing something of a reputation as a public speaker along the way.[42] However, Strong would later counsel his own sons to master the regular curriculum before devoting themselves to literature and debate.[43]

In the 1850s, Yale employed a recitation method of learning in the classroom. Professors generally did not lecture, and students did not ask questions. Instead, students were expected to read their lessons from a textbook and be able to recite them to their instructors in class. As Strong explained it,

> No discussion was permitted at any time. I do not recall that a single question was asked by any student of an instructor during the whole four years of my college course. It was a dead-alive system, which of itself did much to make scholarly work a drudgery and almost nothing to make it attractive. . . . A narrow accuracy was cultivated—breadth was ignored.[44]

The recitation method did little to kindle Strong's academic interests, so for better or for worse, much of Strong's undergraduate educational development took place outside the classrooms of Yale.

Strong developed a number of keen and lasting friendships with faculty members and students alike. As he later wrote, "The good which I got from my college course consisted very largely in the acquaintance which I formed with men, both among the faculty and among the students."[45] Chief among Strong's valued acquaintances was Theodore Dwight Woolsey. A descendant of the famous theologian Jonathan Edwards (1703–58), Woolsey served as president of Yale from 1846 until 1871 and taught Greek at the college for many years. According to Strong, Woolsey influenced him not so much with his teaching as with his character. Disciplined, courageous, and at times wholly inflexible, Woolsey impressed students with his simple Christian manhood. Although by nature very quick-tempered, Woolsey worked hard to control this aspect of his personality, often remaining silent for a moment while he regained his composure.[46] He maintained the highest standards of character, and he expected such in his students. Mainly for this reason Strong concluded, "No man whom I have ever met has so ruled me by his mere character. . . . It was worth going to Yale College to sit for four years under the influence of President Woolsey."[47]

Noah Porter, Woolsey's eventual successor as president of Yale in 1871, was in Strong's day professor of intellectual and moral philosophy. Strong confessed that as a teacher Porter was abysmal. His lack of discipline and easygoing nature made him the exact opposite of Woolsey in many respects. As a general practice, Porter added little if anything to the information in the textbook. He also, unwittingly, often managed to convince his students that the subject at hand was dull and uninteresting. Strong was generally disappointed in Porter as a pedagogue. However, he recalled that on one occasion Porter departed from his usual course and gave a brief lecture on the subject of ethics. This lecture so intrigued

Strong that, for the first time in his college career, he approached the professor after class to discuss the subject. To his surprise, he discovered that the views expressed by Porter were original to him. As a result, Strong began to develop a new measure of respect for his teacher.[48]

Many years later Strong visited Porter after the older man had retired from Yale. During this visit, Strong asked Porter if he had apostatized from the Christian faith, that is, if he had become an idealist. Despite his advanced age, Porter replied with vigor, "Never! If idealism be true, what is the world but a dream?" Although Strong's own ethical monism seemed to some observers to flirt with idealism, he apparently agreed with the implication of Porter's question. In later life, Strong regarded Porter as one of the three individuals who did the most for his intellectual development. In particular, Porter's book *The Human Intellect* (1868) had a more significant influence on Strong than the teacher ever did in the classroom.[49]

Fresh from Andover in Strong's day, George Fisher served as pastor of the Yale college church from 1854 until 1861 and as professor at Yale from 1854 until his retirement in 1901. In Strong's opinion, Fisher was not the most entertaining speaker, and he told of students sleeping by the score while Fisher read his sermons with tears running down his cheeks. Nonetheless, Strong regarded Fisher as a capable preacher and writer and considered his primary strengths his ability to arrange difficult material and craft a lucid argument. Strong considered Fisher the primary instructor who helped him learn to write clearly. Strong also benefited from the personal interest Fisher showed him. He regarded Fisher a lifelong friend and readily acknowledged that Fisher had put him on "a higher order of philosophical and theological reading than [he] had known before."[50] Interestingly, Strong also credited Fisher's lectures on pantheism with giving him an early taste for theology. Years later, after Strong announced his ethical monism in the 1890s, he was accused by many of having embraced pantheism, an accusation he consistently denied.

Despite this interaction with numerous professors of religion, Strong's own religious awakening, as he called it, did not occur until after his junior year in college. Throughout much of his childhood, on Saturday afternoons Strong's mother took him to a dimly lit closet, where she would pray and would attempt to teach him to pray by having him repeat phrases. In later life, he recalled that on the day when he first prayed some stammering words of his own he felt drops upon his cheek and was surprised to discover they were his own mother's tears. Strong's mother also taught him the words to many hymns and in other ways impressed on him the importance of spiritual things. Because his father was a deacon in the local Baptist church and made sure that the family was faithful in church attendance, when Strong headed off to college he thought he might become a minister someday. But by his own testimony, he was still "at heart very far from the kingdom of God."[51] Despite his religious upbringing, Strong considered himself unconverted.

Throughout his first three years at college, Strong gave very little thought to his spiritual condition. Around the time he entered Yale, he received letters from two of his female cousins urging him to become a Christian.[52] Although he was grateful for his cousins' concern, he for the most part ignored their appeals. Having decided that the pursuit of scholarship was not his path and giving little thought to spiritual things, Strong spent his early college years pursuing pleasure and frivolity. He fell into "irregular habits and associations" and in his opinion teetered on the brink of evil.[53] As he later wrote, "My selfish, ambitious, reckless life for three years in college was permitted by God in order to convince me that I was a great sinner and helpless in my sins unless God should have mercy upon me."[54] No one at the college spoke to him about his relationship to God during those early years,[55] but everywhere Strong looked he saw among the faculty and student body men whom he deemed to be his moral superiors. By his junior year, his sense of guilt was palpable and increasing.

One evening near the end of his junior year, Strong was standing outside the old college chapel listening to the bells as they called students to evening prayers. Suddenly Strong felt a hand on his shoulder and he turned to see Wilder Smith, one of his classmates, looking somewhat agitated. With trembling voice, Smith said to him, "Strong, I wish you were a Christian!"[56] Strong was taken back at this statement, but he thanked Smith for his concern, agreed that he did need to become a Christian, and promised to think about it. The brief exchange was an unremarkable event for Smith, but it had a lasting impact on Strong.[57] As Strong recalled, "It was the only word he ever spoke to me, and yet it haunted me until I closed with God's offer of pardon and began an earnest Christian life."[58]

Not long after this encounter with Smith, Strong headed home to Rochester for spring break. It was early April 1856, and evangelist Charles Finney was in town for another series of revival meetings, his third in as many decades.[59] Arriving home in the late afternoon, Strong discovered that his entire family planned to attend one of Finney's meetings that evening. Jenny Farr, one of the cousins who had earlier written to Strong about his spiritual condition, was temporarily staying with the family. Although he had not intended to spend his first evening home at church, at the request of his cousin Strong agreed to attend.

The meeting that night was being held at a Presbyterian church on nearby South Washington Street.[60] After walking to church with his cousin, Strong found that the building was packed and the extra chairs in the aisles were largely filled. Having somehow become separated from the rest of his family, Strong and his cousin managed to find a seat at the end of a pew near the middle of the auditorium. Strong had previously heard Finney preach in Oberlin, Ohio, and he could still remember the evangelist asking him why he was not a Christian. This evening, as the service came to a close, Finney pressed his case once again. Strong later said that he could not recall the topic or much else about the service that night, but as Finney gave the invitation, he felt as if he was struck by a bolt of lightning. With many others, Strong went forward and was led to the church basement where counselors were waiting to talk to those concerned about their souls. When Frank Ellinwood, the pastor of the church, asked Strong if he was a Christian, he replied that he was very far from it. The pastor then asked if he had some feeling on the subject of religion, and Strong said he had none at all. Ellinwood pointed out that by coming forward Strong had indicated that he knew he ought to submit to God. Strong agreed that he ought to do so, but he still remained noncommittal. Ellinwood said that he would go speak to a few other people and then return to see what Strong had decided. As Strong recalled,

> The moments that followed were moments of struggle. I reviewed the past. I saw that I was a miserable sinner, that I had been living a wicked life, that I was in danger of being given over to my wickedness, that if I was ever saved there must be a change, that the chance to change was now given me, [and] that the chance might never come again. . . . Gradually the determination was formed within me that I would put myself into God's hands to do with me what he would.[61]

When the pastor returned, Strong told him that he was ready to submit to God. That night Strong went home and before retiring resolved to begin reading his Bible and praying on a regular basis. As far as he was concerned, the most important day of his life was over—he was converted (though he later acknowledged it was a purely New School conversion).[62]

The next morning Strong told his parents and his cousin Jenny about his decision. Although he began reading his Bible and attending morning prayer meetings, Strong still lacked confidence that he was right with God. He struggled with doubts about his salvation and with continual temptations to sin. He asked Christians to pray for him, but he still felt no closer to God. In his autobiography, Strong described twelve theological lessons that he learned throughout his life. During these three weeks, he learned the first of these, "the depth and enormity of sin."[63] He learned that, despite his attempts to live as a Christian, he was in fact very much a sinner.

When vacation was over, as Strong sat in the train to New Haven, he thought to himself, "This train is taking me to hell!"[64] He knew he would face renewed temptations at Yale, and he feared that his good intentions to live as a Christian might disappear like the morning dew. On the train Strong ran through various scenarios in his mind and determined he would live as a Christian regardless of the consequences or the difficulties it might entail.

Back at Yale, Strong continued to struggle. Although he told other Christian students that he was a Christian, he still often felt that this was not the case, so he determined to search the Scriptures for a reason to believe he was truly converted. One day, while reading 2 Corinthians 6, he came upon a text that said, "I will dwell with them, and walk in them; and I will be their God, and they shall be my people. . . . Saith the Lord, and touch not the unclean thing; and I will receive you, and will be a Father to you, and ye shall be my sons and daughters, saith the Lord Almighty." Strong took this as an indication from God that he was truly and vitally connected to God. Afterward Strong said that his perspective on nature was changed by this realization. He began to look at the world around him as a revelation of God and of his love: "The world outside seemed somehow elevated to the planetary spaces above and to be part of a mighty universe in which dwelt and reigned a present God. . . . I was joined to God forever, and as I looked up to the stars that shone through the trees, I said to myself, 'When those shall grow old and die, I shall dwell with God and shall partake of the life of God!'"[65] Strong's later reflection on this time in his life suggests that even at this early stage he was beginning to develop what would later mature into his ideas of union with Christ and divine immanence in the universe.[66]

At the end of the term, Strong returned to Rochester. He was baptized on August 3, 1856, his twentieth birthday, by J. R. Scott in the First Baptist Church of Rochester. At the time he was not yet fully convinced that Baptist doctrine was correct, but he figured that if he were immersed by Baptists, he would never have reason to doubt the validity of his baptism. Strong was disappointed that his baptism did not bring him any conscious benefit. Apparently he was hoping for some type of subjective feeling to accompany the physical act of baptism.[67]

During his final year at Yale, Strong discovered that he was still very much a sinner. He lost what he called "the joy of [God's] salvation" and fell away from some of his earlier commitments.[68] Strong later concluded that God allowed him to face this trial of his faith to teach him a second theological lesson, that only God can regenerate:

> My willful transgression, after such experience of his forgiving mercy, wrought in me a profound conviction that I was not sufficient to myself. Only God could keep me true to him. My complete dependence upon him for *preserving* grace threw light upon my earlier experience and taught me that I then must have been the subject of *regenerating* grace. If without the help of God I could not *keep* myself in the Christian way, how without the help of God could I ever have *gotten into* that way?[69]

The bonds of Arminian theology were beginning to slacken, and he was starting to move in the direction of moderate Calvinism. From the time of his conversion, Strong felt he was called to preach the gospel. He soon determined to continue his preparation for ministry back in Rochester.

Strong's Seminary Days

From their earliest days the University of Rochester and the Rochester Theological Seminary had a symbiotic relationship. They were, as Strong put it, "twins," though not "organically and inseparably united."[70] Both schools opened their doors to begin instruction on the same day in November 1850, and in the early years the seminary rented space in the university building.[71] According to popular lore, none other than Ralph Waldo Emerson used the university as "an illustration of Yankee enterprise, saying that a landlord in Rochester had a hotel which he thought would rent for more as a university; so he put in a few books, sent for a coach-load of professors, bought some philosophical apparatus, and, by the time green peas were ripe, had graduated a large class of students."[72] Although the university outpaced the seminary in terms of growth, both schools were generally healthy in the 1850s. In fact, among Baptist schools the University of Rochester was second only to Brown University in terms of enrollment.[73]

Although Strong had chosen to go elsewhere for his collegiate instruction, he now decided to return to Rochester for his seminary training. Strong's father had been closely identified with the early history of both the University of Rochester and the Rochester Theological Seminary,[74] but that was not the primary impetus behind his decision. Rochester was his hometown, and he thought it would be good to spend more time with his parents while studying for the ministry. They had, after all, funded his four years of study at Yale. Although Strong was not yet, as he called it, "a firm Baptist," he could think of no other denomination he could safely join, so by default he concluded it would be best to study at a Baptist institution. Most important, Ezekiel Gilman Robinson was then professor of theology at Rochester. Strong viewed Robinson as "the very ideal of a pulpit orator," and he "felt that [he] could have no instructor in theology or homiletics half as competent as Dr. Robinson."[75] Robinson was a big drawing point for Strong to attend the seminary in Rochester.

In stark contrast to the recitation method practiced at Yale, Robinson encouraged his students to think critically and to ask questions in class. As Strong noted, "[Robinson] never was so happy as when he stirred up a hot debate." This change caught Strong completely off guard. Emboldened, however, by the example of older students he gradually, if somewhat timidly, began to participate in classroom discussion. Strong later considered his experience under Robinson "the real beginning of [his] intellectual history."[76]

Robinson not only challenged Strong by his teaching methods, but he also forced Strong to rethink much of what he had learned at Yale. For example, whereas Noah Porter had given his students the impression that metaphysics was an uninteresting topic, Robinson showed Strong the practical value of such subjects. As Strong later acknowledged, "Under Dr. Robinson all my ideas with regard to metaphysics were changed. I began to see that it alone dealt with realities, that, in fact, one could have no firm footing in any other department of knowledge unless he had reached a good metaphysical foundation." Robinson held to a Kantian doctrine of relativity, which Strong adopted and held for more than twenty-five years.[77] Strong later considered some of the actual philosophical ideas he acquired from Robinson to be fetters of a sort, but he credited Robinson with introducing him to the importance of studying philosophy.[78]

Although in Strong's opinion Robinson towered above the other faculty members, he also studied under a number of other capable men. Velona Hotchkiss taught both Hebrew and Greek at the seminary during the 1850s and 1860s. Whereas Robinson was somewhat of a radical, always questioning older views, Hotchkiss was a very conservative thinker. He held that the world was created in six literal days and believed in a worldwide flood in Noah's time. For these reasons, among others, Strong thought him "somewhat narrow."[79] At his funeral in 1882, Strong said of Hotchkiss,

> He was an ardent lover of the Bible, and a profound believer that its every line and syllable were written by holy men of old as they were moved by the

Holy Ghost. In those days, we who were students wondered whether he did not press too strongly and exclusively the divine aspect of the doctrine of inspiration, and whether he made sufficient allowance for the human moulds into which the molten gold of truth has been poured.... He loved the old doctrines, and he held them in their old forms.[80]

Strong recognized the professor's scholarly work was driven by his belief in the infallibility and authority of the Scriptures, and for this he deeply respected Hotchkiss. Still, Strong preferred the questioning Robinson to the more staid and stable professor.

George Northrup was, in Strong's day, professor of ecclesiastical history at the seminary. Like Robinson, he encouraged discussion in the classroom. Conscientious and more mystical than the other professors, Northrup had just completed his undergraduate education when he began teaching, and he was still working through a number of theological issues himself. For this reason, he tended to place himself on level ground with his students. As Strong put it, "His very inexperience compelled him to put himself by our sides as a fellow student, and that stimulated us to think for ourselves as we never would have been stimulated by more advanced and dogmatic instruction."[81] Strong appreciated Northrup's demeanor in the classroom, but Robinson remained the gold standard against which he measured the others.

In addition to his academic work, during his first year at seminary Strong began ministering to a small group of people who met at the Rapids, a small village on the Genesee River three miles south of Rochester. It was a rough area populated largely by canal workers, who spent much of their spare time fighting, drinking, and gambling. The town had three bars, no church, and one run-down schoolhouse. However, the town also had Charlotte Stillson, a woman committed to the spiritual betterment of the community. Throughout the week Stillson would visit folks in the village and encourage them to send their children to Sunday school and to attend services themselves. On Sunday afternoons the neighborhood children were gathered together in the old schoolhouse, where Strong would lead them in singing and speak to them about their souls. Then on Sunday evenings Strong would preach to any adults who came out to hear the young seminary student. Strong described his Sunday schedule during the year and a half he ministered in the Rapids:

On Sundays after I had attended morning service at the First Baptist Church in town and had taught my young women's Bible class in the church Sunday School, I walked my three miles, often through rain and mud, to Mrs. Stillson's house at the Rapids. There I had a cold lunch and soon after went a little farther out on the Chili Road to the tumbledown schoolhouse, where I led singing and superintended the school. We came back to Mrs. Stillson's for supper. After supper, and often with a lantern to light us along the miry road, we repaired again to the schoolhouse, which was dimly lighted with tallow candles and was crowded to its utmost capacity with an audience of seventy-five. There were fellows outside to throw stones through the windows and fellows inside to create every possible disorder. Somehow I managed to secure their goodwill, and they made me no positive trouble, though it was hard for the young women, without a guard, to get back unmolested to their homes. But all the while there was one quiet little woman whose influence was gradually subduing the community, and that was Mrs. Stillson.[82]

During this time in the Rapids, Strong preached simple gospel messages, and he credited this experience with preventing him from becoming caught up with rhetorical display.

One evening, Stillson invited a number of young women to her home for Bible study and prayer. Strong read to them from Isaiah 53 and told them about the atoning work of Christ. That night he believed several of them were genuinely converted, and from this experience Strong learned his third lesson in theology: "The atonement of Christ is the effective and the only persuasive to faith. . . . No man had a right to believe in God as a Savior except upon the ground of the sacrificial death of Jesus."[83] Strong found that it was not enough to tell people that God would forgive them. He needed to explain how God could justly save them from their sins.

Strong later reflected that he may have learned more about theology in the Rapids than he ever learned at the seminary. Ministering to people in a difficult area forced him to ask many questions that he never would have encountered in the classroom. Stillson herself also had a significant impact on his thinking. She planted a theological emphasis that may have laid some of the groundwork for his later ethical monism. Strong wrote of Stillson: "I learned from her example the doctrine of a present Christ. And though I had still much to learn about this present Christ . . . now I began to pray to Jesus my elder brother, my human companion, my present friend."[84] By her example, Stillson taught Strong to emphasize the presence of Christ, that is, the immanence of deity.

During the spring of his second year at the seminary, Strong developed a bad cold that settled in his lungs.[85] After he coughed up blood several times, the family doctor was called, who recommended that Strong end his studies at once and spend an entire year in the open air, else he "might enter the kingdom of heaven" sooner than any of them wished.[86] Heeding the doctor's instructions Strong finished his seminary studies two or three months early and headed to Europe for an extended holiday.[87]

On May 6, 1859, Strong and a companion named Theodore Bacon set sail from New York bound for Liverpool on the steamer *City of Washington*. During his more than fourteen months abroad, Strong engaged in a walking tour, visiting England, Scotland, France, Switzerland, Germany, Italy, Greece, Egypt, and Palestine.[88] Strong heard many of Europe's great preachers, including Robert Candlish, Horatius Bonar, and Charles Spurgeon, and he saw many of Europe's architectural landmarks, such as Westminster Abbey, the British House of Commons, the University of Wittenburg, the Acropolis, and St. Peter's Basilica. After spending three weeks in Rome, Strong later reflected that he "almost longed for a good settled bronchitis which would compel [him] to spend a whole winter in this most instructive and fascinating of all the cities of the world."[89]

The travel and change of pace were certainly good for his health, but Strong also benefited from his interaction with a variety of companions. In addition to his original travel mate, Strong spent quite a bit of his time with Americans he met overseas. Chief among them was Elisha Mulford, who was staying in the city of Berlin, where he spent his days learning German, reading G. W. F. Hegel, and smoking his pipe. A graduate of both Yale and Union, Mulford was a disciple of Anglican theologian F. D. Maurice (1805–72) and was quickly becoming a follower of Hegel as well. Later he attempted to popularize the thought of Maurice and Hegel in his two books, *The Nation* and *The Republic of God*, but at this early stage he was content to spend two or three evenings a week talking with Strong until late into the night. Although these conversations were not Strong's first introduction to Hegel, they likely included some of the most evangelistic appeals he had ever heard for Hegelian philosophy. Strong spent most of October through December of 1859 in Berlin.[90]

During the first half of 1860, Mulford traveled with Strong to Paris, Antwerp, Amsterdam, and The Hague, and at the end of June they sailed from Liverpool back to Boston aboard the steamship *Arabia*. By the time they arrived in Boston Harbor, Strong had been away from the United States for one year, two months, and four days, and he calculated the trip to have cost about $2,400. The trip had been costly and time consuming, but his health had been restored. He had also learned much about foreign language and foreign life, and perhaps most important, he had "found [his] tongue, had acquired ease in conversation, and had learned to mingle with men." He now had quite a store of memories to draw on for conversation and illustrative purposes, but he also noted that his spiritual condition had somewhat worsened during his time abroad. Ministry no longer seemed an inviting prospect but rather a threatening one.[91] He later admitted, "In my European experience the edge of my Christian feeling became dull. I lost the desire and the love for Christian service, although I learned a great deal of German, and got together a library of German books, which was very useful to me afterward."[92] Though spiritually detrimental, the trip had opened his eyes and broadened his perspective on many issues.

Pastoral Ministry in Haverhill, Massachusetts

Shortly after returning from Europe, Ezekiel Robinson asked Strong to candidate at the First Baptist Church of New York City. Having been born and raised in a city, Strong thought New York would provide an excellent setting for ministerial success. He liked the city, and if he were to pastor, he wanted a city church. Strong preached what he considered an excellent sermon, but the church thought otherwise. Strong was surprised when they did not extend a call for him to become their next pastor. In retrospect, he realized that his sermons at that time were overly refined, highly rhetorical, and generally deficient in terms communicating the simple gospel.[93]

Robinson next sent Strong to a smaller church in Haverhill, in the northeast corner of Massachusetts. At the time, the village of Haverhill had only about ten thousand residents, and the church, about three hundred members.[94] Strong's initial impression of the place was unfavorable. He longed for the city and thought this out-of-the-way town would provide little opportunity for advancement, but the people liked his preaching and after the Sunday evening service asked him to accept the pastorate. However, there was one difficulty the church did not anticipate: while in Germany, Strong had decided that immersion was the only valid mode of baptism, but he had not yet determined whether or not baptism must precede church membership and admission to communion. He confessed to the church that he did not yet hold to restricted communion. Believing him a Baptist, the people were shocked by his admission. They replied that, unless he could change his mind about this issue, they would have to withdraw their invitation.[95]

Strong returned to Rochester determined to settle his denominational views. He realized that his view of communion would likely prevent him from being called to any significant Baptist church, so he knew he needed to resolve the question in his own mind. Other issues were also troubling him during this time. Shortly after his return from Europe, Strong had visited an aunt in Oberlin, Ohio, where he met and was smitten by Julia Finney, daughter of evangelist Charles Finney. The two were hastily engaged, but that fall she suddenly broke off their engagement. Strong was devastated by this chain of events:

> Darkness seemed to be closing round me. I had wanted a city church, but the city church did not want me. A country church had wanted me, but I had not wanted the country church. A certain young lady of intelligence and refinement, of musical and social gifts, had seemed to suit me, but now I learned of insuperable obstacles which prevented all hope of securing her. I was at my father's house, pecuniarily dependent when I ought to be earning my own living. . . . I began to be despondent, but I began anew to think and pray.[96]

During December 1860, while walking under a clear night sky, Strong renewed his commitment to follow God and to pursue the truth with regard to both doctrine and ministerial duty.

Soon after this, Strong was invited to fill the pulpit of the North Baptist Church in Chicago. The church was small, with fewer than fifty members and almost no financial resources, but it was a place for Strong to regain his bearings both personally and ministerially. In Chicago he spent much of his time either studying or visiting people in the community. For several months he preached simple, plain gospel messages. Life and ministry, if not ideal, at least seemed stable. Then suddenly everything changed. In April 1861, shots rang out at Fort Sumter, a harbinger of dreadful events to come. As newly elected President Lincoln began calling for troops and the Civil War commenced, the atmosphere in Northern cities was transformed. Strong's preaching, too, was impacted by these national events. He was a Unionist through and through, and his sermons reflected as much. He longed to see a stronger national government that could respond decisively to the threat of rebellion: "I was patriotic, and I did my part in strengthening the hands of the president and in nerving the people to give their money and their sons for the defense of the Union. I declared that 'the powers that be are ordained by God' and that rebellion against just civil government is rebellion against God."[97]

In light of his interim ministry, he also began wishing for a stronger church government. Strong started putting together a more developed understanding of church government and gradually came to see that "as birth must come before food, so . . . baptism, the ordinance that symbolizes birth, must come before the Lord's Supper, the ordinance that symbolizes nourishment." He had finally adopted a Baptist view of communion: "I saw my way to be a thoroughgoing Baptist—I could no longer be anything else."[98] Strong considered his arrival at a Baptist view of the church to be his fourth lesson in doctrine.

About this time, the church in Haverhill contacted Strong again asking if perhaps he had changed his mind regarding communion. He replied that he had come to a Baptist understanding of the ordinance but that he was not sure that it was his duty to pastor that particular church. The Haverhill church responded by inviting Strong to fill the pulpit for an indefinite trial period. This time he accepted, though not without some reservations. He still had no great love for the little town:

> I went only because God sent me. When I set foot there for the second time, I wanted to flee like Jonah. I wanted a larger place, and I wanted a city church. But obeying God's call, I began work there. And I found after a little that the wisdom and plan of God were better than any wisdom and plan of mine. To all eternity I shall never cease to praise him that he did not permit me to have my own way but directed me instead to that little shoe-town in the northeastern corner of Massachusetts.[99]

Although not prone to displays of affection, his New England congregation clearly loved their young pastor from the start, and the trial period was soon made permanent.

Strong was ordained by the church on August 1, 1861. Although the nation was in the midst of great turmoil, Strong found his conservative New England congregation to be the epitome of stability and faithfulness. While not nearly as flattering as the church in Chicago, the sturdy folk in Haverhill were present when the church doors were open, and unlike the big city church, they paid him a generous salary on time every month.[100] When Strong was drafted to serve in the Union army he was ready and willing to head off to war. The congregation, however, believed Strong could do more to help the Union cause by preaching at home, so they raised $350 to secure a substitute for their new pastor.[101]

Shortly after his ordination, Strong took a month's vacation back in Rochester, where he called on Charlotte Stillson in the Rapids. She told him that she wanted him to meet Hattie Savage, a young lady she thought would be a perfect match for him. Stillson invited the two for afternoon tea, and as Strong put it, "I came, I saw, and I was conquered." They began courting immediately, were engaged within the week, and were married on November 6, 1861, less than three months after meeting. Although he later counseled his own children and grandchildren not to proceed so quickly, he included the caveat, "unless they are sure they have found a treasure as great as mine."[102]

Hattie's father, Eleazer Savage, had been the first pastor of the First Baptist Church in Rochester and was involved in reviving about a dozen dying churches over several decades. Raised in a pastor's home, Strong's new bride quickly adapted to her life as a pastor's wife at the church in Haverhill. Strong's ministry appeared to go well: the church loved their young pastor and his wife, and the young couple had come to love their congregation. Then, after two years of preaching two sermons a week, he began to feel as if his "cask seemed to run dry." He found it difficult to prepare sermons and often lay awake at night thinking that his ministry was a waste. Struggling with ill health and depression, Strong and his wife headed back to Rochester for four weeks of vacation in the summer of 1863. Strong determined to read nothing but the Bible during his time in Rochester. As he read the book of Acts, he noticed that the apostles were marked not by despondency but by courage and hope. He contrasted this with his own ministry and concluded that they were full of optimism and power because of "the presence of Christ *in them*." He went back to John's gospel and reread Christ's promises to his disciples. It eventually dawned on him that Christ's promise to be with his disciples and his teaching about the vine and the branches were not merely pictures of Christ's sympathy and friendship but, rather, descriptions of a powerful and vital union between Christ and his followers. For the first time, Strong saw this relationship as "a union in which the Spirit of Christ interpenetrates and energizes ours, a union in which he joins himself so indissolubly to us that neither life nor death, nor height nor depth, nor any other creature shall be able to separate us from him." Previously he had viewed Christ as an external Savior. He now saw Christ as his "very mind and heart" and as a Savior who had "made himself to be a part of me forever." This new understanding of Christ's relationship to the believer had major implications for other areas of his theology and for his ability to correlate and communicate his developing doctrinal system. Strong later wrote, "Regeneration, conversion, justification, sanctification, perseverance, ecclesiology, and eschatology revealed themselves to me successively as mere correlates of this union of Christ with the believer. If I had never had this experience, I never could have taught theology."[103] This fifth doctrinal lesson, which Strong called "union with Christ," was an important step toward what he would later call ethical monism.

Strong returned from his vacation with a new outlook on Christian life and ministry. Whereas he would previously spend days looking at a text of Scripture trying to come up with a simple sermon outline, he now found that in minutes much of the sermon would come to him with little effort. Several notable conversions soon took place in the town, and the church grew even as the nation convulsed and young men, including several from Haverhill, fell silent in the battlefields.[104]

Strong's family, too, was growing. On November 28, 1862, their first child was born, a son they named Charles after Hattie's brother, Charles Savage, who had recently lost his life in the war. Then, on August 29, 1864, they had their first daughter, Mary. If Strong had found it difficult to keep a rein on expenses as a newly married man, he found it even harder as his household expanded. Strong claimed that he would never have left Haverhill for purely financial reasons, but finances surely played a part. He also still wanted a larger field in which to labor in the gospel, and he always felt the Haverhill congregation was a bit too conservative for his liking.[105]

In July 1865, Strong was invited to candidate at the First Baptist Church in Cleveland, Ohio. He initially turned down the offer—he had no desire to move that far west—but agreed to stop in Cleveland and fill the pulpit on his way to vacation on Lake Superior. During their brief time in Cleveland, Strong and his wife were both immediately attracted to the church, and the church seemed to appreciate his preaching—in fact, they compelled Strong to fill the pulpit again on his way back from vacation. That second Sunday in Cleveland, the pulpit committee extended a call to the church, and Strong accepted. He dropped Hattie and the children off in Rochester and returned to Haverhill to resign and pack up their earthly belongings for the move to Cleveland. He announced his resignation on Thursday and by Sunday night had preached his farewell sermon. The church in Haverhill was shocked by his sudden departure, but they did not bear hard feelings against their young pastor, and in subsequent years Strong enjoyed many pleasant visits to the town. He always considered it a place where God had worked mightily in his life by revealing to him the doctrine of the believer's union with Christ: "Haverhill was the place where a change was wrought in my experience more striking than that at my conversion—the place where it pleased God to reveal his Son in me—and therefore Haverhill will always seem to me a veritable house of God and gate of heaven."[106] However, at the time he was more than willing to leave this "gate of heaven" for a larger and potentially more progressive church in Cleveland.

Pastoral Ministry in Cleveland, Ohio

When Strong arrived in Cleveland in the fall of 1865, the city boasted a population of about sixty-five thousand. The city was beautiful and was in the midst of a period of rapid growth.[107] It was just the kind of place Strong was hoping to minister. The auditorium of the First Baptist Church could seat around a thousand, and church membership stood at about six hundred. The church was healthy, but the facilities still included plenty of room for additional growth.

The church initially offered him a salary of $3,000 a year, more than double what he had been making in Haverhill. Several wealthy members also helped him acquire a substantial home with plenty of room for his growing family and his growing library. The increased income and improved domestic conditions gave Strong greater flexibility to perform his duties, and he felt that the larger and better-educated congregation called for some adjustments to his preaching: "I cut myself loose from the fetters of tradition and branched out into new lines of thought and study." Whereas in Haverhill Strong had studied the Bible almost exclusively, in Cleveland he began to examine other subjects he thought might help him become a better interpreter of the Scriptures: geology, mineralogy, microscopy, botany, chemistry, meteorology, astronomy, political economy, and metaphysics. As he studied these subjects his appreciation of natural revelation gradually increased: "The book of nature began to seem a part of God's revelation quite as much as the book of Scripture." His study of these subjects also opened up doors for him to lecture on these topics in a variety of contexts.[108] His growing reputation as a well-informed speaker led to him being offered professorships at Brown University and Crozer Theological Seminary. However, Strong was not yet ready to return to the classroom, so he turned these offers down, feeling he could not leave the pastorate for "any ordinary chair."[109] Still, he was moving in a direction that would eventually draw him away from the church and into the academy.

For a number of years, Strong was content to devote the bulk of his energy to his congregation in Cleveland. Things seemed to be going well in the church. Within his first few months in the city, more than one hundred people had been converted and added to the rolls.[110] Although that level of growth did not continue, the church was actively involved in foreign missions and planting domestic churches and was well regarded in the community. Before Strong came to Cleveland, the various Baptist churches in the city had little to do with each other, but soon he began hosting an informal Baptist ministers' meeting in his office every Monday morning for fellowship and mutual encouragement. This led to the establishment of a City Mission Union whereby the Baptist churches in Cleveland worked together to promote evangelical outreach and denominational expansion.

Strong enjoyed his ministry in Cleveland, but he also began looking beyond the city limits. In 1831, the Ohio Baptist Education Society had founded a college in Granville, Ohio, about 120 miles south of Cleveland. Strong soon became interested in this work, and in 1867 he was elected a trustee of the school, which by this time had been renamed Denison University.[111] Strong especially enjoyed the annual ministers' institutes in Granville in connection with the university. He did some teaching in the institutes and "first began to think that [he] might have gifts for teaching and might enjoy that sort of life."[112]

Strong's time in Cleveland was eye opening in many ways. Through his scientific study he gained a new appreciation for Christ's role as creator, which he later considered his sixth doctrinal lesson. He had not yet developed the idea of ethical monism, but he was slowly moving in that direction. He recalled, "God gave me in Cleveland a wider view of the universe and prepared me to see the larger relations of Christ to the world he had made. . . . The immanence of Christ did not then impress itself upon me as it did afterwards in Rochester. But I was gathering material for broader conceptions." Cleveland also provided Strong with what he called a "healthy objective element that was previously lacking,"[113] This increased understanding of the world through scientific study and interaction with broad-minded people seems to have caused him to view religious authority as less centered in a book such as the Bible.

While in Cleveland, Strong met several people with whom his life would be forever entwined. The most significant of these was John D. Rockefeller Sr. (1839–1937). Contrary to statements found in many sources, Rockefeller was not a member at the First Baptist Church in Cleveland.[114] Rather, he was a lifelong member of a Cleveland church that changed names several times and is today best known as the Euclid Avenue Baptist Church.[115] Exactly when Strong first met Rockefeller is unclear. However, after the Rockefellers' second child died in August 1870, Strong was asked to conduct the funeral because the Rockefellers' own pastor was out of town: "In the absence of his pastor, I was called to conduct the funeral service."[116] This statement by Strong makes it clear that he did not consider himself Rockefeller's pastor.[117] By conducting the funeral, Strong established a definite and memorable connection with the rising businessman—a relationship that would become much stronger, if sometimes tested, in years to come.

During his years in Cleveland, Strong's own family continued to grow. On December 7, 1866, his son John Henry was born, and then on February 10, 1870, twin girls, Cora and Kate. The church continued to provide financially for their pastor and his growing family, but other offers did come in. One of the most attractive came in 1869 when a committee from the Madison Avenue Church in New York City appeared in the congregation one Sunday and afterward asked if he would consider a call from that church.[118] Strong had always loved the city, and he viewed New York as the pinnacle of city life and ministry. Plus, the church was offering a salary of $6,000 a year, significantly more than he was then making. Strong went to New York and preached, and the church promptly extended a unanimous call, but Strong was not yet ready to accept: he had big plans for the church and wanted the church to agree to them before accepting the call. After several months of correspondence and few assurances from the church, Strong finally decided to decline. The church was unwilling to embrace his plans for a mission chapel and, more important, would not agree to follow his leadership on this issue among others.

In 1869, Strong also preached for the Judson Missionary Society at Brown University. He thought he had preached well, but did not expect anything particular to come of the occasion, so he was surprised the next year when he was awarded a Doctor of Divinity degree from the university.[119] Although honorary, this degree recognized his ministerial accomplishments and growing reputation and further set him on course for an academic career.[120]

Returning to Rochester

A few years later, in 1872 Ezekiel Robinson resigned from the presidency of Rochester Theological Seminary. For years tensions had been building around some of his theological tendencies and his corresponding influence on students.[121] A graduate of Brown University, Robinson had first been approached by his alma mater about assuming the presidency in 1867 while on a yearlong sabbatical in Europe, but shortly after returning from Europe he had decided to remain in Rochester. The seminary had graciously allowed him a year off, had struggled in his absence, and now very much needed his administrative leadership. He spent the next several years rebuilding the school and expanding its financial base, but he struggled with ill health and thought the Rochester climate and the official seminary president's house in particular contributed to his difficulties. In the spring of 1871, Brown University renewed its offer, and this time after much coaxing and deliberation, Robinson finally accepted. At the time he considered this transition a "descent to a lower and less useful sphere of labor," but the decision was made, and after almost twenty years of service at Rochester, Robinson returned to his alma mater.[122] Although others would later say similar things about Strong, Strong himself wrote of his former professor, "To Dr. Robinson the institution at Rochester owes more of its character and success than to any single other man."[123]

With Robinson's departure, Rochester lost both its president and its professor of theology. The trustees began to look around for someone to fill the professor's chair and quickly focused their attention on Strong. In addition to being a graduate of the school, he was a successful pastor and had carried a reputation for being well read and for being at home in a variety of academic contexts. An extended series of doctrinal sermons at the church in Cleveland had also bolstered his reputation as a theologically astute pastor. In the spring of 1872, the seminary trustees asked Strong to accept the professorship of theology. Although just thirty-five years old at the time, Strong replied that he could not accept the position unless he was also made president of the seminary, for he said, "I could not work easily unless I had affairs in my own hands."[124] Remarkably, the trustees then offered him both the presidency and the professorship, which he accepted.

In June 1872, Strong preached his final sermon in Cleveland. He then embarked on a three-month tour of Europe before assuming his duties in Rochester. In September, he moved to Rochester and took up the reins as president and professor of theology at the seminary shortly before the new term began. His first year Strong was pleased to find that the seniors had finished their theology during the previous year, so he needed only to teach the middle class, which consisted of just seventeen students. Strong wrote out the content of his first lecture on the morning of the day he delivered it, and he continued this practice for his first two years, until he had worked through the entire system of theology.[125] His predecessor and former professor, Ezekiel Robinson, had written extensive notes for the class, but Strong put these notes aside so he would not be tempted to repeat Robinson's material without giving it sufficient thought.[126] In fact, Strong did not examine Robinson's material at all until about twenty years later, when he was asked to write an evaluation of Robinson's theology as part of a memorial for the older man.[127]

As he prepared his lectures week by week and was forced to work through numerous theological issues, Strong found that he turned more often to German writers than to English-speaking ones: "English and American theologians often evade or ignore difficulties and leave the reader unconscious of their existence.... But German writers aim to cover the whole subject. When they come to a question they cannot answer, they at least recognize it, suggest a tentative answer, or declare it to be for the present unanswerable." Thus, he found himself devouring the writings of such authors as Isaak August Dorner (1809–84), Friedrich Adolf Philippi (1809–82), and Gottfried Thomasius (1802–75) among others.[128]

Although Strong often turned to German writers, he did not by any means abandon American and English authors. Many American and English writers were stressing the doctrine of divine immanence during the second half of the nineteenth century, and Strong drank deeply from their writings as well, even if he sometimes found their draft less satisfying. Although the connections are not always easy to make, Strong's thinking, and especially his eventual adoption of ethical monism, was doubtless affected by his early life and ministry and by philosophers on both sides of the Atlantic.

Chapter 2 explores the writings of several German thinkers who seem to have provided some of the philosophical building blocks Strong used to construct his ethical monism. It also examines the writings of several English-speaking philosophers who emphasized the doctrine of divine immanence and who appear to have pushed Strong's thinking toward ethical monism.

Philosophical Background of Ethical Monism

S TRONG'S THEOLOGY WAS MOVING slowly but perceptibly in the direction of ethical monism long before he came to Rochester. Strong himself acknowledged that many of the major emphases of his later theology were already present, albeit in seed form, when he arrived in Rochester to take up his duties as president and professor of theology.

A glance at the indexes of both Strong's early and later theology texts reveals hundreds of references to philosophers who expressed concepts that bore remarkable similarities to his ethical monism. This is not to say that Strong borrowed his distinctive philosophical approach from others wholesale. However, prior to proposing the concept of ethical monism, Strong was familiar with the theories of philosophers and theologians who taught various forms of philosophical idealism. Although he was at times critical of such men, he seems to have imbibed certain elements of their thought. This chapter surveys key figures in the history of idealism that Strong cited in his published works.

Johann Gottlieb Fichte (1762–1814)

Fichte was the first of the major post-Kantian idealists. Though born in rural Saxony to a family of poor ribbon weavers, Fichte managed to secure a solid classical education before heading off to university in 1780. After studying at Jena, he spent several years working as a private tutor. In 1790 Fichte began studying the works of Immanuel Kant (1724–1804), which soon had a major impact on his philosophical career. When Fichte's first book, *Attempt at a Critique of All Revelation*, was published anonymously in 1792 many people regarded it as the work of Kant himself, so it was initially received as Kant's fourth critique.[1] Once Kant revealed the real author of the volume, Fichte's name became known throughout the universities of Europe, and his reputation as a philosopher was firmly established.

Fichte viewed himself as a faithful heir of Kant's philosophical vision. For example, in the introduction to *The Science of Knowledge*, Fichte wrote, "I have long asserted, and repeat once more, that my system is nothing other than the *Kantian*."[2] However, he differed from Kant on several important issues, and Kant himself would eventually come to regard Fichte's system as distinct from his own. For example, whereas Kant implied that things-in-themselves actually exist and are responsible for the sensory component of our knowledge, Fichte denied the independent existence of things outside the knower and instead argued that the knower is the cause of all such concepts and categories. For Fichte, both the knower and the thing known are ultimately one and the same, because the thing known is a product of the knower's mind.[3] This view of reality suggests some form of monistic idealism.

Fichte also spoke a good deal about what he called the "ego" or the "self-positing I." His use of these terms led many people to assume that he was speaking about the individual self or person, but he was actually referring to the "one immediate spiritual Life," that is, the infinite, or at least unlimited activity, which is the ground of all consciousness.[4] Such rather abstract concepts eventually led to accusations of atheism.[5] Indeed, Fichte did make a number of statements that could be easily misunderstood, for example, "The concept of God as a separate substance is impossible and contradictory."[6] Based on comments like these, one early-twentieth-century writer noted, "It is evident that Fichte's conception of the relation of God to the world is not the ordinary one."[7] This was certainly the case. However, as Frederick Copleston has pointed out, Fichte's philosophy was not so much atheistic as it was subtly pantheistic.[8] Fichte was a transcendental idealist whose philosophical speculations led him very close to pantheistic monism, if indeed such a term does not actually summarize his view of reality.

Strong cited Fichte at least as early as 1867. In a commencement address given at the medical college in Cleveland that year, Strong addressed the subject of "Science and Religion." In his address he quoted Fichte as saying that, "we are all born in faith."[9] It is impossible to know how much Strong was reading Fichte at this early date, but he was at least aware of Fichte by the middle to late 1860s.

In Strong's first printed theology notes (*Lectures on Theology*, 1876), he referenced Fichte only once. In a section discussing the doctrine of creation, Strong stated, "The logical alternative of creation is therefore a system of pantheism, in which God is an impersonal and necessary force." He then quoted what he called "the pantheistic dicta of Fichte," namely, that "the assumption of a creation is the fundamental error of all false metaphysics and false theology."[10] In this context, Strong clearly identified Fichte as a pantheist, and he cited Fichte primarily to disagree with him, but apparently Strong was not ready to set Fichte's works aside altogether.

By the time his lecture notes were expanded and published as his *Systematic Theology* in 1886, Strong had added several more references to Fichte, and none of these were negative. For example, in the early pages of his *Systematic Theology*, while discussing the possibility of theology, Strong quoted Fichte as saying that "we are born in faith."[11] This new addition was an echo of his earlier reference to Fichte at the 1867 commencement address in Cleveland. Although too much should not be read into a brief citation of this sort, contextually this use of Fichte implies that Strong did not consider Fichte completely outside the bounds of the Christian faith. At least, Strong appears to have assumed that Fichte's reference to "faith" was a reference to something they both held in common.

Similarly, in his discussion of the relationship between a renewed heart and the reception of divine revelation, Strong inserted several new quotations from Fichte: "Our system of thought is very often only the history of our heart. . . . Truth is descended from conscience. . . . Men do not will according to their reason, but reason according to their will."[12] Here Strong seems to cite Fichte as if he were a fellow Christian who had made a number of contributions to theological thought.

In Strong's discussion of anthropology, he cited Fichte's remarks about self-consciousness as a distinguishing mark between humanity and mere animals.[13] Once again, Strong referenced Fichte not as a foil but, rather, as a source who supported a point he wanted to make.

Additional references to Fichte appeared in subsequent editions of Strong's *Systematic Theology*, and nearly all of these were positive or at least neutral. Furthermore, references to Fichte in Strong's other writings confirm that Strong was familiar with Fichte's thought by the late 1870s and that he continued to study Fichte in the decades that followed.[14] How much Fichte affected Strong's thinking is impossible to determine, but it appears that Strong was reading Fichte as he updated his *Systematic Theology* every few years between 1886 and 1907.

Friedrich Wilhelm Joseph Schelling (1775–1854)

After Fichte, the next major figure in the history of German idealism was Friedrich Schelling. Born the son of a Lutheran pastor in southern Germany, at the age of fifteen Schelling took up his studies at the Protestant seminary in Tübingen. There he soon became friends with G. W. F. Hegel (1770–1831) and Friedrich Hölderlin (1770–1843), who were both five years his senior but were just a year or two ahead of him in the seminary. The three young men discovered they had a good deal in common and were soon roommates. As it turned out, each of the young students disliked the seminary, each resolved not to enter pastoral ministry, and each gradually turned his eyes from the study of theology to the field of philosophy.[15]

Schelling was a precocious but somewhat unstable philosopher. As Terry Pinkard has written, with just a touch of hyperbole,

> He published his first major philosophical work at the age of nineteen and, by the time he was twenty-nine, he had published more philosophy books than most people could even transcribe in a lifetime. By 1798 (at the age of twenty-three), Schelling became an "extraordinary" professor at Jena and Fichte's successor. Each year, with each new publication, Schelling's system seemed to change, leading Hegel later sarcastically to remark in his Berlin lectures that Schelling had conducted his philosophical education in public. . . . Schelling was ambitious and experimental in temperament, sometimes a bit reckless in his arguments, and he was continually refining and testing out new ideas and ever open to revising old ones.[16]

In addition to succeeding Fichte at Jena, Schelling also taught at Erlangen and Munich before finally settling in Berlin, where he took up the chair of philosophy that had been occupied by Hegel prior to his death. Although he succeeded both Fichte and Hegel in terms of employment, within the field of German idealism Schelling wandered somewhere between the two men. Because of how much his thought developed during his lengthy career, it is nearly impossible to summarize Schelling's philosophy without a good deal of qualification. For example, one is pressed to speak of Schelling's "early philosophy," his "post-Fichtean thought," and so forth.[17]

Although Schelling's earliest works reflect a strong affinity for Fichte's transcendental idealism, he was not content with Fichte's understanding of the ground of identity. Schelling therefore developed what he believed was a more comprehensive way to defend a common basis for nature and the self. This method of thought he labeled the "system of identity," or absolute idealism. In this scheme, Schelling sought to tie consciousness to objects rather than to subjects. He also held that unity of thought and being was maintained by various relationships between objects and subjects.[18]

Despite his differences with Fichte and later with Hegel, Schelling was, like them, a monistic idealist well within the stream of German idealism. For example, in an early series of lectures delivered at the University of Jena in 1802, Schelling declared, "There is actually and essentially only *one* essence, *one* absolute reality, and this essence, as absolute, is indivisible such that it cannot change over into other essences by means of division or separation. Since it is indivisible, diversity among things is only possible to the extent that this indivisible whole is posited under various determinations."[19] Although Schelling's philosophy developed through the decades, his commitment to monistic idealism appears never to have wavered.

Much as with Fichte, Strong cited Schelling prior to coming to Rochester. In a speech delivered at his alma mater in 1868, Strong discussed the "Kantian philosophy," which he noted had been developed by Schelling and Hegel. The idealism of Schelling and Hegel, he argued, "found its consummation in a Pantheistic scheme which confounded the universe with God, and made all human lives and actions but the brilliant bubbles that rise for a moment and then disappear upon the endless current of impersonal and unconscious being."[20] In this context, Strong's chief complaint against Schelling's Idealism was that he believed it ultimately undercut personal existence and responsibility, two things Strong would later try to preserve by arguing for an ethical monism.

When Strong first had his theology notes printed for the benefit of his students, the volume made no mention of Schelling. When those notes were later published as his *Systematic Theology* (1886), they contained only one rather insignificant reference to Schelling.[21] However, Strong was definitely familiar with Schelling's work by the late 1880s.[22] By the time the eighth edition of his *Systematic Theology* was published, Strong had added a number of additional references to Schelling. Most of these citations were relatively insignificant, but Strong identified Schelling, along with Fichte and Hegel, as heirs of Kant's idealism.[23] He clearly was reading Schelling during the 1890s as he revised his theology text.

Georg Wilhelm Friedrich Hegel (1770–1831)

The eldest son of the German treasury secretary, G. W. F. Hegel enjoyed a relatively comfortable childhood. As a youth he attended the Gymnasium in Stuttgart, where he took an early interest in Greek, Latin, and mathematics. Hegel then studied at Tübingen (1788–93), where he was soon joined by Schelling. Then, like Fichte, he served as a private tutor to families in Bern and Frankfurt (1793–1800). After teaching at Jena and several other universities, Hegel succeeded Fichte as chair of philosophy at the University of Berlin in 1818, where he was himself eventually succeeded by Schelling.

Hegel's relationship to Fichte and Schelling is reflected in his earliest philosophical work, a short treatise titled *The Difference between Fichte's and Schelling's System of Philosophy* (1801). In this essay, Hegel argued that Fichte had made a number of improvements on Kant's idealism but that Schelling and he himself had further improved on Fichte. In broad terms, Hegel found Fichte's idealism to be overly subjective, and he thought that Schelling had solved this problem through his philosophy of nature.[24]

Unlike Schelling, Hegel was not particularly precocious. In fact, when Hegel graduated from the seminary in Tübingen, his certificate mentioned "his good character, his fair knowledge of theology and philology and his inadequate grasp of philosophy."[25] Little did Hegel's instructors anticipate that he would become one of the most influential figures in the history of modern philosophy. In fact, as Peter Singer noted, "No philosopher of the nineteenth or twentieth centuries has had as great an impact on the world as Hegel. The only possible exception to this sweeping statement would be Karl Marx—and Marx himself was heavily influenced by Hegel. Without Hegel, neither the intellectual nor the political developments of the last 150 years would have taken the path they did."[26] More specifically, without Hegel, Strong's theology may not have taken the path it did. Strong did not regard himself as a follower of Hegel, and at times he directly disagreed with Hegel's conclusions. However, Hegel surely set some of the philosophical backdrop for Strong's thinking and especially for his ethical monism.

In the various editions of his *Systematic Theology*, Strong cited Hegel more frequently than either Fichte or Schelling, and he demonstrated a thorough acquaintance with Hegel's major writings. In his 1876 *Lectures on Theology*, Strong cited Hegel only a few times,[27] but his use of Hegel had increased significantly by his first edition of *Systematic Theology* a decade later. In the 1886 edition of his *Systematic Theology* many of Strong's citations of Hegel were negative. For example, Strong noted that "religion is not merely, as Hegel declared, a kind of knowing."[28] Strong classified Hegel's idealism as one of the "merely human philosophies" subject to "contradictions and refutations," and he directly disagreed with Hegel's description of man's "Paradisaic condition" as "only an ideal conception underlying human development."[29]

Such references did not disappear from later editions of Strong's *Systematic Theology*, but over time Strong did add a number of positive comments about Hegel. In the final edition of his *Systematic Theology*, Strong referred to Hegel's *Encyclopedia* and positively cited Hegel's *Lectures on the Philosophy of Religion*. Moreover, he thought that Hegel's thesis-antithesis-synthesis paradigm could help explain the inscrutability of God's triune existence.[30] He also quoted Hegel's definition of God as if it were essentially correct.[31]

Strong was still critical of Hegelian idealism and especially Hegel's pantheism. As Strong saw it, Hegel's fundamental error was that "he regarded the

Universe as mere Idea, and gave little thought to the Love and the Will that constitute it."[32] Elsewhere Strong wrote, "Conscience with its testimony to the voluntariness and the damnableness of sin, as it is the eternal witness against Pantheism, is also the eternal witness against the Idealism of Hegel."[33]

Strong was not willing to accept Hegel's idealism, but he appreciated and embraced certain aspects of Hegel's thought, while firmly rejecting others. In an article published in 1888, after comparing the philosophies of Fichte, Schelling, and Hegel, Strong wrote, "If it were not for the fact of sin, and for personal wills that war against the rational and involve themselves in death, the scheme of Hegel would be very attractive. . . . Its monistic basis gratifies the speculative intellect." Even at this early point, Strong apparently found the concept of monism appealing, but Hegel's inability to explain the concepts of sin and guilt to Strong's satisfaction prevented Strong from adopting Hegel's idealism. Strong lamented what he regarded as "the utter inability of Hegelianism to explain or even to recognize the ethical problems of the universe."[34]

Fichte, Schelling, and Hegel shared a number of ideas. As Rolf-Peter Horstmann has recently pointed out, one of these was the belief that "to avoid Kant's dualism, one has to supplement his philosophy with a monistic basis and accept that monism is the only viable alternative to dualism." Horstmann then noted, "It is this belief that made them German idealists."[35] Although Rochester Theological Seminary had a German department in the late 1800s and Strong read numerous German authors, including Fichte, Schelling, and Hegel, he was not a German idealist. He liked the general concept of monism the German idealists argued for, but he thought it failed to account for the reality of sin and moral culpability. In time, he came to believe that a concept he would call ethical monism could overcome these difficulties while preserving what he saw as the major strengths of philosophical monism.

Rudolf Hermann Lotze (1817–81)

Hermann Lotze was born in Bautzen, Saxony, and received his early education at the Gymnasium in Zittau. At the age of seventeen, he entered the University of Leipzig as a medical student and received two doctorates in 1838, one in philosophy and the other in medicine. Despite his training in the life sciences, Lotze was not destined for a medical career. Instead, he soon began lecturing on philosophy and medicine at the University of Leipzig. After teaching for several years at Leipzig, in 1844 Lotze was appointed professor of philosophy at the University of Göttingen, where he remained until shortly before his death.

Lotze's two great interests were science and philosophy. His interest in science prompted him to study medicine, but the realm of philosophy is where he made his most significant contributions. Lotze drank deeply from the wells cultivated by Fichte, Schelling, and Hegel, but he is not usually numbered among the German idealists. He was more of a transitional figure who helped pave the way for a personalist form of idealism.

Unlike most of the German idealists, Lotze regarded God as a personal being. In fact, he argued that the idea of an impersonal spirit was completely contrary to reason.[36] Copleston explains why Lotze differed from the German idealists on this point: "As for the view of Fichte and other philosophers that personality is necessarily finite and limited and so cannot be predicated of the infinite, Lotze replies that it is only infinite spirit which can be personal in the fullest sense of the word."[37] For Lotze, personality is more accurately ascribed to God than it is to any finite being, for God alone is self-existent and therefore perfect personality.[38]

Today Lotze has been largely overshadowed by such figures as Immanuel Kant, Georg Hegel, and Josiah Royce, but in the late nineteenth century Strong considered Lotze to be among the most influential philosophers of his era. In a paper Strong read before the Baptist Congress in Buffalo, New York, in November 1898, he declared: "This conception of evolution is that of Lotze. That great philosopher, whose influence is more potent than any other in present thought." He later preserved this exact wording in the final edition of his *Systematic Theology*.[39]

Strong's own use of Lotze's works increased significantly during his career at Rochester. In the first edition of his *Systematic Theology*, Strong referenced Lotze only a few times.[40] In contrast, in the final edition he cited Lotze in about three dozen different places. Most of Lotze's writings were translated into English during the 1880s, so it is not surprising that Strong's use of them became much more visible during the 1890s. In the final edition of his *Systematic Theology* Strong cited at least four of Lotze's books, each first published in English in the mid-1880s, shortly before the first edition of his *Systematic Theology* appeared: *Metaphysic* (1884), *Outlines of Metaphysic* (1884), *Microcosmus* (1885), and *Outlines of the Philosophy of Religion* (1885).[41]

Strong's opinion of Lotze's philosophy was mixed. He thought that Lotze's "objective idealism" avoided some of the problems associated with what Strong called "materialistic idealism."[42] He also found Lotze's understanding of God more palatable than Hegel's.[43] However, he was also willing to criticize what he perceived as weaknesses in Lotze's views. Against Lotze's assertion that the universe "grasped in its totality, offers an expression of the whole nature of the

One," Strong countered that "the universe is but the finite expression or symbol of [God's] greatness."[44] In other words, Strong believed that the universe could never fully display God's infinite character. He also argued that Lotze was wrong concerning the relationship of holy being to holy willing. Strong claimed that *being* must logically precede *willing*, while Lotze denied this.[45]

In general, however, Strong could agree with much in Lotze. Closely related to the issue of ethical monism is the question of God's relationship to the universe. Strong argued that God's omnipresence is not necessary but, rather, free. He wrote, "We reject the pantheistic notion that God is bound to the universe as the universe is bound to God. God is immanent in the universe, not by compulsion, but by the free act of his own will, and this immanence is qualified by his transcendence." Strong then pointed his readers to Lotze's explanation of God's relationship to the world:

> We are not to picture the absolute [i.e., God] placed in some remote region of extended space, and separated from the world of its creations, so that its influence has to retraverse a distance and make a journey in order to reach things; for its indivisible unity, omnipresent at every point, would fill this space as well as others. Still less ought we, who hold this space to be a mere phenomenon, to imagine a cleft between finite beings and the common foundation of all things, a cleft which would need to be bridged by miraculous wanderings. Wherever in apparent space an organic germ has been formed, at that very spot and not removed from it, the absolute is also present.[46]

Strong then offered the following illustration based on a conversation between a Sunday school student and his teacher: "Is God in my pocket?" "Certainly." "No, he isn't for I haven't any pocket." Strong concluded, "God is omnipresent so long as there is a universe, but he ceases to be omnipresent when the universe ceases to be."[47]

Lotze's influence on Strong's thinking is evident at numerous points, but his influence also extended to American idealists whom Strong cited, such as Borden Parker Bowne and Josiah Royce.

Borden Parker Bowne (1847–1910)

Bowne was an American philosopher and theologian heavily influenced by German writers, especially Hermann Lotze. In fact, Strong once called Bowne "the best expositor of Lotze's system."[48] Bowne was ordained in 1867, about the time he began his undergraduate studies. After studying at New York University, Bowne was invited to become professor of philosophy at Boston University in 1876, where he would remain for more than thirty years. As his reputation grew, Bowne received offers from other schools, including Yale and the newly founded University of Chicago, yet he remained in Boston, where he served as both professor and dean of the graduate school until retiring shortly before his death.

Early in his career Bowne described his philosophy as transcendental empiricism, which appears to acknowledge Kant's impact on his own thought. In a posthumously published work based on his lectures at Boston University, Bowne explained what he meant by transcendental empiricism: "It is transcendental as going beyond the empiricism of sense impressions, but it is empiricism as limiting knowledge to the field of experience. The true view then is neither empiricism nor rationalism of the old type, but criticism which unites and reconciles them"[49] Such terminology accurately described Bowne's early thinking, and he never completely abandoned it, but he eventually decided to call his system personal idealism or simply *personalism*.[50] This change of terminology reflected both the evolution of Bowne's philosophical position over time and his self-conscious staking out of new philosophical ground. As one biographer put it, Bowne avowed "that as a personalist he was the first of the clan in any thoroughgoing sense."[51]

Gary Dorrien has summarized the major themes of Bowne's philosophical personalism as "epistemologically dualistic, metaphysically pluralistic, and ethical in orientation." This last phrase is significant, for the ethical thrust of Bowne's system made it attractive to many who were not overly concerned about parsing the finer points of his philosophy. Bowne himself was interested in preserving the ethical aspect of Christianity regardless of what might become of its actual theology, and his attempt to do so met with a ready audience. Bowne was a Wesleyan by background, but he was well respected by theological liberals and by many who embraced a social Christianity regardless of their denominational identification. As Dorrien has pointed out, "Virtually all liberal Protestant thinkers of his generation looked to him for intellectual leadership."[52] Like many theological liberals of his day, Strong seems to have thought very highly of Bowne, though he of course was interested in the details of Bowne's philosophical system.

Unlike most of the other philosophers mentioned above, Bowne and Strong were contemporaries. Bowne taught at Boston University during the 1880s and 1890s while Strong was teaching in Rochester, and Bowne wrote most of his books during the years when Strong was writing and revising his own works.

Therefore, it is not surprising that Strong's use of Bowne's writings increased significantly between the first and final editions of his *Systematic Theology*.

In the first edition of his theology, Strong cited Bowne's works about sixteen times, nearly all from either Bowne's examination of Herbert Spencer's philosophy or his recently published book on metaphysics.[53] At this relatively early stage in his career at Rochester, Strong was somewhat critical of Bowne. In fact, he found in Bowne a tendency toward pantheism, and he took issue with this. For example, Strong wrote, "To deny second causes is essential idealism, and tends to pantheism. This tendency we find in the recent Metaphysics of Bowne, who regards only personality as real."[54] For Strong, this was Bowne's great weakness as a philosopher. Whether Bowne changed, Strong changed, or, more likely, both did, by the final edition of Strong's *Systematic Theology* in 1907 his use of Bowne had greatly increased and his opinion improved significantly, with references to at least nine of Bowne's books. Many of these had been written during the intervening years between the first and final editions of Strong's *Systematic Theology*, but more important, Strong no longer accused Bowne of having pantheistic tendencies and in fact altered the section where he had made such an accusation. He still viewed Bowne as an objective idealist, but now he stated, "This idealism of Bowne is *not* pantheism, for it holds that, while there are no second causes in nature, man is a second cause, with a personality distinct from that of God, and lifted above nature by his powers of free will."[55] Strong himself had not become a Boston personalist, but his concept of ethical monism bore an important similarity to his new description of Bowne's personalist idealism. Like Bowne, Strong sought to avoid pantheism by emphasizing that human personalities are distinct from the divine personality, and both argued that the reality of such personalities provides the basis for genuine ethical responsibility.

Strong's change of opinion about Bowne's philosophy first appeared in the fifth edition of his *Systematic Theology*. As late as the fourth edition (1893) Strong was still accusing Bowne of having pantheistic tendencies, but in the fifth edition (1896) Strong suddenly removed this accusation and instead inserted the claim that Bowne's objective idealism was not to be confused with pantheism.[56] The fifth edition was also the first edition of Strong's *Systematic Theology* to contain his newly developed concept of ethical monism.

Strong never embraced Bowne's personal idealism, but Strong's opinion about Bowne's relationship to pantheism appears to have changed at about the same time he developed the concept of ethical monism, timing that appears conceptually driven rather than mere coincidence.

Josiah Royce (1855–1916)

Royce was born to immigrant parents in Grass Valley, California, just as the California gold rush was coming to an end. In fact, his parents had been among the wave of "forty-niners" who had made the westward trek some six years earlier.[57] During his early years, Royce was educated primarily by his mother, who opened a small school in Grass Valley a few months before he was born.[58] The gold rush having largely dried up, in the spring of 1866 the family moved to San Francisco. In the rapidly expanding city, Royce attended local schools before entering the recently established University of California at Berkeley in the early 1870s.

Upon graduation from Berkeley, Royce received a grant from a group of local businessmen, which enabled him to spend a little over a year studying in Germany. Royce studied philosophy first at the University of Leipzig and then at Göttingen. While living east of the Rhine, Royce spent much of his time reading Kant, Schopenhauer, and other German idealists. He also sat under the teaching of a number of influential philosophers in the university lecture halls. Among these, Hermann Lotze had the greatest impact on his thinking.[59] By the time Royce left Germany, he was a committed philosophical idealist. As one of Royce's biographers put it, "This year of 1875–76 was the decisive one of Royce's intellectual life. It made him a German romanticist in literature, a German idealist in philosophy."[60] Upon returning to the United States, Royce attended Johns Hopkins University, where in 1878 he became among the first to complete a Ph.D. at the school.[61] He then taught for a few years at the University of California before accepting a lectureship at Harvard in 1882.[62] In 1885, Royce became an assistant professor at Harvard, and in 1892, full professor. Nearly all of his published writings were produced during his years at Harvard.

Although primarily remembered as an idealist philosopher—Cornelius Van Til called him "the first great American idealist"—Royce wrote in a number of different genres, including religious prose, historical narrative, and even fiction.[63] However, it was in the field of philosophy that Royce left his mark.

Royce was deeply interested in religion and ethics. As he wrote in his first book, "The religious problems have been chosen for the present study because they first drove the author to philosophy, and because they of all human interests deserve our best efforts and our utmost loyalty."[64] In this book and others that followed, Royce grappled with the thorny questions of epistemology, individual personality, and the problem of evil.

Most of Royce's major works appeared after the first edition of Strong's *Systematic Theology* was published in 1886. Yet even in that very first edition, Strong indicated that he was familiar with Royce's recently published *Religious Aspect of Philosophy* (1885). At this early point Strong noted that, while Royce's system "seems, in one view, to save God's personality, it practically identifies man's personality with God's, which is subjective pantheism."[65] Having briefly encountered Royce's philosophy, Strong thought that Royce's scheme essentially amounted to pantheism. Interestingly, as was the case with Bowne, this accusation of pantheism later disappeared from Strong's theology text. This time the change came not in the mid-1890s but in the early 1900s. The seventh edition of Strong's *Systematic Theology* (1902) still included the statement suggesting that Royce's philosophy led to "subjective pantheism." However, in the final edition Strong at last removed this statement and instead simply questioned whether or not Royce's view "equally guarantees man's personality or leaves room for man's freedom, sin and guilt."[66] Royce himself never believed that his system was pantheistic or in any way led to pantheism.[67] Apparently Strong finally came to agree with Royce's self-assessment, but why did Strong change his opinion? It is possible that as Strong read Royce's later writings he concluded either that Royce had changed his view or that he had previously misunderstood Royce, but it is also possible that, after proposing the idea of ethical monism, Strong was less willing to accuse others of pantheism unless the evidence was overwhelming. Thus, although Strong changed his evaluation of Bowne simultaneously with his embrace of ethical monism, it may have taken Strong a number of years to reevaluate various philosophers in light of his own changing perspective. Another plausible explanation is that, in a predigital age, Strong's own earlier statement about Royce's philosophy may have escaped his notice when he was revising his theology book in the late 1890s. Regardless of the exact reasons for Strong's changed opinion about Royce and the timing of his revised comments, Strong clearly read and appreciated Royce's works. By the time the eighth edition of his *Systematic Theology* appeared, it contained substantive references to at least five of Royce's books.

However, Royce almost certainly was not a philosophical source that pushed Strong in the direction of ethical monism. After all, most of Royce's books appeared after Strong had already formulated his distinctive philosophical contribution. Still, it seems likely that Strong found in Royce a philosopher who understood and grappled with some of the same issues that led him to the discovery of ethical monism.

Although Royce and Strong traveled in very different circles, the two men shared a number of ideas and experiences. Both men were intrigued by the concept of philosophical idealism. Both were accused of teaching pantheism, and both vigorously denied the accuracy of such charges. Both Royce and Strong were very concerned about preserving the integrity of individual personalities within a monistic scheme—in fact, at times Strong appealed to Royce to argue for such a distinction. For example, on the one hand Strong criticized Spinoza and Hegel because he felt that they "deny self-consciousness when they make man a phenomenon of the infinite," but on the other hand, he noted favorably that "Royce likens the denier of personality to the man who goes outside his own house and declares that no one lives there because, when he looks in at the window, he sees no one inside."[68] Both Royce and Strong saw the futility of such attempts, and both wanted to preserve the idea of real personalities who exist in a monistic universe but are still responsible for their actions. One of Royce's contemporaries once described him as the philosopher who "has gone further in his study of human selfhood, in the attempt to reconcile personality and monism, than any other writer."[69]

In the final analysis, Strong was not and should not be characterized as an open follower of Royce, but he read Royce's books as they appeared at the end of the nineteenth century. In many ways Strong found in Royce a like-minded philosopher who wrestled with many of the same issues that Strong found intriguing.

Conclusion

Strong never cited any particular philosopher or theologian as directly influencing his development of ethical monism. However, various forms of philosophical idealism were in the air that Strong was breathing during the years leading up to his philosophical breakthrough. Strong left behind clear indications that he was reading and thinking about the philosophical systems of Fichte, Schelling, Hegel, Lotze, Bowne, Royce, and others during the years before and, especially in the case of Royce, immediately after he announced his discovery of ethical monism. The references to these men that appear in increasing numbers through the successive editions of Strong's *Systematic Theology* suggest that he viewed them as philosophical sparring partners who sharpened his thinking about issues related to human responsibility, personal existence, and ultimate reality—in short, about what he called ethical monism.

Strong's ethical monism developed not in an ideological vacuum but, rather, in the mind of a thoughtful theologian who was reading philosophical idealists of many stripes during the late nineteenth century. Although ethical monism was Strong's distinctive contribution to theology, it was in some ways also a new shade that Strong added to the philosophical idealist's palette.

CHAPTER 3

Ethical Monism as Both a Conclusion and a
Starting Point for Theology

WHEN STRONG RETURNED TO Rochester in September of 1872, he assumed his new role as president and professor of theology at the seminary. At this point, he was not an ethical monist. In fact, although the term *ethical monism* had been used by a handful of writers before Strong, he probably would not have recognized the phrase as a distinct philosophical term, much less have embraced it as his own.[1]

Strong's decision to adopt both the concept and the terminology of ethical monism was not the result of an overnight conversion—like most ideological shifts, his personal journey took place over time. In fact, although this chapter discusses Strong's earliest references to ethical monism, it is difficult to pin down exactly when he first embraced the idea. Strong himself never pointed to a eureka moment, yet a real change took place in his thinking. Although his journey to ethical monism was incremental and the seeds of ethical monism were planted years before he announced his discovery, at some point Strong experienced a genuine change of mind.

Strong's Early Rejection of All Types of Philosophical Monism

Several years before Strong became an ethical monist, he wrote several articles arguing against any kind of philosophical monism. Although Strong's theology was developing, he apparently did not envision that he would soon adopt and somewhat adapt the language of monism as he attempted to resolve lingering tensions within his own theological system.

While *Bibliotheca Sacra* has had a tendency to relocate, it was fairly stable during most of Strong's academic career. Beginning in the mid-1880s, the journal was published by Oberlin College, and it remained there throughout the balance of Strong's tenure at Rochester.[2] Although Oberlin was nominally Presbyterian, the school was more than happy to publish essays by prominent Baptists such as

46

Strong. In January 1888, for instance, the journal included an article by Strong titled "Modern Idealism," in which Strong described modern idealism as "the method of thought which . . . regards ideas as the only objects of knowledge and denies the independent existence of the external world."[3] Strong traced this idealistic "method of thought" back to English philosopher John Locke (1632–1704), and he discussed its development through the writings of Berkeley, Schelling, Fichte, Hegel, and others.

At this point in his career, Strong was opposed to the kind of idealism he saw becoming increasingly popular in academic circles, so he put forward a number of reasons for rejecting idealism as a valid explanation of the world. For example, Strong claimed that idealism is inconsistent with itself because it is forced to grant the existence of something "before ideas, and more than ideas, namely, the self."[4] Modern idealism, Strong argued, describes ideas as the only real objects of knowledge, but noted that those ideas could not possibly exist apart from a previously existing self that is able to think those ideas and is not itself merely an idea. According to Strong, such idealism is unable to hold together because it cannot live within its own terms. It is essentially self-refuting, or at least internally inconsistent.

Strong further noted that idealism confuses the conditions of external knowledge with the objects of that knowledge. Sensations and ideas are necessary conditions of external knowledge, but such things should not be confused with being the only real objects of external knowledge. Then, most interestingly, Strong argued against modern idealism by pointing out that it "is monistic in its whole conception of the universe."[5] Strong believed that modern idealism was intrinsically monistic, and without explaining why, he cited this as a good reason for rejecting it out of hand. In the late 1880s, Strong seems to have viewed philosophical monism as inherently and self-evidently erroneous.

In another article, published a few years later, Strong rejected the concept of monism in even clearer terms. In an article titled "Modern Exaggerations of Divine Immanence," Strong contended that an overemphasis on God's immanence inevitably leads to a whole host of theological problems. One, he suggested, was a tendency to undermine the reality of sin as a genuine moral evil. If God is too closely identified with the physical universe, then this would seem to undercut the biblical doctrine of sin and the concept of human responsibility: "Here we have the proof that monism is false. God and man are not of the same substance, else moral evil had been impossible. Every monistic system breaks in pieces when it attempts to deal with the fact of sin."[6] If God and humans are ultimately of the same substance, then it seems impossible for humans to sin lest the divine substance also be party to that sin. At this point Strong seems to have rejected, as he put it, "every monistic system" because of its inability to explain the reality of sin. As late as 1890, he saw this inability to explain the existence of sin in the world as one of the fatal weaknesses inherent in philosophical monism.

Strong's early dismissal of philosophical monism also appeared in the first edition of his *Systematic Theology* (1886). In a chapter discussing flawed explanations of the universe, Strong addressed what he believed to be three erroneous views: materialism, materialistic idealism, and pantheism. He gave reasons for rejecting each of these positions, but his discussion of pantheism is the most interesting. Strong defined pantheism as "that method of thought which conceives of the universe as the development of one intelligent and voluntary, yet impersonal, substance, which reaches consciousness only in man." He noted that pantheism "identifies God, not with each individual object in the universe, but with the totality of things." Strong admitted that pantheism contains several elements of truth, such as its affirmation of the intelligence of God and his immanence in the universe. However, he noted that pantheism's main weakness is its denial of God's personality and his transcendence over the created universe.[7]

Strong listed a number of other specific objections to pantheism based primarily on human experience and reason. Among these, he noted that pantheism assumes a unity of substance that not only is without proof but also is contrary to the natural sense of most people. Humans intuitively know that they are not God or parts of God but, rather, distinct personal beings. The "unity of substance" that Strong detected as inherent to pantheism is essentially philosophical monism. Pantheism is unavoidably and unequivocally monistic. Strong then went on to state that "any system of monism contradicts consciousness."[8] In Strong's mind, pantheism was necessarily monistic, and this was a major part of pantheism's undoing. At this point in his theological development, Strong still viewed every form of philosophical monism as conflicting with what humans innately know to be true about themselves. As he saw it, human self-consciousness effortlessly refutes "any system of monism."

Strong's all-inclusive public denial of monism held steady up through the fourth edition of his *Systematic Theology* (1893). In the fifth edition (1896) the first to incorporate the concept of ethical monism—Strong replaced his previous statement ("*any* system of monism contradicts consciousness") with a more qualified one: "*Many* systems of monism contradict consciousness; they confound harmony between two with absorption into one."[9] The change was a fairly subtle one—from "any" to "many"—but this rewording was necessary to avoid undercutting his own newly discovered key to theology. This use of less comprehensive terminology reflected the fact that Strong no longer believed that all forms of monism were to be rejected. Sometime in the early 1890s, Strong had changed his mind about philosophical monism.

Strong's Continuing Theological Development Leading to His Embrace of Ethical Monism

Strong's theology developed in a number of areas during his early years at Rochester. Chapter 1 discussed the first six of Strong's twelve theological lessons. Strong himself mentioned these lessons at appropriate points throughout the first two hundred pages of his autobiography. He then went back and summarized these six lessons before revealing lessons 7 through 10:

> My first doctrinal lesson, with regard to the depth and enormity of sin, was the result of contrasting myself with him [Christ]. The second lesson I learned, that only God can regenerate, was really the lesson that only Christ can make man like himself. The third truth I attained to was the truth that Christ's atonement is the only ground of acceptance with God and the only effectual persuasive to faith. The doctrine of the church followed next in order, for the church is, in the fourth place, composed of only those who believe in Christ. This faith is not an external matter of life; those who believe are joined inwardly to the Savior; union with Christ was the fifth great principle which I apprehended. Then [sixth] I began to see that this same Christ who had recreated believers had also created nature and that all science was the shining of his light.[10]

Strong's seventh doctrinal lesson had to do with the practice of prayer. He discovered that "prayer is an entering into the mind and will of Christ, so that the believer becomes partaker of his knowledge and power."[11] This lesson, like many of the others, focused on the person and work of Christ and how the believer relates to the second person of the Trinity.

Strong's eighth, ninth, and tenth theological lessons were directly related to his gradual embrace of ethical monism. As Strong readily admitted, the endeavor to comprehend Christ's deity, his atoning work, and his relationship to the world was an important part of his theological development. For a time, as he wrestled with the fact of Christ's deity and his atonement, Strong found it difficult to understand and reconcile these two concepts.[12] He agreed with Ezekiel Robinson's "realism in explaining the justification of the believer by virtue of his vital union with Christ and the condemnation of the race by virtue of the derivation of its life from Adam."[13] For Strong, such realism explained the "how" of imputation, but it did not really answer the question of divine justice. It still left questions in Strong's mind about how the sin of the human race could be justly imputed to Christ. In time, Strong came to see Christ's immanence in the human race as the foundation for Christ's bearing of human guilt. Initially, he saw this connection as stemming from Christ's incarnation, but eventually, Strong came to the conclusion that Christ's union with the human race must have predated his incarnation in order for the imputation of human sin to be just. As he put it, he came to see that "imputation resulted from a prior vital union." Though it took Strong a while to work out the exact nature and timing of this union, Strong believed this concept was one of his major contributions to theology. He wrote,

> If I have added anything to theological science, it is by my application of the realistic principle to the atonement.... I removed the imputation to Christ of the sin of the race from the region of arbitrariness and put it within the realm of reality and order. If Christ took our nature, he must have taken it with all its exposures and liabilities. Though the immaculate conception freed him from depravity, it still left him under the burden of guilt.[14]

Strong believed this application of the realistic principle to the atonement could help explain the relationship between Christ's personal holiness and his ability justly to bear the sin of the human race. Strong regarded this discovery to be his eighth theological lesson.

Having laid out this understanding of the atonement, Strong anticipated some criticism at the hands of dissenting theologians, yet it occurred to him that his application of the realistic principle to the atonement did not go far enough. In his autobiography, Strong wrote, "There flashed upon me with new meaning the previously acknowledged fact of Christ's creatorship." Strong began to draw conceptual lines between the creation of the human race and the doctrines of Christ's incarnation and atonement. In his ninth theological lesson, Strong came to believe that Christ's creation of humanity established a vital union between the Creator and his creatures that existed from the time of creation. This union, Strong now realized, had far-reaching theological implications. As he explained it, "Christ's union with the race in his incarnation is only the outward and visible expression of a prior union with the race which began when he created the race." Strong's ninth theological lesson was that Christ, because of his creation of the human race, is the very life of humanity, and through this connection to humanity, Christ is involved in the responsibility for human sin. Therefore, Strong concluded, Christ's atoning work is not merely possible but also necessary.[15]

Strong regarded his ninth theological lesson as his "second new and original contribution . . . to theology," but he still was not done fleshing out all of
the implications of his new understanding of Christ's relationship to humanity.
Strong's tenth theological lesson was closely related to the previous two, but it
took Christ's relationship to the human race a few steps further. Strong concluded that "Christ . . . is the life of humanity only as he is the life of the whole
universe." In other words, Christ's relationship to humanity stemming from
Creation is but a reflection of his vital relationship to the entire created order.
Strong explained this important transition in his thinking:

> I quickly saw that I must take another and a final step and must see in
> Christ not only the life and light of men but also the omnipresent and
> immanent God. . . . This general doctrine of Christ's identification with
> the race because he is the Creator, Upholder, and Life of the universe, I
> called ethical monism. . . . And this ethical monism is the last, and the most
> important, addition which I have made to theology. It is the tenth distinct
> advance step in my doctrinal thinking.[16]

In Strong's opinion, his final and most important theological lesson was his discovery of ethical monism.

Strong's Earliest Affirmations of Ethical Monism

Strong's writings do not provide a precise date when he first came to hold what
he eventually called ethical monism. In his autobiography, Strong states that the
concept of ethical monism "was so radical and novel that I hesitated long before
I ventured to publish it to the world."[17] Yet publish it he did, albeit in stages.

Prior to publishing directly on the subject, in early 1892 Strong mentioned his
growing interest in philosophical monism in a private letter to fellow Northern
Baptist leader Alvah Hovey (1820–1903). Hovey had recently published a book
addressing, among other things, the relationship of God to nature.[18] Hovey was
concerned about what he saw as a theological drift toward monism, and his book
was in part a rebuttal of theological revisionism.

In a letter dated February 7, 1892, Strong wrote to Hovey about Hovey's rejection of all forms of monism and philosophical idealism:

> Dear Dr. Hovey, I thank you heartily for the copy of your new book of
> "Studies in Ethics and Religion." I congratulate you on its handsome ap-
> pearance. I am under special obligations for the second essay, which I have

read with unusual interest. The subject of the relation of God to nature has been and upon which I have had very anxious thought. Your treatment is very helpful and suggestive. I am trying to work my way through it and still come out an orthodox believer, but I see much to attract in the doctrine of Lotze and Schurman. It seems to me more and more that this doctrine, in its philosophical and theological aspects, is the great speculative question with which we shall have to deal with for the next twenty years. I find all the recent philosophers ranged on one side. . . . If we wish to be popular, I am afraid we shall have to be Monists. Ah, if it were not for sin, and for the Holy Spirit who convinces us of sin, I almost think we might be! I wish I could talk this matter over with you. With revered thanks, I am, ever faithfully yours, A. H. Strong.[19]

Interestingly, at this point Strong noted the potential for monism to lead one away from orthodox belief, and he thanked Hovey for his helpful discussion of the subject. Yet within a short time Strong began publishing ideas that signaled his own affinity for a somewhat new monistic understanding of God's relationship to nature.

"Christ in Creation" Article (1892)

In the fall of 1892 Strong wrote an article titled "Christ in Creation" that was published in both the *Examiner* and the *Magazine of Christian Literature*.[20] In this article, Strong did not use the term *ethical monism*, but he laid out most of its basic elements.[21] For example, Strong described Christ as "the life of man," and he wrote about the importance of understanding Christ's "relation to the universe of which we form a part." Strong knew that he was venturing into theologically uncharted waters: "Some of the views I present may be thought new; but the unfolding of the subject will certainly enlarge our conceptions of the unsearchable riches of Christ." In fact, he began the article by noting, "Theology is a progressive science, not because the truth itself changes, but because human apprehension and statement of the truth improve from age to age."[22] Strong believed that his own apprehension of the truth had improved and that this article was a more accurate statement of important theological truths.

Even at this early stage, Strong seems to have realized that his ideas bore some similarities to both philosophical idealism and pantheism, so he sought to distinguish his understanding from these two theories. He presented his new understanding of Christ's creatorship not only as different from subjective idealism and pantheism but also as an antidote to both of these wrong ideas. Strong, in fact, claimed that "the moment we recognize Christ as the principle of self-consciousness and of self-determination in God, we clear ourselves from Pantheism as well as from a will-less and soul-less Idealism."[23] With this statement and others, Strong preemptively tried to show the dissimilarity between his new theological discovery and both pantheism and philosophical idealism.

Strong also acknowledged that "evolution is a great truth," explaining that "nature is the living garment of the Deity," "nature is the omnipresent Christ manifesting God to creatures," and Christ himself "is the principle of evolution."[24] Most of the major features of Strong's ethical monism appear in this 1892 article. The only important thing missing from the article is Strong's name for his new idea.[25]

Having expressed the main features of ethical monism in print, Strong then waited for two years, as he put it, "trembling on the brink," before using the term *ethical monism* to announce more formally his theological discovery to the world. Strong later explained both his initial hesitation and his final decision to go public with his theological discovery: "At last I concluded that intellectual honesty required me to disclose my views even if they cost me my position as theological teacher. I felt that I could make no further progress without printing the conclusions I had already reached."[26] Strong realized his ethical monism would be perceived as both novel and controversial, and he apparently thought this new idea might cost him his job at the seminary, yet he decided to publish his views.

"Ethical Monism" Articles (1894)

In 1894 Strong finally gave his new idea a name when he published a series of three articles titled "Ethical Monism."[27] In these articles, Strong pointed out that modern thought was moving steadily in the direction of monism, and he illustrated this trend with examples from the fields of science, literature, theology and philosophy.

For his first example, Strong cited Thomas Chamberlin (1843–1928), who was then head professor of geology and dean of the College of Science at the newly established University of Chicago.[28] Working in one of the hard sciences, Chamberlin had come to embrace the principle that any supreme Being that exists must necessarily be confined to the universe rather than outside of it in any way. Although Strong did not think Chamberlin intended to espouse pantheism, he rightly thought that Chamberlin failed to place enough emphasis on the doctrine of divine transcendence.[29] Strong cited Chamberlin not because he agreed with the exact way in which Chamberlin expressed the concept of monism—he did not. For Strong, Chamberlin provided clear evidence that leading scholars in the natural sciences were beginning to embrace a form of monism.

For his next example, Strong pointed to the writings of the recently deceased poet Robert Browning (1812–89). Strong regarded Browning as a monist of the best sort: "[Browning] is a monist, but an Ethical Monist; a believer that God and man are of one substance; but a hater of pantheism, which denies God's transcendence and separate personality."[30] Although not completely uncritical of the famous poet, Strong was in basic agreement with Browning on the issue of monism.[31] According to Strong, even an English poet had come to see this new truth about God and his relationship to the world.

For his third example, Strong cited Lutheran theologian Isaak August Dorner (1809–84). Strong quoted Dorner as saying that "the unity of essence in God and man is the great discovery of the present age. . . . The characteristic feature of all recent Christologies is the endeavor to point out the essential unity of the divine and the human."[32] This sounded a lot like pantheism, yet Strong regarded Dorner to be not a pantheist but, rather, "a great name in modern theology."[33] Apparently some of the great theologians had embraced a form of monism.

For his final example, Strong pointed to German idealist Rudolf Hermann Lotze (1817–81) as proof that monism was the leading philosophy of the day. Strong claimed that "no thinker of recent times has had greater influence in this direction than has Lotze. He is both a monist and objective idealist. Yet he holds with equal tenacity to the distinction between the divine personality and the human personality." Once again, Strong did not find Lotze's monism to be particularly troubling. He asserted that Lotze "intends his monism to be an Ethical Monism, by which I mean simply a monism that conserves the ethical interests of mankind."[34]

In offering these examples from various fields of endeavor, Strong had managed to label at least two of these men (Browning and Lotze) proponents of ethical monism. Strong believed he had demonstrated that great minds involved in the pursuit of truth from different angles were now coming to similar conclusions—conclusions that essentially affirmed his own discovery of ethical monism.

Having cited these four examples, Strong concluded, "It is not too much to say that the monistic philosophy, in its various forms, holds at present almost undisputed sway in our American universities. Harvard and Yale, Brown and Cornell, Princeton and Rochester, Toronto and Ann Arbor, Boston and Chicago, are all teaching it." He realized that monism was becoming increasingly popular within the world of academia, and he feared that the church would miss the opportunity to shape "the ruling idea of our time." Addressing believers and especially Christian preachers, Strong asked two revealing questions:

> This universal tendency toward monism, is it a wave of unbelief set agoing by an evil intelligence in order to overwhelm and swamp the religion of Christ? Or is it a mighty movement of the Spirit of God, giving to thoughtful men, all unconsciously to themselves, a deeper understanding of truth and preparing the way for the reconciliation of diverse creeds and parties by disclosing their hidden ground of unity?

Strong knew many thoughtful Christians viewed every form of monism as part of a "wave of unbelief" that threatened the Christian faith. His second question proposed an alternative understanding of this modern trend toward monism, and Strong indicated that the second question represented his own view of the opportunity that now lay before the church: "I confess that I have come to believe the latter alternative to be possibly, and even probably, the correct one, and I am inclined to welcome the new philosophy as a most valuable helper in interpreting the word and the works of God." Then with increasing boldness Strong went on to explain what he thought was as stake: "Monism is, without much doubt, the philosophy of the future, and the only question would seem to be whether it shall be an ethical and Christian, or a non-ethical and anti-Christian monism."[35]

Strong believed that Christians needed to embrace this new philosophy, and he warned of dire consequences should the church reject what was quickly becoming "the ruling idea" in many leading universities:

> If we refuse to recognize this new movement of thought and to capture it for Christ, we may find that materialism and pantheism perversely launch their craft upon the tide and compel it to further their progress. Let us tentatively accept the monistic principle and give to it a Christian interpretation. Let us not be found fighting against God. Let us use the new light that is given us, as a means of penetrating more deeply into the meaning of Scripture. Let us see in this forward march of thought a sign that Christ and his kingdom are conquering and to conquer.[36]

No doubt this statement includes a bit of hyperbole, but it also reveals Strong's conviction about the importance of this issue and his optimism about the good that might come if the church embraced a Christian, in other words an *ethical*, form of philosophical monism.

Strong explained ethical monism by contrasting it with "forms of monism which do not conserve man's ethical interests." He felt that any kind of monism that emphasized God's immanence in the world, to the exclusion of his transcendence, failed to preserve both human freedom and responsibility for sin.[37] In contrast to this, Strong described ethical monism as "a monism which maintains both the freedom of man and the transcendence of God."[38] Strong recognized that monism apart from divine transcendence necessarily leads to some form of pantheism in which God is "only an impersonal and necessary force." In such a system, humans do not possess any kind of real freedom or personal responsibility. In contrast, "The Ethical Monism, then, for which I contend, is not deterministic monism; it is the monism of free-will, the monism in which personality, both human and divine, sin and righteousness, God and the world, remain."[39]

Strong rightly thought that some Christians would oppose monism no matter how he qualified it, but he tried to explain why such Christians should consider the possibility that ethical monism might be true. He pointed out that human apprehension of truth changes over time; older theories are eventually replaced by newer ones, which people come to deem superior. He offered the following illustration: "Modern astronomy supplanted the ancient by showing that the heliocentric theory gave a simpler and more complete explanation of the movements of the solar system than the geocentric did." He then drew the comparison: "So the monistic philosophy rests its claim to acceptance upon its ability to solve the problems of nature, or the soul, and of the Bible, more simply and completely than the theory of dualism ever could. The test of truth in a theory . . . is not that it can be itself explained, but that it is capable of explaining other things."[40] Strong believed that his ethical monism helped explain physical, intellectual, and moral problems better than more traditional and perhaps more orthodox understandings of the universe ever could.

Strong thought ethical monism supplied helpful answers to some difficult questions, but he also knew that monism raised some questions of its own. He wanted to answer some questions he anticipated, such as, "How can there be any finite personality or freedom or responsibility, if all persons, as well as all things, are but forms or modifications of the divine?" To put it more directly, "How can we be monists, and yet be faithful to man's ethical interests?" In keeping with several of his key doctrinal lessons, Strong found the answer to these questions in the person of Christ. He pointed out that Christ "is of the substance of God, yet he possesses a distinct personality." He then answered these questions with a question of his own: "If in the one substance of God there are three *infinite* personalities, why may there not be in that same substance multitudinous *finite* personalities? No believer in the Trinity can consistently deny the possibility of this."[41] Strong himself saw this as more than a possibility. It was the heart of his ethical monism. Strong believed that since God is a single substance but three distinct persons, those who affirm the doctrine of the Trinity have already conceded the theoretical possibility that the universe and all the persons it contains could be part of that one substance as well. As Strong explained it, "God has limited and circumscribed himself in giving life to finite personalities within the bounds of his own being."[42] This was a clear departure from the traditional, orthodox understanding of God, and Strong knew it, but he believed the time had come for theology to take a new step forward in keeping with the progress of doctrinal development.

Despite Strong's comment about the possibility of "multitudinous finite personalities" within the one substance of God, in his more direct treatments of the doctrine of the Trinity Strong remained essentially orthodox. Ethical monism never seems to have actually corrupted his understanding of the Trinity to the degree that it logically might have.[43]

As he came to the end of this first series of articles, Strong summarized his new and rather controversial idea: "Let me then sum up my monistic doctrine by saying: There is but one substance—God. The eternal Word whom in his historic manifestation we call Christ, is the only complete and perfect expression of God. The universe is Christ's finite and temporal manifestation of God." Then once more he contrasted ethical monism with pantheism:

> This is not pantheism, for pantheism is not simply monism, but monism coupled with two denials, the denial of the personality of God and the denial of the transcendence of God. My doctrine takes the grain of truth in pantheism, namely, its monistic element, while it maintains in opposition to pantheism the personality of God and the personality of man, though it regards the latter as related to the former, somewhat as the persons of the Trinity are related to the one all-inclusive divine personality.[44]

Strong was confident that his ethical monism embraced the truth that could be found in pantheism while rejecting the aspects of pantheism that were false. He believed that his discovery of ethical monism was nothing short of a Copernican revolution that needed to be embraced by the Christian community. This doctrine would change the way people thought about theology, philosophy, and humanity's relationship to God through Christ.[45] It was something that his fellow theologians needed to accept and incorporate into their theological systems.

"Ethical Monism Once More" Articles (1895)

About a year after publishing his first three-part series on ethical monism, Strong wrote another three-part series on the subject, titled "Ethical Monism

Once More." A number of readers had, in Strong's opinion, misunderstood his earlier discussion, so Strong again tried to clarify exactly what he meant by *ethical monism*.

Strong explained that this was in fact a *dualistic* monism. The terms *dualism* and *monism* have often been contrasted with each other,[46] but Strong saw the former term as an important modifier of the latter: "Whatever else we may be, or may not be, we must be dualists through and through, and we must never give up our dualism, because dualism is not only the necessary condition of ethics, but is also inseparably bound up with many, if not all, of those great truths which constitute the essence of the Christian scheme."[47] Strong's ethical monism did not completely rule out the concept of dualism. In fact, it necessarily included dualism, and Strong sensed the need to emphasize this point.

Strong believed in two kinds of dualism: a dualism of matter and mind and a dualism of man and God. Both kinds of dualism involved postulating the existence of a soul—in distinction from matter in the one case and in distinction from God in the other. He saw such distinctions as reflections of the truth he called "psychological dualism." Strong asserted that psychological dualism was completely compatible with philosophical or metaphysical monism because the two terms addressed different kinds of existence. He attempted to resolve the apparent tension in the phrase *dualistic monism*:

> Dualistic monism is not a contradiction in terms, because the dualism and the monism are asserted of different things. . . . While dualism truly asserts that matter and mind, man and God, are two, not one, monism with equal truth asserts that matter and mind, man and God, have underground connections and a common life, because all things, humanity included, live, move, and have their being in God.[48]

For Strong ethical monism was a kind of dualistic monism that acknowledged the existence of personality in distinction from matter. Further, his ethical monism acknowledged the existence of multiple personalities while affirming the existence of a single substance: God.

As he had in the earlier set of articles, Strong once again sensed the need to emphasize the differences between ethical monism and pantheism: "This Ethical Monism is not pantheism, because it maintains the separate personality of man and the absolute transcendence of God. . . . Pantheism is indeed monism, but monism is not necessarily pantheism." Strong believed this last statement was true precisely because his ethical monism was a *dualistic* monism and pantheism rejected the dualism his system entailed. Strong laid out the differences between ethical monism and pantheism largely in terms of pantheism's denial of the dualistic element that ethical monism required: "Pantheism ... does not admit dualism into its system; Ethical Monism embraces it as of the very essence of truth."[49]

Strong also faulted pantheism for viewing the universe as coterminous with God and thus confining God to the universe while denying his freedom. Strong himself was willing to describe the universe as a manifestation of God, but he did not actually identify the universe, or any being or thing in the universe, with God. As he put it, "God is not any single thing in the universe, nor is he the whole universe put together, but he is infinitely above all and he infinitely transcends all."[50] Although to some Strong's ethical monism might seem to obliterate any kind of Creator-creature distinction, Strong ostensibly affirmed such a distinction.

Strong believed that some readers had misjudged his earlier articles on ethical monism because they misunderstood what he meant by the word *substance*. When Strong used this word, he did not mean it in any materialistic sense. In fact, concerning those who thought ethical monism meant that God occupied space and divided himself into parts, Strong replied that such an interpretation was completely against what he intended. Instead, Strong used the word *substance* in a nonmaterial sense: "There is but one substance, one underlying reality, the infinite and eternal Spirit of God, who contains within his own being the ground and principle of all other being." For Strong, this one substance, God, is a spirit being in whom all things exist. All things that exist in the universe are manifestations of God, but they are not God or parts of God in any sense. Rather, God is the ground of their existence in much the same way that human volitions are manifestations of a human mind without being parts of that mind.[51]

After briefly discussing how secondary causes operate in the universe, Strong noted that all secondary causes are actually the work of the one great First Cause. He then explained that ethical monism finds this First Cause in Christ himself. Christ is, in fact, the one who alone makes this world a universe.[52]

As he had mentioned in the earlier series of articles, Strong once again pointed to various advances in science as confirming Christian doctrines. For example, he thought that advances in the study of heredity helped explain the doctrine of original sin. More broadly speaking, he believed that evolution enabled believers better to understand the development of the human race. Unlike many of his potential readers, Strong viewed Darwin and Huxley not as enemies of the faith but, rather, as helping explain some of the great truths found in Scripture. To those who might look with suspicion at his understanding of the relationship between evolution and the Christian faith, Strong asked, "Why should we

regret the publication and acceptance of the doctrine of evolution, if it reveals
to us the method of Christ's working both in nature and in grace?" He then
reaffirmed his conviction that "Nature reveals a present God, and evolution is
the common method of his working."[53] By viewing evolution as God's means
of bringing about his will in the universe, Strong embraced the basic principles
of Darwinism and, in fact, saw evolutionary principles as compatible with and
confirming of his ethical monism.

Strong recognized that some of his critics feared that his doctrine of ethical
monism tended to identify God with every stick and stone in the universe, not to
mention with depraved humans and even the devil himself. He pointed out that
such fears were completely unnecessary, asserting that the plants, animals, and
even fallen beings in the universe are but "varied manifestations of [God's] creative wisdom or of his punitive justice."[54] He then drew an important distinction
between such manifestations of God and the incarnation of God. He explained
that God has been incarnated in Christ alone. All other things and beings in the
universe are manifestations of God's will, but they are not to be equated with
the incarnation of God.[55] Strong saw this distinction between manifestation and
incarnation as lying behind the fact that humans remain fully responsible for the
physical and moral evil in the universe.[56] Although in Strong's view the universe
is evolving according to God's plan, human individuals remain responsible for
all that is wicked in this world. Thus, in Strong's thinking, ethical monism maintains the ethical responsibility of all humanity.

Having argued that the universe in only a manifestation of God, Strong then
asserted that "God's regular volitions . . . constitute nature."[57] He suggested that,
in place of the "old theory" that God *created* nature and even violent persons and
animals, one should embrace the fact that God has chosen to *manifest* himself in
nature and such creatures. For Strong, God's manifestation of himself in nature
and even violent creatures is best understood in light of ethical monism and the
Darwinian explanation of evolutionary progress.

Strong thought that his ethical monism helped provide a thoroughly Christian explanation of evolution. Nonetheless, he confessed that, at the end of the
day, he accepted ethical monism not because of how it helped explain evolution
but, rather, because of the light it shed on the doctrine of the atonement. Over
time Strong had become increasingly uncomfortable with the idea of the imputation of guilt from one person to another. He spoke disdainfully about "an
external and mechanical transfer" of guilt, which seemed to him unjust. Eventually Strong had come to a new understanding of the atonement: "It was a great
day for me when I first saw that there was a natural union of Christ with all men

which preceded the incarnation—that all men in fact were created and had their being in him, and that therefore he who was the ground and principle of their life, though personally pure, must bear their sins and iniquities."[58] This view was quite different from the more common understanding of the atonement, and Strong fully recognized this fact.

Strong noted that three main objections had been presented against his understanding of the atonement. First, some argued that Strong's view made the atoning work of Christ compulsory rather than free. In reply, Strong pointed out that his view simply moved the time of Christ's original commitment to the atonement further back, making it contemporaneous with creation. In other words, in Strong's view the atonement was just as free as in the more traditional view; his view merely connected Christ's free decision to provide atonement to the act of creation, rather than to the act of incarnation. The freedom of the decision remained the same; only the timing of that free decision changed. Strong believed this change resulted in a more consistent understanding of the atonement: "I am persuaded that only when we regard Christ's suffering for sin in the flesh as the culmination and expression of his natural relation to humanity can we deliver his atonement from the charge of arbitrariness or claim for it the confidence of thoughtful men."[59] In Strong's opinion, his view made the atonement more certain and more attractive to modern sensibilities.

Second, some critics objected that, by disconnecting the atonement from the incarnation, Strong's view made the atonement both eternal and universally effective for both men and angels. To this, Strong replied that he affirmed that the atonement was in some sense eternal or perpetual. As he saw it, a loving and holy God must always suffer due to the existence of sin. Speaking more personally, he confessed, "I need a present atonement as much as the patriarchs did. The knowledge that Christ now suffers for my sin is the strongest motive to keep me from my sin." Concerning the possible atonement of demons, Strong admitted that Christ suffers on account of both wicked men and demons because he is the ground of their being and the source of their life.[60] Yet, he did not believe that any demons would actually be redeemed. His explanation for why demons would not be saved amounted to an acknowledgment of God's free choice to save whomever he wishes.

The third objection posed against Strong's understanding of the atonement was that his view made the atonement itself impossible, because it made Christ no more divine than any other man.[61] Strong answered this objection by reaffirming his belief in the full deity of Christ and by arguing that his own view greatly simplified the doctrine of the person of Christ: "We need now no complicated theory of the two natures and of the union between them. We have at the same time and in the same Being complete and sinless humanity combined with suffering and atoning divinity."[62] No doubt for many of Strong's readers this statement raised more questions than it answered,[63] but Strong believed that with this and other replies he had answered the main objections others had raised against his view of the atonement.

Strong concluded this second series of articles on ethical monism by summarizing the doctrine of ethical monism. He described it once more as "psychological dualism combined with metaphysical or philosophical monism." He also expressed his hope that he had convinced his readers that ethical monism was "thoroughly Christian" because it honored Christ by recognizing him as Lord of all.[64]

Early Responses to Strong's Ethical Monism

Responses to Strong's announcement were not long in coming. Strong's first series of articles had appeared in November 1894. The following month, the editor of the *McMaster University Monthly* wrote, "The rumor that Dr. Strong, of Rochester Theol. Seminary, had adopted Monism and was adapting his theology to this new view has been confirmed by three articles from his pen in the *Examiner* on Ethical Monism." The writer then offered a number of quotes from Strong's recent articles that he thought both summarized Strong's position and proved it to be untenable before concluding that "both philosophic and theological mists hang over [Strong's] view, and these must be cleared away by much careful thinking, before many will be inclined to adopt it." Interestingly, he also noted that Strong's ethical monism was not completely original because its roots could be found in German thought.[65] This early mention of Strong's ethical monism was necessarily brief. In many ways, however, it indicated the kind of response Strong could expect.

In December 1894, Alvah Hovey (1820–1903) wrote a series of three short articles in response to Strong's articles of the previous month.[66] By 1894, Hovey was near the end of his long career as president of Newton Theological Institution, and as one of his biographers put it, "probably no other American Baptist ever spoke with more *ex cathedra* influence than he."[67] Hovey was a conservative theologian of solid New England stock; his influence and his orthodoxy were unquestionable—and he found Strong's announcement about ethical monism alarming.

From the outset, Hovey expressed his admiration for Strong, for example, "In respect to the essential principles of the Christian religion he [Strong] has always been firm as a rock." Hovey also rightly recognized that Strong's embrace of ethical monism sprang from a "strong desire to set the truths of Christianity in a clearer rational light, and to establish them on surer philosophical foundations."[68] However, although he admired Strong's intention, Hovey did not share Strong's optimism about the benefits that would flow from a widespread adoption of ethical monism. In his three articles, Hovey discussed four main difficulties he believed monism, including Strong's ethical monism, necessarily entailed. Taken together, these difficulties ultimately led Hovey to reject Strong's ethical monism.

The first of these difficulties stemmed from the fact that monism seems to depict God as both infinitely complex and internally conflicted.[69] Rather than a God who is unified and ultimately simple, monism envisions a deity whose substance extends throughout the material world and includes all things.[70] Hovey noted that if the entire universe is composed of divine volitions, then such volitions are necessarily conflicted because some elements of the universe are inherently antagonistic toward other elements in the universe. Thus, God himself must be internally conflicted. Hovey also pointed out that such a vision of God as substantially extended throughout the universe might easily provide an excuse for idolatry: if everything is part of God's substance, the worship of material objects may just be another way of worshipping the deity.

Hovey's second difficulty with monism was that, in his opinion, monism does not really view Christ as "the complete and perfect expression of God." Hovey pointed out that, if the divine substance is divided into myriad finite beings and things, then everything is an expression of God, and Christ no longer holds the unique position afforded to him in the Gospels:

> If then the monistic philosophy is true, it cannot be said of the historical Saviour that He was "a complete expression of God," and the words of Jesus must be understood in a non-natural sense as referring to the invisible Word as well as the incarnate Logos, or, in a very restricted sense, as meaning, perhaps, that he who has seen me, as thou hast, has seen God in so far as He is a Father to mankind (or to me).[71]

This tendency of monism to deny the unique position to Christ as the perfect and complete expression of God seems in conflict with the biblical record.

Hovey's third difficulty with monism was that monism envisions created things as divine volitions, and finite spirits as circumscriptions of the divine substance, and this ultimately leads to significant problems with one's understanding of sin and human responsibility. Hovey believed monism necessarily implied that "things are divine volitions, regular and habitual, but finite spirits are the divine substance, circumscribed and individualized, yet acting freely and often wickedly." Hovey explained this another way: "The divine life as a whole, moving in volitions which represent the one all-embracing consciousness, is seen in the changes of nature, but the divine life circumscribed and acting as finite spirits is free, and brings strife and sin into the life of God." He argued that, even if monism were the trend in modern philosophy, it needed to be rejected because it did not exalt or improve one's view of God, and it did not help resolve the problem of sin.[72]

Hovey admitted that by tacking the qualifier *ethical* in front of *monism* Strong was attempting to avoid these kinds of problems. However, he thought that the overall tendency of monistic philosophy was too strong to be held in check by a mere adjective: "We cannot easily suppress a fear that the logical tendency of monism is to deny human responsibility by referring it to God, the only real being. . . . The more strictly the human spirit is identified with the divine substance or life, the more difficult will it be to imagine it guilty of wrong doing."[73] In the end, Hovey thought that the tendency of monism to swallow everything up in God made it impossible to hold humans guilty of sin. Monism, even as qualified by Strong, could not be reconciled with biblical statements about human responsibility and guilt.

Hovey's fourth difficulty with monism was more general. In his final article, Hovey claimed that monism lacked biblical support and was, in fact, inconsistent with biblical teaching.[74] He thought it was clear that Strong had come to embrace ethical monism not by way of Scripture but by means of philosophy, yet Strong had put forward a few biblical texts that he thought favored monism. Hovey examined three of these texts (John 1:3–4, 15:5–6; Col 1:16–17) and concluded that none of them actually supported a monistic interpretation of the world.

He pointed out that Strong had misread the Greek punctuation in John 1:3–4 and therefore had misappropriated the text. In John 15:5–6, Hovey noted that the branches attached to the vine were not all inclusive of everyone or everything in the universe. Instead, in this passage Christ was speaking about his disciples, or at least those who professed to be his disciples. Concerning Colossians 1:16–17, Hovey argued that Paul was talking about Christ's creation of the world. The apostle was saying that the world came into existence through Christ and is held together by him. This had nothing to do with philosophical monism. As Hovey commented, "Dr. Strong is therefore right in insisting upon *creation*, though it is difficult to grasp his notion of the act, if it is anything more than a series of modifications in the One Divine substance." With regard to the Colossians passage he also wrote, "Monism seems to be off its true base when it proposes to vindicate the fact of creation. It would be better for it to drop the word and satisfy itself with teaching the reality of change or modification in the substance of the self-existent and only being."[75] At the end of his third article, Hovey concluded that not a single passage of Scripture put forward by Strong ultimately supported monism and that the consistent message of Scripture seemed to place an infinite gulf between the Creator and the things created. Although Hovey respected Strong as a fellow laborer in the Gospel ministry, he believed that Strong had made a significant misstep in his adoption of ethical monism.

Strong appears never to have replied directly to Hovey's criticisms in any of his published works. However, just a few years after Hovey's articles appeared, Strong delivered an interesting address in honor of Hovey's fifty years of ministry at Newton Theological Institution. In this speech, Strong surveyed the changes in the field of theology over the past fifty years. The presence of Hovey and the occasion notwithstanding, Strong held little back as he took the opportunity to press once again his views on ethical monism. Without using the exact phrase *ethical monism*, Strong asserted that the current generation was coming to recognize the great truth of God's immanence in the world. He claimed that, while the theology of fifty years ago had virtually forgotten about the immanence of God, recent theologians had rediscovered this doctrine in the past half century. In recent decades, he asserted, believers had come to realize afresh that God is immanent in the world and that this immanent God is none other than Christ himself. Therefore, there exists a Christian form of monism.[76] One can only wonder what Hovey thought as he listened to Strong use a speech in his honor to argue for ideas that he had criticized in print just a few years earlier.

The summer after Hovey's last article appeared, another critical but even-handed response to Strong's first three articles appeared in the *Methodist Review*.[77] Adolphus J. F. Behrends (1839–1900) had graduated from Rochester Theological Seminary shortly after Strong, and the two men had known each other for some three decades. In fact, when Strong left the First Baptist Church of Cleveland in 1872, to take up the post as president of the seminary, the church called Behrends as their next pastor.[78] In his article evaluating ethical monism, Behrends indicated that he knew and respected his ministerial predecessor, but he spoke freely about his concerns regarding Strong's ethical monism.

Behrends described Strong's articles as "startling in their significance." He noted, "That they have been read with incredulous amazement is very plain;

and that their influence is regarded with alarm, as likely to be very injurious, is evident from the criticism which they have already received." No doubt this last statement was a reference to the articles by the editor of the *McMaster University Monthly* and by Alvah Hovey. Behrends pointed out that Baptists have not historically demonstrated any inclination toward philosophical pantheism, and he viewed Strong's writings as having the potential to begin a theological revolution among Baptists.[79]

Behrends readily confessed that Strong was not a pantheist, and for this much he was thankful, but he believed that pantheism was the logical and inevitable outcome of Strong's ethical monism. He summed up Strong's theory as including four major ideas: (1) there is but one substance—God; (2) there are no second causes in nature; (3) as in the Trinity, there are three infinite personalities in one substance, so in the same numerical substance there may be multitudinous finite personalities; and (4) Christ is the natural life of humanity, that is, its substance, and it follows that he was responsible for the sin committed by his own members. In reply to such statements, Behrends objected, "When [Strong] says that he is not a pantheist I believe him; but . . . I am constrained to assume that his language does not fit his thought, and that he would and must repudiate the inevitable implications of his statements."[80] Behrends then examined each of these ideas in some detail, pointing out where each went astray, and concluded,

> One thing is plain—he who accepts the monism commended in these articles must be prepared to pay a heavy price. There are many things in the articles which are superbly said and which every devout man will most heartily indorse. But there is a dead fly in the precious ointment. . . . I cannot regard them as anything but subversive. I dread their influence upon our young men, who will not stop where the author does.[81]

In the end, Behrends appreciated Strong's desire to give unity to thought and his desire to see a stronger ethical connection between God and humanity—in fact, he did not even object to the term *ethical monism*. However, he believed that the ground of unity between God and humans should be found in God's will rather than in his substance. Behrends thought that Strong was pursuing the right general idea but that he had wrongly linked the concept of monism to the substance of God. As Behrends said in the final line of the article, "I like the text, but I do not like the sermon."[82] In this Behrends was not alone. Many others who heard "the sermon" went away shaking their heads and thinking that the preacher had somehow missed the mark.

Ethical Monism in Strong's *Systematic Theology*

Appearing about the same time that Strong began to embrace ethical monism, the fourth edition of Strong's *Systematic Theology* (1893) contained no trace of his new theological discovery. This soon changed, however, as subsequent editions appeared.

In the preface to the fifth edition of his *Systematic Theology* (1896), Strong indicated that this new edition contained a number of minor corrections and a few additional references, but the substance of the volume "remain[ed] unchanged," as he put it, "with four exceptions . . . where the principle of Ethical Monism is adopted."[83] Strong indicated that the changes reflecting his adoption of ethical monism appeared on pages 51, 203, 205, and 413.

The first of these changes appeared at the beginning of a chapter titled "Erroneous Explanations of the Facts."[84] In this chapter in subsequent editions Strong directly discussed ethical monism as a way of understanding the universe and its relationship to God. In an introductory paragraph, Strong listed four major theories addressed in the chapter: materialism, materialistic idealism, pantheism, and ethical monism. In this initial summary, Strong defined ethical monism as follows:

> Universe = Finite, partial, graded manifestation of the divine Life; Matter being God's self-limitation under the law of necessity, Humanity being God's self-limitation under the law of freedom, Incarnation and Atonement being God's self-limitations under the law of grace. Metaphysical Monism, or the doctrine of one Substance, Principle, or Ground of Being, is consistent with Psychological Dualism, or the doctrine that the soul is personally distinct from matter on the one hand and from God on the other.[85]

Although Strong laid out this preliminary definition of ethical monism and discussed the other three theories (materialism, materialistic idealism, and pantheism) at length in the pages that followed, for some reason he ended the chapter without ever returning to the topic of ethical monism. This apparent oversight continued until the eighth edition of his *Systematic Theology* (1907), when he finally added a separate discussion of ethical monism at the end of the chapter, now retitled "Erroneous Explanations, and Conclusion."

This chapter, as it appears in the final edition, contains Strong's mature and carefully crafted discussion of ethical monism.[86] Here Strong defines ethical monism as "that method of thought which holds to a single substance, ground, or principle of being, namely, God, but which also holds to the ethical facts of God's transcendence as well as his immanence, and of God's personality as

distinct from, and as guaranteeing, the personality of man."[87] In affirming the
existence of "a single substance," this definition maintains a form of ontological
monism. However, Strong believed that his insistence on the personality of man
as distinct from God's personality was why his philosophical perspective could
rightly be called *ethical* monism.[88]

Strong thought that biblical passages about God's omnipresence by implication taught his own view of divine immanence. Therefore, Strong believed that
support for his understanding of divine immanence could be found throughout
Scripture. He cited texts such as Psalm 139:7, Jeremiah 23:23–24, and Acts 17:27–
28 as examples supporting his position.[89] Strong then cited a few biblical passages
he thought implied an understanding of divine transcendence similar to his own,
including 1 Kings 8:27, Psalm 113:5, and Isaiah 57:15.[90] In addition to Scripture,
Strong claimed that revered theologians such as Augustine and Anselm also
supported his understanding of God's relationship to the universe.[91] Although
he did not actually claim that Augustine and Anselm taught ethical monism,
he implied that they embraced the essence of his philosophical position. Strong
then discussed ethical monism under four main points, each treated below: (1)
metaphysical monism is qualified by psychological dualism; (2) the universe is a
manifestation of the divine life; (3) divine immanence guarantees individuality
in the universe; and (4) Christology is the key to understanding the universe.[92]

Metaphysical Monism Is Qualified by Psychological Dualism

In his first point, Strong confessed that ethical monism bore some similarity to
pantheism in that both philosophical positions hold that "God is in all things
and that all things are in God." For Strong this was the one great element of
truth in pantheism, but he also argued that this "scientific unity" is consistent
with the facts of ethics, namely, with the fourfold concept of "man's freedom,
responsibility, sin and guilt." In Strong's mind this meant that "Metaphysical
Monism, or the doctrine of one substance, ground, or principle of being, is necessarily qualified by Psychological Dualism, or the doctrine that the soul is personally distinct from matter on the one hand, and from God on the other."[93] In
other words, ethical monism acknowledges a kind of natural unity between God
and humanity, but it also sees a personal and moral distinction between the two.

As he had in earlier articles, Strong once again cited various authors to demonstrate that the overwhelming trend in modern thinking was toward a monistic
understanding of the world. While older theology emphasized individuality and
strong distinctions between God and humanity, Strong thought his forbears had
largely overlooked the solidarity he and many other modern thinkers perceived

in the universe. If Christian theology did not adapt to this modern understanding of the world, it risked being left behind as hopelessly outdated, and perhaps just as important, theology would fail to move forward to a new and better understanding of God and His relationship to the universe.

Employing picturesque language, Strong explained how individuals related to one another within his system:

> The individuality of human beings, real as it is, is not the only reality. There is the profounder fact of a common life. Even the great mountain-peaks of personality are superficial distinctions, compared with the organic oneness in which they are rooted, into which they all dip down, and from which they all, like volcanoes, receive at times quick and overflowing impulses of insight, emotion and energy.[94]

For Strong this emphasis on the common life of all humans, which they ultimately share with God, had been largely missing in earlier theology. He aimed to grasp this truth from the clutches of pantheism and redeploy it in the service of a more perceptive and more culturally acceptable Christian theology.

The Universe Is a Manifestation of the Divine Life

In his second point, Strong provided a more positive explanation of the key differences between ethical monism and pantheism. He began by stating, "In contrast then with the two errors of Pantheism—the denial of God's transcendence and the denial of God's personality—Ethical Monism holds that the universe, instead of being one with God and conterminous with God, is but a finite, partial and progressive manifestation of the divine Life." Strong then offered an interesting though controversial analogy: "The universe is related to God as my thoughts are related to me, the thinker."[95] Within ethical monism, God is viewed as a being that is greater than the universe while the universe itself is seen as a manifestation of God.

Once again, Strong pointed to various writers who supported his philosophical proposal. This time he focused on poets who seemed to show a measure of sympathy for ideas similar to ethical monism. Quite tellingly, several of the poets he cited were not known for their orthodoxy.[96] As was the case with his first point, he cited no scriptural texts in support of his position.

Divine Immanence Guarantees Individuality in the Universe

In his third point, Strong argued against another misunderstanding of ethical monism:

The immanence of God, as the one substance, ground and principle of being, does not destroy, but rather guarantees, the individuality and rights of each portion of the universe, so that there is variety of rank and endowment.... While God is all, he is also in all; so making the universe a graded and progressive manifestation of himself, both in his love for righteousness and his opposition to moral evil.[97]

Strong noted that some critics had claimed that ethical monism led to moral indifference because it eliminated all distinctions between God and humans. He responded by pointing out that such a charge might rightly be laid at the feet of pantheistic monism, but it could not rightly be attributed to ethical monism. As Strong put it, "Ethical monism is the monism that recognizes the ethical fact of personal intelligence and will in both God and man, and with these God's purpose in making the universe a varied manifestation of himself."[98] In Strong's mind, his critics had confused ethical monism with pantheistic monism and had wrongly attributed the errors of the latter to his view.

Christology Is the Key to Understanding the Universe

In his fourth and final point, Strong described the person and work of Christ as the key to understanding the universe:

Since Christ is the Logos of God, the immanent God, God revealed in Nature, in Humanity, in Redemption, Ethical Monism recognizes the universe as created, upheld, and governed by the same Being who in the course of history was manifest in human form and who made atonement for human sin by his death on Calvary. The secret of the universe and the key to its mysteries are to be found in the Cross.[99]

Having omitted any reference to the Scriptures in his first three points, Strong at last cited a number of biblical passages he thought supported his view of Christ and Christ's relationship to the universe: John 1:1–4, 14, 18; Ephesians 1:22–23; Colossians 1:16–17; 2:2–3, 9; and Hebrews 1:2–3. While orthodox scholars generally agree that these verses indicate that Christ created and currently sustains the universe, it is not readily apparent how they might support ethical monism, and Strong did not explain. In fact, Strong moved on to what really lay behind his ethical monism: "This view of the relation of the universe to God lays the foundation for *a Christian application of recent philosophical doctrine.*"[100]

Strong thought that his ethical monism fit very nicely with the findings of modern science and the direction contemporary philosophy seemed to be heading. Ethical monism offered an explanation of the universe that Strong believed many thinkers would find attractive, yet he believed it offered a genuinely Christian explanation of the universe. He proposed that "the system of forces which we call the universe is the immediate product of the mind and will of God; and, since Christ is the mind and will of God in exercise, Christ is the Creator and Upholder of the universe." For Strong this meant that "Nature is the omnipresent Christ, manifesting God to creatures."[101]

Strong then teased this idea out a bit. He identified Christ himself as "the principle of cohesion, attraction, interaction, not only in the physical universe, but in the intellectual and moral universe as well." This meant that some of the so-called discoveries of modern science were really just names for the Christ who lay behind them and, more important, that Christ is the foundation for ethics and logic. Strong explained, "As the attraction of gravitation and the principle of evolution are only other names for Christ, so he is the basis of inductive reasoning and the ground of moral unity in creation."[102]

Once again Strong found it necessary to emphasize that ethical monism affirms the truths contained in pantheism and deism while rejecting the errors present in these philosophical systems. In other words, ethical monism provides a better philosophical explanation of reality than either of these systems. Strong ended his discussion of ethical monism by asserting that ethical monism provides the basis for a new and better explanation of many different philosophical and theological issues. As he confessed in the preface to the final edition of his *Systematic Theology*,

> During the twenty years which have intervened.... My philosophical and critical point of view meantime has also somewhat changed. While I still hold to the old doctrines, I interpret them differently and expound them more clearly, because I seem to myself to have reached a fundamental truth which throws new light upon them all.... This view implies a monistic and idealistic conception of the world.[103]

Chapter 4 discusses how ethical monism fit with, and in several cases influenced, key areas of Strong's theology.

Ethical Monism and Its Impact on
Other Areas of Strong's Theology

S TRONG'S DISCOVERY OF ETHICAL MONISM had important reper-
cussions for his overall theology.[1] He admitted as much when he stated
that ethical monism "furnishes the basis for a new interpretation of many
theological as well as many philosophical doctrines."[2] The impact of ethical
monism on Strong's larger theology is best seen in his later discussions of three
doctrinal areas: (a) Scripture and experience, (b) evolution and miracles, and (c)
sin and the atonement. This chapter discusses each of these in turn.

Ethical Monism and Strong's View of Scripture and Experience

Strong's doctrine of Scripture changed significantly during his long career at
Rochester Theological Seminary. He always considered himself to be thoroughly orthodox, and he consistently affirmed the inspiration and authority of
the Scriptures. However, over the years, and especially during the 1890s, Strong
began to alter how he spoke about the Scriptures and the nature of inspiration.

Strong's Earlier Views on the Scriptures

Early on in his academic career, Strong held what most theologians would consider a fairly conservative view of Scripture. In his *Lectures on Theology* (1876),
Strong began his discussion of inspiration by offering the following definition.
He defined inspiration as "that special influence upon the minds of the Scripture
writers, in virtue of which their productions, apart from errors of transcription,
and when rightly interpreted, together constitute an infallible and sufficient rule
of faith and practice." Then, having defined inspiration, Strong both explained
and refuted three mistaken theories concerning the inspiration of the Scriptures:
the intuition theory, the illumination theory, and the dictation theory.[3] Strong's
refutation of each of these views sheds light on his own position.

Strong described the intuition theory as the idea that inspiration is just a way of speaking about exceptional natural abilities. According to Strong, those who hold to the intuition theory believe that the Bible is a product of inspiration in the sense that a great work of art is a product of inspiration. He rejected the intuition theory for at least four reasons. First, the intuition theory necessarily leads to "inspired" self-contradictions because various books allegedly written under such inspiration disagree with one another. Second, it makes religious truth essentially subjective because the truths in question all originated in the minds of mortals. Third, it logically denies the reality of a personal God who reveals himself to his creatures. If inspiration is just a way of speaking about exceptional artifacts of strictly human production, then apparently no self-revealing God exists. Fourth, the intuition theory basically explains inspiration by denying inspiration. In other words, by attributing inspiration to natural human abilities, it makes inspiration virtually meaningless as a religious term.[4] For these reasons, Strong viewed the intuition theory as an untenable explanation of inspiration.

Strong then addressed what he called the illumination theory of inspiration, the idea that "regards inspiration as merely an intensifying and elevating of the religious perceptions of the Christian, the same in kind, though greater in degree, than the illumination of every believer by the Holy Spirit." In this theory, the Bible is not to be described as inspired or as the Word of God itself. Rather, the writers of Scripture were inspired, and the documents they produced now contain the Word of God. Strong offered four reasons for rejecting this position. First, he thought the illumination theory was insufficient to account for all the relevant facts. Since illumination gives no new truth but only enables those who are illumined to understand previously revealed truth, the original communication of truth must be different in kind from illumination. Second, in this theory the writers of Scripture would not have been prevented from "frequent and grievous error." This view seems to assume that the existence of errors in Scripture does not pose a serious problem. Third, Strong feared that this kind of inspiration still left humanity without any authoritative word from God. Much like the intuition theory, this view seems to deny the actual existence of divine revelation. Fourth, Strong thought that this theory necessarily meant that human reason must determine which parts of Scripture to accept and which parts to reject. Therefore, human reason rather than Scripture would be the ultimate determiner of truth.[5] As was the case with the intuition theory, Strong believed that the illumination theory fell far short of the correct understanding of inspiration.

The third theory Strong ultimately rejected was the dictation theory, the idea that the writers of Scripture were so passive in the production of the sacred text that they were essentially mere pens, not penmen. In this view, the writers of Scripture were recorders of the sacred text, but they were not really authors of a divine message. Strong offered four reasons for rejecting this position. First, the dictation theory wrongly assumed that God's occasional method of revealing truth was his universal method. Strong acknowledged that in some places God had directly dictated truth to the writers of Scripture but noted that it was illegitimate to infer from such instances that this was the method God used in the production of all Scripture. Second, this theory does not account for the clearly human element the Scriptures contain. If the dictation theory were true, seemingly there would be no stylistic differences between the various writers of Scripture, yet such differences are impossible to deny. Third, Strong argued that it was unlikely God would dictate information that the writers of Scripture already knew or could easily discover. Fourth, he thought that mechanical dictation seemed to contradict how that God normally works in the human soul: the work of God does not usually bypass the human faculties but, rather, makes full use of them.[6] It seemed to Strong that the production of Scripture would follow this pattern. Although the dictation theory was a more "conservative" approach to the question of inspiration than the other two options, Strong ultimately rejected it as an inadequate explanation of how the Scriptures came into being.

Having rejected these three theories, Strong then presented his own view on the inspiration of the Scriptures, the "dynamical theory," by contrasting it with the other views he had just refuted:

The true view holds in opposition to the first of these theories [intuition], that inspiration is not a natural but a supernatural fact, and that it is the immediate work of a personal God in the soul of man.

It holds in opposition to the second [illumination], that inspiration belongs not only to the men who wrote the Scriptures, but to the Scriptures which they wrote, and to every part of them, so that they are in every part the word of God.

It holds in opposition to the third theory [dictation], that the Scriptures contain a human as well as a divine element, so that while they constitute a body of infallible truth, this truth is shaped in human moulds and adapted to ordinary human intelligence.

In short, inspiration is neither natural, partial, nor mechanical, but supernatural, plenary and dynamical.[7]

When describing his understanding of inspiration at this early stage in his career, Strong preferred terms such as *supernatural, plenary,* and *dynamical,* but as he discussed the topic of inspiration from various angles, he also sometimes spoke about it as being *verbal* in its effects.

During the 1870s and 1880s, Strong occasionally used the term *verbal* to describe the inspiration of the Scriptures. However, even at this early stage he appears to have been somewhat conflicted about exactly what verbal inspiration entailed.[8] While discussing the union of the divine and human elements in inspiration, Strong offered the following explanation of verbal inspiration:

> Inspiration did not always or even generally involve a direct communication to the Scripture writers, of the words they wrote.
>
> Thought is possible without words and in the order of nature precedes words. The Scripture writers appear to have been so influenced by the Holy Spirit that they perceived and felt even the new truths they were to publish, as discoveries of their own minds, and were left to the action of their own minds, in the expression of these truths, with the single exception that they were supernaturally held back from the election of wrong words, and when needful were provided with right ones. Inspiration is therefore verbal as to its result, but not verbal as to its method.[9]

Although Strong did not like to speak about the method of inspiration as being verbal, he did affirm that the Scriptures themselves were verbally inspired. Throughout his early career Strong held a fairly high view of the Scriptures, which included a belief that the Bible is the verbally inspired Word of God.

Strong noted that one of the most common objections to the doctrine of inspiration was the idea that the Scriptures contain errors in some places where they address certain secular matters. Strong replied to this assertion by suggesting that, if such errors could be proven to exist in Scripture, they would not necessarily undermine the doctrine of inspiration. Rather, those errors would simply push Christian theologians to place more emphasis on the human component in Scripture. However, early in his career Strong did not believe that such errors had been proven to exist. He specifically denied that the Bible contains any errors when it addresses matters of science, and he spent a fair bit of space discussing how the problem of alleged "errors" of various sorts should be handled.[10] When he began teaching theology at Rochester, Strong apparently held to the inerrancy of the Scriptures. At the very least, he did not believe that any actual errors existed in the original manuscripts of the Bible.

Strong's views on the inspiration and inerrancy of Scripture appear to change somewhat during the 1890s, but for the most part his public statements about the Scriptures held fairly stable until the seventh edition of his *Systematic Theology* (1902).

Strong's Later Views on the Scriptures

In the seventh edition of his *Systematic Theology* (1902), Strong retained his original definition of inspiration. However, he added a new section to his discussion of the union of divine and human elements in inspiration, which he began by stating, "We may now venture upon a series of statements more definite and explicit than we have hitherto been justified in making. These statements have respect to the method, rather than to the fact, of inspiration."[11] These new statements that were "more definite and explicit" filled the next two pages.

Although Strong had not abandoned his "dynamical" theory of inspiration, he now downplayed the importance of holding any particular theory concerning the inspiration of the Scriptures. He claimed, "No theory of inspiration is necessary to Christian faith. . . . The fault of many past discussions of the subject is the assumption that God must adopt some particular method of inspiration, or secure an absolute perfection of detail in matters not essential to the religious teaching of Scripture."[12] If Strong himself had made such assumptions in his own past discussions of inspiration, he no longer made them.

As Strong explained his new understanding of inspiration, it became clear that his own view had changed in several significant ways. In earlier editions of his theology text, Strong had denied that the Scriptures contain errors of any kind. For example, he wrote, "It is noticeable that the common objections to inspiration are urged not so much against the religious teaching of the Scriptures, as against certain errors in secular matters, which are supposed to be interwoven with it. . . . But we deny that such errors have as yet been proved to exist."[13] In 1876 and into the 1890s, Strong denied the existence of any actual errors in the biblical text, but by 1899, he had apparently changed his position: that year in an address Strong told his listeners, "Inspiration was like grace; it was not infallible nor impeccable. The first covenant was not faultless, and for the hardness of their hearts God gave his people statutes that were not good."[14] These comments seem to stand in stark contrast to some of his earlier statements. They also seem in conflict with those of the Psalmist who wrote, "Your statutes are wonderful; therefore I obey them. . . . The statutes you have laid down are righteous; they are fully trustworthy" (Ps 119:129, 138). Strong's statements questioning the infallibility and inerrancy of the Scripture do not appear to have been a one-time slip of the tongue. In the seventh edition of his *Systematic Theology*, Strong proposed, "God can use imperfect means. As the imperfection of the eye does not disprove its divine authorship, and as God reveals himself in nature and history in spite of their shortcomings, so divine inspiration does not guarantee inerrancy in things not essential to the main purpose of Scripture."[15] Apparently Strong now believed in a kind of limited inerrancy. Although he had not yet removed all of his earlier references to the infallibility of Scripture, Strong had clearly changed his position on the question of inerrancy.

In the final edition of his *Systematic Theology*, Strong's modified view became even more pronounced. For the first time, he included a completely new definition of inspiration: "Inspiration is that influence of the Spirit of God upon the minds of the Scripture writers which made their writings the record of a progressive divine revelation, sufficient, when taken together and interpreted by the same Spirit who inspired them, to lead every honest inquirer to Christ and to salvation."[16] Gone from this new definition was any reference to the Scriptures as infallible or as being the believer's "sufficient rule of faith and practice."[17]

Strong's revised chapter on inspiration also revealed that he no longer wanted to speak of inspiration as being *verbal* in nature. In his original *Lectures on Theology*, Strong had asserted that "inspiration is therefore verbal as to its result, but not verbal as to its method."[18] Strong retained this sentence through the first seven editions of his *Systematic Theology*.[19] However, in the final edition of his theology text, Strong replaced this sentence with the following statement: "Inspiration is therefore not verbal, while yet we claim that no form of words which taken in its connections would teach essential error has been admitted into Scripture."[20] Thus, Strong denied the verbal inspiration of the Scriptures. Furthermore, his use of the phrase *essential error* also provided a hint that Strong now believed the Bible might contain errors in matters that could be deemed nonessential.

In the final edition of his *Systematic Theology*, Strong attempted to redefine inerrancy to accommodate his belief that the Scriptures contained some errors: "Inerrancy is not freedom from misstatements, but from error defined as 'that which misleads in any serious or important sense.'"[21] Apparently Strong's new understanding of inerrancy meant the Bible might contain errors as long as those errors did not mislead readers "in any serious or important sense." This was not the normal meaning of inerrancy, and Strong knew it,[22] but he had come to believe that the Scriptures contained some inaccuracies, so he needed to shape the language of orthodoxy to fit his revised theology.

At several different places in his chapter on inspiration, Strong made it clear that the Scriptures should not be regarded as being completely free from all errors. At one point he confessed, "While we admit imperfections of detail in matters not essential to the moral and religious teaching of Scripture, we claim that the Bible furnishes a sufficient guide to Christ and to salvation." Then with even greater confidence Strong asserted, "Inspiration did not guarantee inerrancy in things not essential to the main purpose of Scripture."[23] Strong was not willing to concede that the central message of Scripture had been corrupted in any way, but he was now ready to admit that errors might be found among what he deemed the nonessential details, which included, among other things, some elements of the historical narratives recorded in Scripture. For example, Strong asserted,

> While historical and archaeological discovery in many important particulars goes to sustain the general correctness of the Scripture narratives, and no statement essential to the moral and religious teaching of Scripture has been invalidated, inspiration is still consistent with much imperfection in historical details and its narratives "do not seem to be exempted from possibilities of error."[24]

Strong thought he had identified incidents in the Old Testament where scriptural authors had exaggerated numbers and suppressed information that might undermine their own positions.[25] Although Strong acknowledged that some errors had entered the Scriptures during transcription, in his opinion such examples were so numerous that they could not all be attributed to copying and were present in the autographs themselves.

Experience and Ethical Monism

A number of reasons lay behind the changes in Strong's views about the Scriptures. Two of the primary catalysts, somewhat intertwined, were the expanding role of experience in Strong's thought and his adoption of ethical monism as a governing principle of theology.

Strong's move from an authority-based to a more experience-based theology can be seen in his earlier and later definitions of *inspiration*. As noted above, Strong's earlier definition stressed the fact that the Scriptures "constitute an infallible and sufficient rule of faith and practice."[26] In other words, because the Scriptures are inspired by God, they are authoritative. His later definition described the Scriptures as "sufficient, when taken together and interpreted by the same Spirit who inspired them, to lead every honest inquirer to Christ and to salvation."[27] This later definition was more functional and less objective than the earlier statement. Instead of describing what the Scriptures are, it explained how the Scriptures work. The later definition also suggested a more subjective basis for interpreting the Scriptures. The Scriptures were to be interpreted by the Holy Spirit who inspired them.[28] Strong's view of inspiration had been altered by experience, and he now approached the task of interpretation of the Bible from a more subjective basis.

Ethical monism also clearly played a role in Strong's developing views about the Scriptures. As Strong confessed in an appendix he added to his autobiography in 1908,

> My later thought has interpreted the Bible from the point of view of the immanence of Christ. As I have more and more clearly seen him in human history, I have been led to recognize an evolutionary process in divine revelation.... As Hebrew history is the work of Christ, so is Hebrew Scripture. As the history is his work in spite of its imperfections, *so the Scripture is his work in spite of its imperfections.* ... Inerrancy in matters not essential to their moral and religious teaching is not to be claimed.[29]

By about 1900, Strong was willing to concede the existence of errors in the Scriptures, and apparently these errors were attributable not to later copyists but, rather, to the original authors themselves.

Not everyone who detected the developments in Strong's theology was troubled by those changes. William Adams Brown (1865–1943), a Presbyterian theologian of a more liberal bent, wrote a fairly positive review of the first volume of the final edition of Strong's theology.[30] Brown's main purpose in reviewing Strong's work was to note and evaluate the changes that appeared in the new edition. He pointed out that the most important changes were in Strong's discussions of miracles and Scripture. He noted that an insistence on inerrancy had disappeared from Strong's newer treatment of Scripture, and he cataloged places where Strong had scaled back his defense of Scripture from the charge that it contained some errors. Strong now allowed that Scripture contained errors or misstatement of facts that did not affect its essential religious message. Brown believed that these changes were "far-reaching in importance" and observed that they involved "the entire shifting of the basis of authority from an external and dogmatic basis to one which is spiritual and inherent."[31] In other words, Brown believed that Strong's basis of authority had shifted from the Scriptures to personal experience.

Ultimately, Brown welcomed these changes in Strong's thinking about Scripture, but he also thought that Strong had not come far enough. Brown detected lingering inconsistencies in Strong's theology that he believed were remnants of

an older theology Strong no longer really held. Interestingly, Brown also identified what he thought stood behind these changes in Strong's theology: "The
explanation of the changes, so far as they affect the structure of Strong's thought,
and not simply the form, is to be found in the section on ethical monism." Again,
after discussing Strong's new view of Scripture, Brown correctly observed that
"the explanation of the change of position is to be found in Strong's conception
of the immanent Christ." From his office at Union Theological Seminary, Brown
looked across the denominational and cultural chasms that separated Rochester
from Union, and he noted with evident pleasure that Strong had taken a few steps
in his direction. Strong still regarded himself as eminently orthodox, but he had
unwittingly loosened his grip somewhat on certain important aspects of biblical orthodoxy. Brown drew his review to a close by discussing the nature of the
theological enterprise and by pointing out the inevitability of additional changes
in Strong's theology: "It is one of the misfortunes of theology as of all philosophical disciplines, that one cannot make a change at any point of his system without being logically committed to corresponding changes in all. We cannot but
feel that more is involved in Dr. Strong's principle of the immanent Christ than
has yet received full expression, even in his revised system."[32] Indeed, as Brown's
comment suggests, Strong may never have fully perceived all the implications of
ethical monism or have completely integrated the implications he did discern.

Ethical Monism and Strong's View of Evolution and Miracles

Strong's understanding of how God created and currently works in the universe changed over time, and ethical monism was the primary influence on how
Strong described God's method of working in the world. This is most clearly
seen in Strong's views concerning the concept of evolution and the meaning
of miracles.

Evolution as the Method of God

Strong's acceptance of some type of theistic evolution predated his discovery
of ethical monism by at least two decades. In *Lectures on Theology* (1876), he
described his understanding of the creation account as a "pictorial-summary
interpretation."[33] Strong used this phrase throughout his academic career to distinguish his view from other theories, including in each revision of his *Systematic
Theology*, even the final edition.[34]

For Strong, a pictorial-summary interpretation meant that the Genesis
account of creation is "true in all its essential features" but was "presented in

graphic form suited to the common mind and to earlier as well as later ages." In other words, he believed that the Scriptures are flexible enough that they can adapt to the ever-changing views of modern science without compromising the fundamental truth of creation. Strong held that the creation account was given "in pregnant language, so that it could expand to all the ascertained results of subsequent physical research." In Strong's mind, the Scriptures could themselves evolve to keep pace with the findings of science. During an address he gave to the Alumni Association of Union Theological Seminary in May 1901, Strong explained that the Scriptures had evolved and were still evolving much like the findings of natural science: "As evolution in nature is still going on, so is the evolution of Scripture. As a book, the Bible is complete; but the meaning to us of the truth of the Bible is constantly changing, just as the meaning of nature, under scientific scrutiny, is constantly changing."[35] The Scriptures, Strong believed, had evolved and were still evolving to meet the changing canons of the scientific community.

Having explained this flexibility of meaning, Strong then gave "an approximate account of the coincidences between the Mosaic and the geological records." In his early *Lectures on Theology*, Strong worked his way through the various stages of the geological record as understood by contemporary science and sought to explain how statements in chapter 1 of Genesis corresponded to the scientific consensus. He described various classifications of the plant and animal kingdoms as fitting into specific stages of geological progress and concluded that man as "the first being of moral and intellectual qualities, and the first in whom the great design has full expression, forms in both the Mosaic and the geologic record, the last step of progress in creation."[36] For Strong, there was no question that human beings appear as the pinnacle both of creation and of the geological record. Geology and the Scriptures therefore agree about humanity's status in the spectrum of living creatures.

Strong did not view humankind as a product of "unreasoning natural forces" but rather as deriving its existence from a creative act of God. This belief did not automatically rule out the possibility that humans had evolved from lower life forms, because "the Scriptures do not disclose the method of man's creation." For this reason, "whether man's physical system is, or is not, derived by natural descent, from the lower animals, the record of creation does not inform us." At this early stage in his career, while admitting the possibility that humanity's "physical system" was a product of evolution, Strong preferred to see both man's body and soul as results of immediate creation.[37] However, this would eventually change.

Some twenty years later, after Strong had embraced ethical monism, he felt comfortable describing humans as having evolved from lower life forms. In a paper delivered in 1898 before the Baptist Congress in Buffalo, New York, Strong stated, "The dust from which the body of Adam was made was animate dust; lower forms of life were taken as the foundation upon which to build man's physical frame and man's rational powers; into some animal germ came the breath of a new intellectual and moral life."[38] After accepting ethical monism, Strong saw the creation of human beings as a special work of God in which he fashioned humans from "animated dust" or "the highest preceding brute."[39]

On July 23, 1878, Strong delivered an address before the Literary Societies of Colby University, titled "The Philosophy of Evolution."[40] In this speech Strong critiqued the atheistic views of Herbert Spencer (1820–1903) but considered himself an evolutionist of sorts:

> We are ourselves evolutionists then, within certain limits, and we accept a large portion of the results of Mr. Spencer's work. We gratefully appropriate whatever science can prove. . . . We know that gravitation does not take the universe out of the hands of God, but only reveals the method of the divine working. So, the day is past, in our judgment, when thoughtful men can believe that there was a creative fiat of God at the introduction of every variety of vegetable and animal life. God may work by means, and a law of variation and of natural selection may have been and probably was the method in which his great design in the vast majority of living forms was carried out.[41]

Prior to embracing ethical monism, Strong's system attempted to reconcile the creation account with the claims of modern science, but he lacked a means of bringing the two together in a consistent fashion. His discovery of ethical monism in the 1890s provided a hermeneutic that enabled him to more consistently integrate contemporary views about evolution into his theological system.[42]

For years Strong had argued that theistic evolution should not be viewed as a threat to the Christian religion, but now he presented his case with greater conviction. He had found a better way of explaining how the Christian faith incorporated and even helped explain the idea of evolution: "Evolution has new light thrown upon it from the point of view of Ethical Monism. It is disarmed of all its terrors for theology the moment it is regarded as only the common method of Christ our Lord. It is only the scientific expression of a great Christian truth."[43] In Strong's view, evolution in no way undercut belief in the existence of God: "Evolution does not make the idea of a Creator superfluous, because evolution is only the method of God," and "Evolution does not exclude design when we once see in it the method by which the Son of God has been imparting his own life and so manifesting the Father."[44] Strong now saw evolution as God's method of creating, fashioning, and sustaining the world by means of the immanent Christ, who is the very life of the universe.

To those who questioned his orthodox credentials because of his position on evolution, Strong replied,

> I do not deny creation; I believe in it with all my heart. The world has had a beginning, and it is the work of God's sovereign power in Christ. But I no longer conceive of the successive acts of creation as the bringing into being out of nothing new substances that are outside of and different from God. I believe in creation, but I have a new conception of the method of creation.[45]

Strong held that the concept of evolution could not be properly defended apart from belief in God. Naturalism could never account for the existence of life and such a variety of life forms in the universe. Strong believed that his ethical monism could help explain evolution more fully and more accurately than science alone.

In his earliest published discussion of ethical monism, Strong had noted ethical monism's main implication for evolutionary thought: "Darwin was able to assign no reason why the development of living forms should be upward rather than downward, toward cosmos rather than chaos." Strong believed that Darwin's great weakness was that he lacked the essential truth of ethical monism: "If Darwin had recognized Christ as the omnipresent life and law of the world, he would not have been obliged to pass his hands across his eyes in despair of comprehending the marks of wisdom in the universe." The answer to Darwin's dilemma was recognizing the immanent Christ as the power and the guiding force behind evolutionary progress.[46]

In ethical monism, Strong had found a new way to reconcile the Christian faith with modern ideas about evolution. Strong believed that, by viewing the immanent Christ as working through evolution, he could explain why evolution was taking place in the world. In the end, Strong assigned a new role to Christ: "Christ, the wisdom and power of God, is the principle of evolution, as he is the principle of gravitation and induction."[47] If ethical monism had helped Strong reconcile evolution and theology, it had done so only by significantly altering both.

Miracles More Accurately Defined

Strong's understanding of miracles also evolved under the influence of his ethical monism. For Strong, much like ethical monism helped explain how evolution had shaped the world, ethical monism could shed light on the nature of miracles.

When Strong published his lecture notes in 1876, he provided the follow-ing definition: "A miracle is an event palpable to the senses, produced for a religious purpose by the immediate agency of God; an event therefore, which though not contravening any law of nature, the laws of nature, if fully known, would not be competent to explain."[48] This definition clearly depicted miracles as something above and beyond the laws of nature and inexplicable apart from divine activity.

At a pastors' conference just two years later, Strong gave a somewhat different definition: "A miracle is an event in nature, so extraordinary in itself and so coinciding with the prophecy or command of a religious teacher or leader, as fully to warrant the conviction, on the part of those who witness it, that God has wrought it with the design of certifying that this teacher or leader has been commissioned by him."[49] While not denying the supernatural character of a mir-acle, this newer definition both envisioned miracles as taking place "in" rather than "above" nature and gave the functional purpose of miracles as certifying the credibility of a messenger of God.[50]

The first of these definitions appeared in all eight editions of Strong's *System-atic Theology* and seems to have been the one he preferred for a number of years. The second definition Strong initially proposed in a speech delivered in 1878, more than a decade before he embraced ethical monism. That speech, printed in the *Baptist Review* the next year, for the most part went unnoticed by Strong's theological peers.[51] And this second definition was completely absent from the first seven editions of his theology text.

When theologians reviewed the final edition of Strong's *Systematic Theology*, they often pointed out two significant changes: his revised understanding of inspiration and his new definition of miracles.[52] In the final edition Strong re-peated his original definition of miracles almost verbatim, but designated as only a "preliminary definition." He then included the second definition and labeled it an "alternative and preferable definition" of a miracle.[53] Although Strong had formulated both definitions early in his theological career, he now embraced the second definition as superior. The preferable definition of miracles left out all reference to the laws of nature and the immediate agency of God and instead simply emphasized the "extraordinary" nature of the event. These changes better reflected Strong's later understanding of God's relationship to nature in light of ethical monism.

Strong gave five reasons why this new definition of miracles was superior to the earlier one. Most of these reasons were in some way related to ethi-cal monism:

a. It recognizes the immanence of God and his immediate agency in nature, instead of assuming an antithesis between the laws of nature and the will of God.

b. It regards the miracle as simply an extraordinary act of the same God who is already present in all natural operations and who in them is revealing his general plan.

c. It holds that natural law, as the method of God's regular activity, in no way precludes unique exertions of his power when these will best secure his purpose in creation.

d. It leaves it possible that all miracles may have their natural explanations and may hereafter be traced to natural causes, while both miracles and their natural causes may be only names for the one and self-same will of God.

e. It reconciles the claims of both science and religion: of science, by permitting any possible or probable physical antecedents of the miracle; of religion, by maintaining that these very antecedents together with the miracle itself are to be interpreted as signs of God's special commission to him under whose teaching or leadership the miracle is wrought.[54]

Because Strong had come to see God as ontologically identified with nature, he no longer viewed miracles as a supernatural work of God from without.[55] Instead, Strong now saw miracles as extraordinary acts of the immanent God who is constantly working out his will by means of natural laws. For Strong, natural laws were the ordinary expression of God's will, and miracles were just the extraordinary expression of his will. Miracles and natural law were two sides of the same coin.

In an address Strong delivered at a Methodist Episcopal church in 1903, he stated,

> Even though all miracle were proved to be a working of nature, the Christian argument would not one whit be weakened, for still miracle would evidence the extraordinary working of the immanent God, who is none other than Jesus Christ. . . . Our unreadiness to accept this naturalistic interpretation of the miracle results wholly from our inveterate habit of dissociating nature from God, and of practically banishing God from his universe.[56]

Far from "banishing God from his universe," Strong saw the universe itself as a manifestation of God. Most of Strong's reasons for preferring a new definition of miracles related directly to his understanding of ethical monism. He did not view miracles as either a violation or a suspension of natural law, nor did he see them as the supernatural work of a Creator who is distinct from his creation. Instead, Strong held that miracles should be understood as belonging to a higher order of nature, not separate from the immanent God but, rather, part of his divine will. Strong did not develop a completely new definition of miracles after his acceptance of ethical monism, but he did alter his *Systematic Theology* to reflect his new preference for a definition that more readily fit a strong emphasis on divine immanence.

Reviewers of the final edition of Strong's *Systematic Theology* noted the inconsistency between the two definitions that sat in the text just a page apart. William Adams Brown criticized Strong for still including the older definition at all: "The extent of the distance traversed between this point of view and that which is marked by the earlier definition is apparent to all. The only question which suggests itself is why, since Professor Strong has so firmly planted himself upon the new ground, he should any longer retain in his text evidence of the discarded position."[57] Brown thought it odd that Strong included the earlier definition of miracles in the final edition of his theology text when he clearly preferred a different definition, but Strong never fully expunged all vestiges of his theology before ethical monism. Strong had embraced ethical monism in the 1890s, but even in 1907 traces of his earlier theology stood alongside evidence of his new approach. More than a century later, these conflicting elements remain in the final edition as testimony to the changes in Strong's thinking about miracles and other important theological issues.[58]

Ethical Monism and Strong's View of Sin and the Atonement

Although Strong held a form of theistic evolution throughout his career, he consistently affirmed the existence of an original pair of humans from which all humanity had descended. However, Strong believed that humanity's evolution had also entailed an important degeneration or devolution of sorts.[59] Although human bodies had evolved upward under the guiding hand of God, Strong acknowledged that sin had entered the human race and that humanity had fallen from its original state. Such a fall necessarily entailed guilt and a corresponding liability to punishment. Beginning in the 1890s, Strong's ethical monism led him to affirm several rather unorthodox ideas about divine suffering and Christ's relationship to human guilt.

Sin as a Corporate Responsibility

Prior to formulating the concept of ethical monism, Strong boldly asserted that "every monistic system breaks in pieces when it attempts to deal with the fact of sin."[60] In the early 1890s, Strong rightly recognized the difficulty posed by trying to reconcile any kind of monism with the biblical doctrine of sin and the undeniable reality of evil in the world. However, within just a few years of making this statement, Strong had found a way to reconcile them. In fact, ethical monism ultimately reinforced and helped explicate Strong's own distinctive view of sin.

Many aspects of Strong's doctrine of sin and his concept of humanity remained stable throughout his career. For example, in both his early and later theology Strong affirmed that the entire human race had descended from a single pair of humans.[61] His changing opinion about the origin of the human body did not affect this belief. Strong realized that, apart from the existence of a single pair of humans at the beginning of the race, a coherent doctrine of original sin would be impossible.[62]

Strong also held steady in his belief about what sin actually is. He consistently defined sin as "lack of conformity to the moral law of God, either in act, disposition or state," and he unswervingly identified selfishness as the fundamental principle of sin.[63] In Strong's thinking, love for God was the essence of all virtue, and love of one's self was the heart of all sinfulness.

Strong further believed that Adam's fall meant that his descendants would be born depraved, guilty, and under the just condemnation of God. The question of how depravity and guilt could justly be communicated to all humanity has been debated by orthodox theologians for centuries. Strong's explanation was fairly simple. Almost a decade before he embraced ethical monism, Strong asserted that "Adam and his posterity are one, and, by virtue of their organic unity, the sin of Adam is the sin of the race."[64] For Strong, the corporate unity of the race in Adam meant that all humanity bore responsibility of Adam's sin.

Strong rejected Pelagian, Arminian, and New School theories concerning the imputation of Adam's sin. He also argued against the theory of mediate imputation and the federal theory, which he pejoratively called the "Theory of Condemnation by Covenant." Strong instead preferred what he called the Augustinian theory or the theory of Adam's natural headship. Strong held this view of imputation both before and after he announced this discovery of ethical monism. As Strong's name for his theory suggests, this view finds its roots in Augustinian theology, and Strong was happy to count the bishop of Hippo among the earliest proponents of this position. Strong also pointed to Samuel J. Baird (1817–93) and William G. T. Shedd (1820–94) as contemporary representatives of this view.[65]

Strong explained the theory of natural headship as meaning that "God imputes the sin of Adam immediately to all his posterity in virtue of that organic unity of mankind by which the whole race at the time of Adam's transgression existed seminally in him as its head."[66] This view tied imputation to seminal headship rather than a covenantal relationship.

In support of the natural headship theory, Strong originally proposed four arguments, which held steady through the first seven editions of his *Systematic Theology*. In the final edition, Strong added a fifth: the support of "the conclusions of modern science." Strong believed that even biological research had come to support his understanding of the imputation of Adam's sin to all humanity. Though not a scientist himself, Strong claimed that the theory of natural headship was "an ethical or theological interpretation of certain incontestable and acknowledged biological facts." Among his support for this assertion, Strong included a statement by Borden Parker Bowne: this proponent of personal idealism claimed that "all real existence is necessarily singular and individual." Strong believed that modern science and his own understanding of ethical monism both offered new support to the theory of natural headship that he had held for years.[67] As Myron James Houghton correctly pointed out, although Strong continued to argue for natural headship on the basis of biblical exegesis, ethical monism became an even more important factor in his decision to continue holding this view.[68]

Although ethical monism did not push Strong to embrace the theory of natural headship, ethical monism fit very well with the way Strong had long understood the imputation of Adam's sin. Far more integral to Strong's ethical monism was his view of the atoning work of Christ.

The Atonement as a Necessary Suffering

Strong's later discussions of evolution, miracles, and sin reflected his embrace of ethical monism, but it most significantly impacted Strong's view of the atonement. In 1904 Strong announced, "We must acknowledge also that our conceptions of Christ's atonement have suffered some change. . . . That change has been in the nature of a more fundamental understanding of the meaning of the atonement, and its necessity as a law of universal life."[69]

The relationship between ethical monism and the atonement in Strong's thinking was a two-way street. In fact, by Strong's own account, it was the doctrine of the atonement that actually pushed him in the direction of ethical monism: "I accept Ethical Monism because of the light which it throws upon the atonement rather than for the sake of its Christian explanation of evolution."[70]

In his earliest theological notes, Strong described his understanding of the significance of Christ's death as the "ethical theory of the atonement."[71] He summarized his view as follows:

> This holds that the necessity of an atonement is grounded in the holiness of God. There is an ethical principle in the divine nature, which demands that sin shall be punished. . . . There is an ethical demand of God's nature that penalty follow sin.
>
> . . . The atonement is therefore a satisfaction of the ethical demand of the divine nature by the substitution of Christ's penal sufferings for the punishment of the guilty.[72]

Although Strong embraced the ethical theory of the atonement throughout his career and continued to speak about it using the words just quoted, he later explained his view quite differently.

Strong felt very keenly the charge that the suffering of the innocent Savior in place of the guilty is unjust. In one of his earliest attempts to answer objections to ethical monism, Strong admitted, "For many years my classes propounded to me the question: How could Christ justly bear the sins of mankind? The theories which held to a mechanical transfer of guilt became increasingly untenable." In a posthumously published book Strong wrote, "To me it has been the greatest problem of theology, to explain *God's imputation to Christ of the sins of the whole race.*"[73]

Early in his career Strong shared William Shedd's realistic view of the transmission of sin, so he consulted Shedd privately about how to resolve the tension created by Christ's suffering on behalf of sinners. According to Strong, Shedd simply told him that it was a "mystery of God." Strong, dissatisfied with this answer, kept looking for a satisfactory solution. Eventually he discovered it in ethical monism. Reflecting back on his own theological development, Strong wrote,

> I wanted to find some union of Christ with humanity which would make this imputation also realistic and biological. I have found it, and have expounded it in my book entitled, *"Christ in Creation."* It is my chief contribution to scientific theology . . . it is by my explanation of God's imputation of all human sin to Christ that my theology must stand or fall.[74]

The full title of that book was of course, *Christ in Creation and Ethical Monism*. By his own account, Strong viewed ethical monism and its explanation of the atonement as central to his later theology.

On the basis of ethical monism, Strong no longer simply spoke of the atonement as a substitution. He now spoke of it as both a substitution and a sharing:

> To our fathers the atonement was a mere historical fact, a sacrifice offered in a few brief hours upon the Cross. It was a literal substitution of Christ's suffering for ours, the payment of our debt by another, and upon the ground of that payment we are permitted to go free. . . . All this is true. But it is only part of the truth. . . . We must add to the idea of *substitution* the idea of *sharing*. Christ's doing and suffering is not that of one external and foreign to us. He is bone of our bone, and flesh of our flesh; the bearer of humanity; yes, the very life of the race.[75]

This statement included more changes to Strong's view of the atonement than may at first meet the eye. By speaking about the atonement as a sharing, Strong meant that he saw Christ not as bearing foreign guilt but, rather, as bearing his own guilt. In fact, as the life of the humanity, Strong believed that Christ was necessarily "responsible with us for the sins of the race."[76]

In the 1880s, Strong tied Christ's inheritance of human guilt to the incarnation. He held that, when Christ became incarnate in the Virgin Mary, the sinless Son of God became a part of the fallen human race and therefore became subject to human guilt for sin. At this early stage, Strong believed that Christ theoretically could have avoided human guilt in a couple of ways:

> [Christ] might have declined to join himself to humanity, and then he need not have suffered. He might have sundered his connection to the race, and then he need not have suffered. But once born of a Virgin, and possessed of the human nature that was under the curse, he was bound to suffer. The whole mass and weight of God's displeasure against the race fell on him, once he became a member of the race.[77]

At this point, Strong still saw Christ's inherited guilt as a necessary by-product of Christ becoming a member of the human race. Later, after accepting ethical monism in the 1890s, Strong understood Christ as united to the human race prior to the Fall of Adam. As he explained it, "Christ's union with the race in his incarnation is only the outward and visible expression of a prior union with the race which began when he created the race."[78] In Strong's later thinking, the incarnation was a revelation of a relationship between Christ and the human race that began when the first pair of humans was created.

Strong also saw Christ's suffering for sins as beginning at the Fall: "So through all the course of history, Christ, the natural life of the race, has been afflicted in the affliction of humanity and has suffered for human sins. . . . This suffering has been an atoning suffering, since it has been due to righteousness." For Strong this meant that the atonement itself began before the incarnation of Christ: "Christ therefore, as incarnate, rather revealed the atonement than made it." In Strong's later view, Christ's death on the cross was not itself the atonement but was merely "the revelation of the atonement." He believed that Christ's atonement began when the Fall occurred and continued up through his death on the cross, which was primarily a revelation of Christ's age-long suffering for sins.[79]

Strong's later view of the atonement was a novel attempt to explain how the sinless Son of God could justly bear the sins of guilty humans. By tying Christ's union with humanity to creation rather than to the incarnation, and by viewing Christ as organically united to the race as its very life, Strong could argue that Christ had justly inherited the guilt (though not the depravity) of human sin when the Fall occurred. On these same bases, he could also argue that Christ began atoning for human sins long before his incarnation. Ethical monism had provided Strong with a new way to answer difficult questions about the justice of imputation and the necessity of the atonement. Such challenging questions had largely driven him to embrace the idea of ethical monism.

Conclusion

As a number of his contemporary critics observed, ethical monism significantly affected several major areas of Strong's theology. However, the relationship between ethical monism and these other areas was often a reciprocal one. Strong's early thinking about such important theological concepts as miracles, evolution, and the atonement included gaps and unanswered questions that seemed to call for an idea like ethical monism. After Strong enthroned ethical monism as a fundamental principle of his theology, to varying degrees it reshaped his thinking about these and other theological issues.

CHAPTER 5

Contemporary Responses and the
Legacy of Strong's Ethical Monism

S TRONG'S ETHICAL MONISM SHAPED, reshaped, and occasionally offered new support and clarification to other areas of his theology, as chapter 4 demonstrates. By the time the final edition of his *Systematic Theology* rolled off the presses between 1907 and 1909, Strong's theology—both the actual text and what he believed—had taken on its settled form.[1] This chapter explores how other theologians viewed Strong's final theology and how Strong's theological journey affected them.

Contemporary Responses to Strong's Ethical Monism

Although philosophical monism remained an influential idea among philosophers and theologians during the early 1900s, Strong's specific brand of monism never gained a large following.[2] Contemporary observers took note of his innovative theological concept, but for the most part they rejected it. Many of Strong's more conservative critics accused Strong of flirting with, if not secretly embracing, a form of philosophical pantheism. Few things called forth louder protestations from Strong than accusations of pantheism. He consistently denied that his ethical monism had anything to do with pantheism and often claimed that such observers did not really understand his position. If such accusations were built on misunderstanding, then quite a few of Strong's readers misunderstood what he intended to communicate about God's relationship to the world.

A number of reviewers took note of the first four editions of Strong's *Systematic Theology*, and most of the reviews that appeared in evangelical publications were quite positive. For example, in discussing the first edition, an anonymous reviewer writing for the *Methodist Review* quibbled with Strong over a few points but in the end concluded that Strong's work was "thoroughly biblical and eminently evangelical" and that Strong had left the entire church in his debt.[3] Writing for the same publication a few years later, another anonymous reviewer praised Strong's second edition and, despite Strong's Calvinistic tendencies, which the writer did not share, concluded, "In view of its general modern character, its evident breadth of learning, its omission of none of the essential doctrines of theology, its logical acumen in defense of truth, and its pronounced affiliation with the orthodoxy of the Christian Church, we welcome this treatise to our table, and commend its use to those who aspire to be theologians."[4] Calvinists, too, greeted early editions of Strong's *Systematic Theology* with general praise and occasional comments that the volume was, if anything, not Calvinistic enough.[5] Early responses to Strong's work consistently noted his orthodoxy. When reviewers criticized some aspect of Strong's theology, almost without exception they did so over denominational distinctions or the Calvinism-Arminianism issue. The first four editions of Strong's theology text did not call forth any major, unanticipated criticisms.

The fifth edition of Strong's *Systematic Theology* (1896) was the first to incorporate the concept of ethical monism. Not surprisingly, this change marked a turning point not only in Strong's thinking but also in how his theology text was received by others. Benjamin Breckinridge Warfield (1851–1921), longtime chair of theology at Princeton Theological Seminary, was one of the first to review the new edition of Strong's work. Because he was reviewing a fifth edition, he focused on what was unique to this new edition. Warfield noted, "A particular interest attaches, however to his new edition of the book from a surprising *volte face* which has been executed by its author, in the interval between the issues of the fourth and fifth editions, on one of the most fundament questions which can underlie a system of theology. We refer to his adoption of the theory of the universe which he calls 'ethical monism.'" Warfield was puzzled by Strong's change of mind, and he pointed out the irony of the fact that Strong had directly opposed philosophical monism as late as 1888 but now seemingly embraced it with both hands. Warfield briefly mentioned a few ways in which Strong's adoption of ethical monism had begun to affect other areas of his theology. He also expressed his surprise that ethical monism had not yet had a greater impact on Strong's system. Warfield feared that such an impact would inevitably take place in the years to come if Strong did not abandon ethical monism. In the end, Warfield offered the following evaluation of Strong's new position. He wrote, "Strong's 'ethical monism' is pantheizing idealism saved from its worst extremes by the force of old habits of thought."[6] Such was the lion of Princeton's initial evaluation of ethical monism.

A few years later, Warfield reviewed Strong's *Christ in Creation and Ethical Monism* (1899). Once again he noted "a somewhat radical change of fundamental conceptions" in Strong's thinking. Expressing his disagreement with Strong's ethical monism, Warfield confessed his relief that the new idea had still not affected Strong's overall theology as much as might be expected.[7]

As Warfield anticipated, the effects of ethical monism on Strong's larger system became more pronounced in subsequent editions of his *Systematic Theology*. In 1908, Caspar Wistar Hodge Jr. (1870–1937) reviewed the first two volumes of the final edition of Strong's work. Hodge was the grandson of Charles Hodge (1797–1878), the nephew of Archibald Alexander Hodge (1823–86), and the son of Caspar Wistar Hodge (1830–91). Like his forbears, Hodge also taught at Princeton for many years. He was an orthodox Presbyterian, and he came from a long line of conservative theologians.

Hodge's lengthy review focused primarily on Strong's ethical monism and its implications for other areas of Strong's theology. Hodge saw nothing good coming from Strong's ethical monism: "We cannot agree with Dr. Strong that his 'idealistic' and 'monistic' conception of God and the world has worked or can work any improvement in his statement of Christian doctrine." In fact, Hodge made it clear that he believed ethical monism had pushed Strong's theology in a very unhealthy direction. He admitted that Strong had tried to distinguish his ethical monism from idealistic pantheism, but Hodge saw the distinction as overly fine, unable to hold up to close scrutiny: "If the universe and humanity are each God's 'self-limitations', it is difficult to see how any doctrine of Creation can be maintained or how idealistic pantheism, with its destruction of Christian doctrine, can be avoided." In the closing paragraph of his review, Hodge tried to soften his theological barrage by assuring his readers that his overall attitude was not "simply one of adverse criticism."[8] His need to make such a statement says much about the overall tone of his review. The bulk of Hodge's review focused on ethical monism, leaving no doubt about his opinion. Like Warfield, Hodge believed Strong had unwittingly embraced a subtle form of pantheism and that his theology had been significantly harmed by it.

When the third volume of the final edition of Strong's *Systematic Theology* appeared in 1909, Hodge took up his pen to review it as well. He spent much of the review pointing out what he perceived as problems in Strong's treatment of the order of God's decrees. Hodge rejected Strong's hypothetical universalism and thought Strong had been inconsistent in his discussion of lapsarian views. Near the end of his review, Hodge included a few lines that must have stung Strong as he read them: "We would not conclude this notice without calling attention to what, in our estimation, greatly enhances the merit of this third volume . . . namely the apparent absence from this volume of the 'ethical monism' which

Dr. Strong advocated in volumes I and II." The main reason for this absence was, of course, not because Strong had abandoned ethical monism but because the subjects addressed in that volume were not significantly impacted by ethical monism. Hodge then recalled that, when he reviewed the earlier volumes, he had "sought to show that the ethical monism and the Christian supernaturalism of the author stood often side by side, unharmonized and incapable of being harmonized."[9] In Hodge's mind, the third volume was superior to the earlier volumes precisely because it did not reflect Strong's belief in ethical monism. Even though the subject did not appear in volume 3, Hodge wanted to make clear to his readers that he strongly disagreed with Strong's ethical monism.

Shortly after Strong died, his final book appeared in print, a little primer on theology titled *What Shall I Believe?* (1922). Hodge reviewed this work as well. In his review, Hodge described Strong's theology as "Augustinianism combined with idealistic monism." He once again pointed out that monism and Augustinian theology could not be combined very well.[10] Likely because Strong had recently died, Hodge tried to avoid being overly critical. He praised Strong's loyalty to the Scriptures and admitted that Strong had done an admirable job of trying to work out a theistic form of monism. In the end, however, Hodge confessed he found it much easier to conceive of monism on a pantheistic than on a theistic basis. Even in discussing Strong's final published work, Hodge spent the bulk of the review pointing out the weaknesses of Strong's ethical monism.

Princeton's conservative Calvinists were not the only reviewers to take note of Strong's decision to adopt ethical monism. Milton Valentine (1825–1906) was a broadly conservative Lutheran educator and one of the editors of the *Lutheran Quarterly*. In 1900, he reviewed Strong's *Christ in Creation and Ethical Monism*. The opening sentences of Valentine's review indicated his overall opinion of Strong's new position. He wrote, "Dr. Strong here appears in a new role—as an 'Ethical Monist.' It does not seem to us, however, that in this he appears at his best." Valentine suggested that Strong's new idea was not, in fact, really new. He also pointed out that monism "has always been rejected by Christian theology as irreconcilable with Scripture teaching and the interests of religion and morality." Valentine spent much of his review letting Strong speak for himself by including numerous quotes. Near the end Valentine noted that Strong had taken great pains to distinguish his own view from pantheism but that he believed Strong's ethical monism was ultimately unable to avoid affirming some form of pantheism:

> Despite our admiration of the high ability of the author and of his loyal aim to serve Christianity, the very outcome of this effort to construct an

adequate and consistent theory confirms our long established belief, that
no monistic scheme has ever been or ever can be framed that can be legit-
imately sustained, either before the court of reason, where the realities of
the universe are witnesses, or in the court of Scripture, where the testimo-
nies of revelation are to determine the view.[11]

Valentine continued to respect Strong as a fellow laborer in the ministry, but he
believed that Strong had unwisely embraced and was now unwittingly promot-
ing the old error of pantheism in slightly different dress.

Several theologians of a more liberal bent soon published reviews of Strong's
later writings as well. In 1900, W. Douglas Mackenzie (1859–1936) evaluated
Strong's *Christ in Creation and Ethical Monism* (1899). Mackenzie was a Congregationalist, and at the time he was professor of systematic theology at the
Chicago Theological Seminary. Mackenzie spent most of his review discussing
Strong's ethical monism. He believed that Strong had managed to distinguish
his view from materialistic monism and from idealism with varying degrees of
success. He also believed that Strong had been careful to avoid identifying God
with the universe in any kind of pantheistic way. Unlike the Princeton theologians, Mackenzie was not overly critical of Strong's ethical monism, but he
did believe that Strong had to make a number of theological and philosophical
"leaps" to sustain his novel position.[12] Reading between the lines, Mackenzie
made it rather clear that he had not really been convinced by Strong's many
arguments for ethical monism.

Writing about this same time, Lyman Abbott (1835–1922) offered a somewhat shorter but franker assessment of Strong's *Christ in Creation and Ethical
Monism*. As a former Congregationalist pastor and an outspoken proponent
of the social gospel, one would hardly expect Abbott to find much in common with Strong,[13] yet he did agree with Strong on a number of important
issues: like Strong, he accepted theistic evolution; like Strong, he was interested
in a wide variety of social and philosophical topics; and most important, like
Strong, Abbott embraced a form of philosophical monism.[14] However, Abbott
found a number of Strong's ideas outdated and somewhat offensive: "Holding
to monism as we do, we regard its combination with such theories [as the fall of
Adam and eternal punishment] as a portent of their ultimate disintegration."
He found Strong's formulation of ethical monism philosophically inconsistent
and wished that monism would evidence an even greater impact on Strong's
thinking. The result, as he put it, would be that Strong's theology would be
"purged of all pessimisms."[15]

As mentioned in chapter 4, William Adams Brown (1865–1943) wrote a generally positive review of Strong's *Systematic Theology* (1907, vol. 1). Brown was a Presbyterian theologian who taught at Union Theological Seminary between the 1890s and 1930s. He was no pantheist, but neither was he a conservative theologian.[16] Brown described Strong's ethical monism as "a type of theism which lays greater stress upon the divine immanence than has commonly been the case in traditional theology." He noted that the latest edition of Strong's *Systematic Theology* provided "an interesting example of the way in which the new view-point affects a scheme of doctrine originally wrought out under very different presuppositions."[17] Unlike most conservative theologians, Brown welcomed Strong's new emphasis on the "immanent Christ" as a step in the right direction, and he gave no indication that he thought Strong was in danger of becoming a pantheist. In fact, Brown might not have viewed pantheism as a real danger to be avoided. His main criticism of Strong was not that he had embraced ethical monism but that Strong's ethical monism had not yet had enough impact on several areas of Strong's theology. Brown thought that the consistent integration of ethical monism would ultimately move Strong further from the canons of traditional orthodoxy.

For the most part, Strong's more liberal reviewers thought that his ethical monism was a step in the right direction but that he had not quite gotten it right and had not fully realized how much ethical monism undercut his earlier theology. By the early 1900s, Strong found himself being criticized from both the right and the left: neither conservatives nor liberals believed his ethical monism was the key to theology that Strong thought it was, and neither side thought he had successfully integrated ethical monism into his theological system.

For the most part, Strong let the negative reviews stand unanswered. However, there is some evidence that Strong was particularly bothered by the repeated accusations of pantheism. Writing to Edgar Young Mullins (1860–1928) of the Southern Baptist Theological Seminary in 1905, Strong complained, "I could wish that you had not confounded monism with pantheism. There is, as I think a Christian monism. Pantheism is to be rejected, not for its monism, but for its two denials, of personality in God and man, and of transcendence in God."[18] Several years later, Strong once again wrote to Mullins about his ethical monism, in anticipation of an upcoming address Mullins would soon be presenting:

In your references to me in your address I hope you will not make the common mistake of supposing that my "Monism" makes men "parts of God". Men are no more *parts* of God than my thoughts are *parts* of me. Men are *products* of God's mind and will, as my thoughts are *products* of my mind and will. But my "Monism" is *ethical*—that is what my critics ignore. . . . My Monism is not Pantheism because it holds to God's transcendence and his separate personality—the two great truths which Pantheism denies.

Apparently Mullins honored Strong's request, for less than two weeks later Strong wrote to Mullins thanking him for how he had described ethical monism in his speech.[19]

Writing for a broader audience, Strong discussed the various responses his ethical monism had elicited: "While there was much favorable notice of my work and I received scores of letters assuring me that it was almost a new revelation, there were many ignorant denunciations of it, and I was called a pantheist and a Buddhist. It was the severest ordeal through which I ever passed."[20] Although Strong was hurt by some of the accusations, he offered very little by way of public reply. Timothy Christian has suggested a partial explanation for Strong's virtual silence, speculating that personal reasons may have prevented him from replying to reviews of the first and second volumes 1907 *Systematic Theology*.[21] About the time such reviews were appearing, Strong was on a leave of absence from the seminary. Strong's wife was experiencing poor health, and they spent September 1908 through May 1909 traveling in Europe. Unfortunately, the time abroad did not cure Strong's wife, and she continued to decline. In fact, her poor health ultimately forced them to return to Rochester four months earlier than originally planned. By that time Strong was in his early seventies, his wife's health was steadily deteriorating, and he had been away from the seminary for almost a year[22]—responding to critical book reviews was probably low on his list of priorities.

Whatever the reasons for Strong's limited response to his critics, he never wavered under their torrent of disapproval, and he remained steadfastly convinced that ethical monism had done nothing to diminish his orthodoxy.

Strong's Legacy

Theology impacts practice. What people believe often has a significant bearing on what they do and how they do it. Such was the case with Strong's ethical monism. Although at times the connection between ethical monism and Strong's actions was not crystal clear, ethical monism, the major development in Strong's theology while at Rochester, definitely had an impact on his larger theology and on his work as president of the seminary. Strong's presidency was a transitional one—the school was a much different place when Strong retired in 1912 than it had been when he arrived there in 1872. Strong was bothered by some of the changes that took place under his leadership, but he was largely responsible for setting those changes in motion through his decisions as its president.

John and Charles Strong

Augustus and Hattie Strong had six children: two sons and four daughters. Both sons would eventually attend the seminary in Rochester, but their later lives could hardly have been more different. One became a wealthy skeptic who turned his back on the Christian faith. The other remained a relatively unknown pastor and a seminary professor of modest means. Grant Wacker suggested that, in terms of disposition, each of Strong's sons seem to have embodied exactly half of their father's personality.[23]

John Henry Strong (1866–1960) largely followed in his father's footsteps. After completing A.B. degrees at both the University of Rochester and Yale, John returned to Rochester to study for the ministry. In 1893, he graduated from the seminary just as his father began publishing his views on ethical monism. At his seminary graduation, John delivered an address on "Union with Christ," a topic close to his father's heart.[24] Although he wrote fairly little, John appears to have embraced many of the main contours of his father's theology but was generally less interested in theology or philosophy.

Following graduation from seminary, John went on to pastor Baptist churches in Ohio and Connecticut. Then, after spending a year studying in Europe, John returned to Rochester to teach New Testament.[25] Although John served the seminary under his father's leadership, he never picked up his father's mantle within the Baptist denomination, and when his father retired from the seminary, John once again returned to the pastorate. Unlike his father, John was more reticent to speak his mind. He never became a celebrated scholar, and if he embraced his father's ethical monism, he appears to have left behind no evidence.

Late in life, Strong described his son as follows: "John is a son after my own heart, in that his affections give him access to theological truth, so that he sheds abroad the influence of an evangelical faith and a spiritual life." As a fellow minister of the gospel and teacher of seminarians, John brought his father much joy. He remained thoroughly evangelical and steadfastly committed to the faith. He was a faithful scholar and pastor, but on several occasions Strong confessed that John did not possess the keen insight or the rigorous intellectual abilities of his older brother.[26] John embraced and held on to his father's faith, but he lacked the creativity, the philosophical curiosity, and the drive to engage in theological speculation that his father possessed.

In contrast to his younger brother, Charles (1862–1940) was not only a source of great pride for his father but also a source of great sorrow. Charles was apparently the more capable of the two brothers, but he also brought his parents the most heartache, due to his eventual rejection of the Christian faith.

As the eldest of the Strong children, Charles initially followed in his father's footsteps. He studied hard, and he came to love the study of philosophy. Like his younger brother, Charles also received two A.B. degrees, one from the University of Rochester (1884) and the other from Harvard (1885).[27] Charles's time at Harvard proved an important turning point in his intellectual life. While there, Charles studied under psychologist and pragmatist philosopher William James (1842–1910). James's impact on Charles was more than might be expected, given that Charles only spent a year at Harvard: James kindled in Charles a lifelong love of philosophical speculation. Charles's enduring respect for James is reflected in his decision to dedicate one of his books, *The Origin of Consciousness*, to the memory of his former teacher. James, too, thought very highly of his onetime student. In 1905, James spent some time visiting with Charles in Europe. James wrote to his wife describing his former student: "I never knew such an unremitting, untiring, and monotonous addiction as that of his mind to the truth. He goes by points, pinning each one definitely, and has, I think, the cleverest mind I ever knew. . . . I suspect that he will outgrow us all."[28]

During his Harvard days, Charles also became friends with fellow student George Santayana (1863–1952). This relationship, too, would prove to be a lifelong one. The two men founded the Harvard Philosophical Club and spent many hours discussing the nature of knowledge and ultimate reality.[29] These conversations, along with Charles's formal studies in philosophy, tended to undercut the Christianity of Charles's youth. As his father put it, "The Harvard atmosphere was very liberal, and I soon found that my son was beginning to question the faith in which he had been brought up." Interestingly, Strong then confessed, "At that time [1884–85], I was myself less open to modern ideas than I have been since."[30]

After graduating from Harvard, Charles began studies at Rochester Theological Seminary in keeping with his father's request, but after just one year he withdrew from the seminary. His father, who was then president of the school, later described Charles's seminary experience as an unmitigated disaster: "His seminary course was very unsatisfactory both to him and to me. I am doubtful now whether, with his disposition to question the old statements of doctrine, it was not an error in judgment on the part of both of us for him to enter the seminary at all."[31] In light of Charles's questions about the Christian faith, he found studying for the ministry much less attractive than the pursuit of philosophy. He longed to travel, to meet interesting people, and to explore the deeper things of life apart from the confines of biblical orthodoxy. He would soon get his wish.

In 1886, Charles traveled to Berlin in the company of Santayana. The two men shared a James Walker Fellowship from Harvard, which covered their expenses.[32] If Charles had begun to question the Christian faith during his college days and had found himself unable to resolve those questions at Rochester, he now encountered a whole new set of questions that effectively erased whatever semblance of faith he still had. Charles's time abroad seems to have been the final stage in his decision to abandon the faith of his father. By the time Charles returned to the states, he had rejected the Christian faith and had given up the idea of a ministerial career.[33]

For several years, Charles taught philosophy at Cornell University (1887–89). In 1889, he married Bessie Rockefeller (1866–1906), the eldest daughter of John D. Rockefeller Sr. (1839–1937). Charles then returned to Europe, where he spent his time pursuing further studies in philosophy at Berlin, Paris, and Freiburg. Although he would teach for a number of years, his marriage to a Rockefeller eliminated the need for him to work and provided him with the time and resources to live and study wherever he wanted without regard to expenses.

In 1890, Charles took a position as docent at the recently founded Clark University in Worchester, Massachusetts. A couple of years later, he was appointed to teach psychology at the newly established University of Chicago. Charles remained in Chicago for a few years, but Bessie's health was unable to handle the Chicago climate, so in 1895 Charles began teaching psychology at Columbia University in New York, where he remained until 1910.[34]

In the midst of these career changes and travels abroad, something rather important took place back in Rochester that brought the elder Strong a great deal of grief both at the time and for many years after. In view of his son's evident departure from the Christian faith, in 1891 Strong urged the First Baptist Church of Rochester to exclude Charles formally from its membership. In the fall of 1891 the church excommunicated Charles, and Charles himself was apparently in full agreement with the decision. Some twenty-five years later Strong would regret this action. In fact, in 1916 he even went so far as to ask the church to reverse its earlier decision. Once again, the church complied with Strong's request.[35]

What is most significant for this study of ethical monism is not the church's later reversal or even Strong's change of heart but the timing and nature of

Charles's departure from the faith, which culminated in the decision of First Baptist Church to exclude him from membership. Charles began studying philosophy in earnest during the mid-1880s, and by about 1887, he had decided to reject the Christian faith. Apparently Strong held out hope for his son during the late 1880s, when Strong wrote several articles arguing against every form of philosophical monism and warning others of the dangers inherent in embracing unbiblical philosophy. In 1891, Strong finally admitted to himself and to others that his elder son had abandoned the faith, and that year Charles was finally removed from the church where the Strongs had been prominent members for decades.

Charles's departure from the faith took place in the years immediately preceding Strong's "discovery" of ethical monism. Although Strong possessed a keen interest in philosophy prior to his son's departure, Strong's new way of blending modern philosophical monism with the Christian faith followed closely on his apostate son's decision to follow philosophy away from the faith. A direct connection cannot be determined with certainty, but the timing of these events is remarkable: one year after Strong finally confessed that his son had left the Christian faith for the study of speculative philosophy, he published his "Christ in Creation" articles that laid out the basic outline of his new understanding of God's relationship to the world, an idea he would soon call ethical monism.[36]

Although a definite causal relationship between Charles's departure from the faith and Strong's decision to embrace ethical monism cannot be established, it seems plausible that at least part of the motivation behind Strong's decision to accept monism, a key element of modern philosophy, was his desire to see his son won back to the faith. If such was the case, Strong's effort failed completely. Charles never returned to the Christian faith. Instead, he remained a skeptic for the rest of his life.[37]

Rockefeller and the Quest for a Baptist University

Most likely Strong first met Rockefeller in Cleveland sometime in the mid to late 1860s. Rockefeller had lived in Cleveland since the early 1850s, and Strong had moved there in 1865 to assume a pastorate. As mentioned in chapter 1, although Strong was never Rockefeller's pastor, he preached the funeral for Rockefeller's infant daughter in 1870.

In 1872, when Strong moved about 250 miles northeast to Rochester to become president of the Rochester Theological Seminary, distance did not bring his relationship with Rockefeller to an end. Rockefeller had been impressed by Strong's ministry in Cleveland, and having become acquainted with the wealthiest Baptist in the nation, Strong was not about to let such a potential source of capital slip through his fingers. The continuing relationship between the two men enriched Strong in several ways. According to one of Rockefeller's biographers, over the next few decades the multimillionaire supplemented Strong's income, paid many of his vacation expenses, and gave approximately $500,000 to Rochester Theological Seminary.[38] Strong's connection to Rockefeller obviously brought great benefits both to him and to the institution he led. However, Rockefeller never gave Strong what he wanted above all else: a world-class Baptist university located in New York.

Although he was president of Rochester Theological Seminary, Strong entertained big plans for the future of Baptist education that went far beyond his job description, plans that depended on Rockefeller's resources. Around 1880, Strong began writing to Rockefeller about establishing a Baptist university in New York. Strong believed that God had uniquely placed and equipped him to appeal to Rockefeller for the funds necessary to see such a project brought to pass, and in fact, Strong believed that God had called him to pursue this goal: "I felt especially sent by God upon this errand."[39] Throughout the 1880s, Strong tried to convince Rockefeller to fund a new, world-class university that would serve the Baptist denomination as no other school in his day. This university, Strong believed, should be located in the thriving metropolis of New York City. As one of Rockefeller's biographers noted, this vision became Strong's "monomania throughout the 1880s," and "he badgered Rockefeller about it at every turn."[40]

Strong envisioned a great university in the heart of New York City. He expected to fill the role of its president, with William Rainey Harper (1856–1906) as his vice president.[41] Strong was anxious to see Rockefeller sign on to his plan, partly owing to fear that Rockefeller would be convinced by someone else to fund a university in another location. At the time, Baptists already had a number of colleges and universities to their name, including the University of Rochester (est. 1850).[42] Some ambitious Baptist leaders hoped to see the Baptist equivalent of Harvard or Yale established with the help of Rockefeller's millions, and numerous locations for such a university had been suggested by various people,[43] a few with strong arguments in their favor.

Chicago was consistently one of the most formidable competitors to Strong's New York plan. Baptists had first established a university in Chicago in the 1850s. The closure of this university, now known as the Old University of Chicago, in 1886 due to financial difficulties did nothing to diminish the perceived need for a Baptist university in the area. By the late 1880s, Chicago was the second largest city in the nation and one of the fastest growing.[44] Strong did not want to see his university lost to Chicago, so he lobbied aggressively on behalf of New York.

Strong, of course, did not see himself as badgering Rockefeller. At least, he did not see himself doing anything other than what God would have him do to help encourage a wealthy fellow Baptist contribute to the advance of Baptist education. But Rockefeller did not like to be pushed when it came to money. Like most people, he wanted to be free to use his resources in whatever way he pleased. Rockefeller's personal respect for Strong and the growing relationship between their children, which would culminate in the marriage of Charles Strong and Bessie Rockefeller in 1889, gave Strong an unusual amount of leverage with Rockefeller. In the end, however, it would not prove to be enough.

Sometime in the mid-1880s, Rockefeller told Strong to stop pestering him about the university. For a time, Strong obeyed this request, but in January 1887, Strong wrote to Rockefeller telling him that he felt he must raise the topic once more. Rockefeller then suggested that they spend the summer traveling in Europe with Charles and Bessie. Strong viewed this trip as a golden opportunity to sell Rockefeller on his plan. He would show Rockefeller the great universities of Europe and whet his appetite for a similar, though distinctively Baptist, institution in New York.[45]

While in Paris, Strong laid out his case, and on the ship back to New York, he exhorted Rockefeller rather forcefully. Strong later wrote, "I told him that the Lord had blessed him with financial prosperity greater than that of any other man upon the planet—he had made more money in a single lifetime than any other man who ever lived, and if he did not do more for God than any other man who ever lived, he could never stand in God's judgment." Strong then described what happened next: "[Rockefeller] turned red, and he looked very angry. But I had delivered my message, and I left the result with God."[46] Concerning this incident and Strong's overall approach to Rockefeller, Ron Chernow rightly noted in his biography of Rockefeller,

> [Strong] completely misread Rockefeller's psychology. Where Rockefeller preferred a modest approach, Dr. Strong was often overbearing, as if trying to bully him into endorsing the project. He committed an unforgiveable sin by suggesting that Rockefeller could sanitize his reputation by funding the university. . . . This argument miscarried on several counts: Rockefeller resented any references to his infamy, felt no need to cleanse his reputation, and rebelled against any insinuation that his charity was selfishly motivated.[47]

Strong had also made the mistake of presenting Rockefeller with an overly ambitious, if fairly accurate, price tag for the project: $22 million.[48] Rockefeller would not be pushed, and he was not ready to commit that much money to such an endeavor. In fact, at the time he did not have that much available in liquid assets.[49] Strong had committed several tactical errors.[50]

For a number of years, Thomas Wakefield Goodspeed (1842–1927) had enjoyed access to Rockefeller's ear, and Goodspeed was far better at reading the rich oilman than Strong ever was. Goodspeed, a graduate of Rochester Theological Seminary, was by the 1880s a trustee of the Baptist Union Theological Seminary in Chicago. During the mid-1880s, Goodspeed had begun telling Rockefeller about the advantages of establishing a great Baptist university in the growing city of Chicago. William Rainey Harper, too, joined this call for a new university in Chicago. In January 1887, just as Strong was again broaching the forbidden topic with Rockefeller, Harper wrote in a letter to Rockefeller, "There is no greater work to be done on this continent than the work of establishing a University in or near Chicago." Together, Goodspeed and Harper convinced Rockefeller of the merits of establishing a new Baptist university in Chicago, and Strong's plan for a Baptist university in New York came crashing to the floor. Strong later wrote, "After all I had done for fifteen years, my New York University was gobbled up and transferred to Chicago. . . . It was a sore trial to me to have my work seemingly come to naught and to have others reap the benefit of the seed I had sown."[51]

In 1890, the University of Chicago was established as a Baptist university, with Harper as its first president. As Strong wished, Rockefeller had committed himself to funding a world-class Baptist institution of higher learning. However, Strong had failed to secure either the location or the presidency of this institution, and his disappointment was severe. He consoled himself in two ways. In his autobiography, Strong noted that Rockefeller consistently attributed the idea of a great Baptist university to him. If Strong could not lead the new university, at least he could take credit for the idea. More significant, perhaps, Strong later claimed that he thought it was best that the administration of the new school fell to others because it left him time to work out solutions to certain theological problems.

Ethical monism was certainly one of the solutions he had in mind: Strong's plans for a Baptist university in New York fell apart shortly before he discovered ethical monism. Moreover, having lost the opportunity to lead a great new Baptist university, Strong seems to have been looking for another way to leave his mark on Baptist theology. Ethical monism may have been, in part, an attempt to engage in a little theological legacy building.

Rochester after Strong

In his forty-year career at Rochester, Strong added many new individuals to the seminary faculty. Some of these new hires were conservatives, but many were not.[52] LeRoy Moore Jr. has argued that Strong oversaw essentially three different faculties during his time as president, corresponding to distinct phases in Strong's theological development.[53] In general, Strong became increasingly willing to hire more liberal faculty members as his theology became more influenced of modern philosophy. Strong's embrace of ethical monism began near the middle of his presidency, and he hired more liberals after adopting ethical monism than he had during the first half of his presidency.

By the time Strong retired in 1912, the faculty of Rochester Theological Seminary was much less conservative than he was.[54] Strong's retirement left two significant vacancies at the school: president and professor of theology. Strong hoped to see his younger son, John, selected as the next president, but by this time the seminary's board of trustees was more to the left than it had been four decades earlier. The board was interested in hiring a president who was even more open to modern thought than Strong was, and so John was far too conservative for their liking.[55]

For several years after Strong's departure, Joseph W. A. Stewart (1852–1947) served as acting president of the seminary. Stewart had come to New York from Canada, initially called in 1887 to serve as pastor at the First Baptist Church in Rochester. In 1903 Stewart resigned the pastorate and became dean of the seminary. While serving as acting president (1912–15) Stewart largely continued the policies of Strong. He was not, strictly speaking, a conservative, and he was willing to hire faculty members who were even less conservative than he was. Stewart was basically a mediating figure who found it easy to compromise to secure consensus.

In a move that was somewhat counterintuitive, the seminary board decided to find someone to fill Strong's position as professor of systematic theology before securing a permanent president. In 1912, George Cross (1862–1929) was proposed for the professorship. When first interviewed, Cross declined to say whether or not he believed in the preexistence, deity, virgin birth, miracles, objective atonement, physical resurrection, or omnipresence of Christ.[56] This had initially given the nominating committee pause, but Stewart secured a statement from Cross that eventually satisfied the committee, and Cross was appointed.

Strong viewed this decision as an enormous mistake: "I regard that election as the greatest calamity that has come to the seminary since its foundation. It was the entrance of an agnostic, skeptical, and anti-Christian element into its teaching, the results of which will only be evil." Strong described Cross's view of Scripture as "only the record of man's gropings after God instead of being primarily God's revelation to man." Strong believed that such a view made systematic theology impossible and turned any such endeavor into merely a history of doctrines rather than an attempt to correlate God's truth and present it in systematic form.[57] On top of these theological shortcomings, Cross was also a product of the University of Chicago—the school that had brought Strong's dreams of a Baptist university in New York to an end. For Strong, the appointment of Cross as his replacement in the theology department was a sign that his own legacy at Rochester was not the direction the school would take.

In 1915, the trustees appointed Clarence Augustus Barbour (1869–1937) president of Rochester Theological Seminary. A graduate of both Brown University and Rochester Theological Seminary, Barbour had served as pastor of the Lake Avenue Baptist Church in Rochester for eighteen years (1891–1909).[58] His success at the church in Rochester had led to a position with the YMCA, then near its height. For much of his six years with the YMCA (1909–15), Barbour traveled the country attempting to build bridges between the organization and local church congregations.[59] The personal connections Barbour established during this time no doubt helped when he took over the president's responsibilities at Rochester. Although Barbour's background was varied and not particularly academic, in 1915 he was called upon both to lead the seminary and to teach homiletics.

Although Barbour had been a trustee of the seminary since 1896 and had served as president of the board from 1913 to 1915, his appointment was not without controversy.[60] In early 1915, Barbour wrote to Strong asking the longtime president to approve of his appointment. Strong replied that he could not grant the approval Barbour hoped for. In fact, in view of Barbour's recent leadership of the seminary board, Strong expressed concern about the direction Barbour would take the school:

> You are too much under the influence of the Chicago School of Theology. It is said that recent appointments to professorship are all men who are unwilling to say that they believe in the preexistence, deity, virgin birth, miracles, physical resurrection, objective atonement, omnipresence of Jesus Christ. The Chicago men, it is said, are practical Unitarians, and that the seminary has already gone over to the unevangelical wing of Christendom. Since you have not stemmed the tide, but have helped it on, you are under suspicion as thinking more of the temporal popularity of the institution than of its conformity to the Scriptural model.[61]

Strong doubted whether Barbour "with his compromising spirit" would be able to prevent the school from drifting into full-blown apostasy.[62] As it turned out, Barbour proved to be the consummate politician. He was personally a little more conservative than some of his faculty, but he managed to play the more conservative ones against the more liberal ones while retaining the favor of both. As Moore put it, "Barbour was a skilled manipulator as well as a theological liberal . . . who made a great deal of experienced religion and very little of the subtleties of dogma."[63]

During Barbour's tenure as president, the seminary continued its slide away from evangelical orthodoxy toward a modernist form of Christianity. Some decried this trend while others welcomed it. For example, in his address to the Pre-Convention Conference on the Fundamentals in 1920, William Bell Riley identified Rochester as being among the seminaries that were "hot-beds of skepticism." On the other hand, in the so-called Kelly report on the state of theological education, published in 1924, Robert L. Kelly praised Rochester for having made "marvelous development during the last half century in its struggle to meet the needs of changing conditions." Specifically, Kelly noted that the curriculum at Rochester had made "a great break from the dogmatic to the scientific, from the theoretical to the practical, and from the ecclesio-centric to the socio-centric point of view." By the early 1920s, both the faculty and the curriculum at Rochester had transitioned from older orthodoxy focused on serving the church to modern thought focused on meeting perceived social needs. As a recent history of the school declares, under Barbour's leadership the school's "transition into a progressive institution was completed."[64]

Near the end of his tenure, in 1928 Barbour oversaw the merger between Rochester Theological Seminary and the Colgate Theological Seminary. He then presided over the combined Colgate Rochester Divinity School for a year before leaving to assume the presidency of Brown University, a position he held until his death in 1937. In 1970, the Crozer Theological Seminary merged with Colgate Rochester to form the Colgate Rochester Crozer Divinity School. Today, the faculty describe the school as "rooted in biblical faith and in the lived traditions of the church" but also as "shaped by the witness of the Social Gospel movement, by the traditions of the Black Church, by the voices of women in church and society, and by Christian responses to religious pluralism and issues of gender, each as critically interpreted and embodied by those who both cherish the past and are open to the future."[65] Although the modern-day school reflects fondly on the leadership of its longtime president Augustus Hopkins Strong, it clearly stands well to the left of Strong's own theological commitments and vision for the school.

Strong's attempt to wed certain aspects of modern thought with Christian theology did not create a stable platform for the seminary's future. Strong's ethical monism was in some ways emblematic of his attempt to bring together orthodoxy and modernism in the seminary faculty. Such a balancing act did not work well in his theology, and it did not work well for the seminary either. The entrance of skeptical thought that began in earnest under Strong's leadership set a trajectory away from its evangelical heritage. Strong's legacy at the seminary was much like his theological legacy: mixed—neither his school nor his theological system emerged unscathed from his attempt to combine ideas that ultimately proved incompatible.[66]

Conclusion

As noted in the first half of this chapter, both liberal and conservative reviewers detected the incongruity in Strong's later theology. More conservative theologians expressed their hope that Strong would eventually abandon his ethical monism and return to a more consistent form of orthodoxy. More liberal theologians thought that Strong had taken a few steps in the right direction but still needed to throw off the traces of orthodoxy that lingered in his theology. Neither those to Strong's right nor those to his left believed that ethical monism could be successfully blended with evangelical theology. In this, both sides were agreed, and both were correct.

Conclusion

A FULL CENTURY AFTER HIS DEATH, Augustus Hopkins Strong remains a puzzling figure in many ways. His theology and his leadership at Rochester involved a number of seeming contradictions. On the one hand, Strong considered himself a pillar of orthodoxy and a defender of the faith. In fact, he thought his discovery of ethical monism strengthened and better explained the Christian faith. On the other hand, Strong hired liberal professors to teach at Rochester, and his promotion of ethical monism led several of his prominent peers to accuse him of pantheism. Thus, Strong left behind a rather mixed legacy.

Solving the Riddle of Augustus Hopkins Strong

Strong was converted under the ministry of Charles G. Finney in 1856, near the end of his junior year at Yale. Upon graduation, Strong enrolled at the Baptist seminary in his hometown, Rochester, New York. After graduating from Rochester Theological Seminary in 1859, Strong pastored churches in Haverhill, Massachusetts (1861–65), and Cleveland, Ohio (1865–72). He later recorded a number of theological lessons he learned during his pastoral ministry, several involving concepts that later provided a foundation for his ethical monism. While pastoring in Cleveland, Strong became acquainted with famous oil magnate John D. Rockefeller, and to some extent, their lives became entwined from that point on.

Strong had originally decided to attend seminary in Rochester largely because of Ezekiel Gilman Robinson, then professor of theology and president of the school. Robinson resigned from the presidency of Rochester Theological Seminary in 1872, more than a decade after Strong had graduated from the institution. After a short search, the trustees invited Strong to fill the chair of theology. However, he refused to take the position unless he also was made president of the seminary. Surprisingly, the board acquiesced, and in the fall of 1872, Strong began his forty-year career teaching theology and serving as president of Rochester Theological Seminary.

Even before returning to Rochester, however, Strong's theology was moving gradually in the general direction of ethical monism. Strong himself acknowledged that several of the major emphases of his later theology were present in his thinking before he became president of Rochester.

Strong was a lifelong student of philosophy. His published works reveal that he read, admired, and occasionally parleyed with the writings of the philosophical idealists of the eighteenth and nineteenth centuries. Although Strong never pointed to any particular philosopher as having influenced his discovery of ethical monism, he was clearly familiar with various forms of philosophical idealism for many years before he embraced it. Comparison of the various editions of his *Systematic Theology* suggests Strong was actively studying the writings of Johann Gottlieb Fichte, Friedrich Schelling, G. W. F. Hegel, Rudolf Hermann Lotze, Borden Parker Bowne, and Josiah Royce, among others, during the decades he revised his theology text. Although Strong criticized most of these men at some point, he also absorbed some of their basic ideas, and his ethical monism bore significant similarities to the philosophical idealism of his day.

When Strong returned to Rochester as president and professor in 1872, he was not an ethical monist. In fact, up through the late 1880s Strong explicitly rejected philosophical monism altogether. Then sometime in the early 1890s, Strong changed his mind. He concluded that monism was the philosophical trend of the future and that if properly interpreted it could be used to bolster rather than undermine the Christian faith. Strong realized that his embrace of monism would be controversial, so he initially hesitated to publish his new beliefs. In the fall of 1892, he finally published an article that revealed the main contours of his new philosophical position. In 1894, Strong gave his new idea a name when he published a series of three articles titled "Ethical Monism." The next year, he followed up this series with another three-part series of articles titled "Ethical Monism Once More." In 1896, in the fifth edition of his *Systematic Theology* Strong incorporated ethical monism into his larger theological system.

Early responses to Strong's ethical monism were mostly negative. Men like Alvah Hovey and Adolphus J. F. Behrends considered Strong a friend, but they considered his embrace of ethical monism misguided and somewhat dangerous. Strong was generally unmoved—he continued to believe his ethical monism provided new and better explanations of a number of difficult philosophical and theological issues.

Questions Answered

This study began by asking what role ethical monism played in Strong's theology and ministry. Clearly, the answer to this question is complex. Ethical monism was in some ways a product of preexisting tensions in Strong's theology. It also bore significant resemblance to the concept of monism that was popular in nineteenth-century philosophy and the emphasis on divine immanence that was common in the liberal theology of his day. It also gradually affected Strong's larger theology and, to some degree, his ministry at Rochester Theological Seminary and the school's future trajectory.

In his later life, Strong believed that his spiritual experience had long been building toward his discovery of ethical monism. He saw ethical monism as something of a culmination of his spiritual journey. He also saw it as the solution to some of theology's thorniest problems.

For many years prior to his discovery of ethical monism, Strong wrestled with a number of unanswered theological questions. For example, in the earliest edition of his theology text, Strong defended his view of the atonement, which he called the ethical theory, and criticized competing ideas. Despite his arguments, Strong struggled to see how the sin of humanity could be justly imputed to Christ. In looking for an answer to this dilemma, he eventually recognized ethical monism as the solution.

Similarly, Strong's early embrace and discussions of theistic evolution seemed to call for greater explanation. Many people, Christians and skeptics alike, believed that the concept of evolution undermined the authority of the Scriptures and the basic message of Christianity. Strong was aware of these charges, and he eventually found in ethical monism a new and better way to explain evolution in what he thought was a distinctively Christian manner.

Ethical monism seems to have played a double role in Strong's theology. It not only helped resolve tensions that had bothered him for years but also shaped other areas of his theology in ways which he seemingly did not anticipate. Ethical monism became for Strong "the key to theology." It was a concept that helped explain many issues related to sin, the atonement, and God's overall relationship to the world.

A number of Strong's theological peers reviewed his later books, after he presented his ethical monism to the world and attempted to integrate it into his larger theological system. Conservative theologians like Benjamin Breckinridge Warfield and Caspar Wistar Hodge Jr. saw nothing good coming from Strong's new idea. They thought he was flirting with pantheism, and they believed that as time progressed ethical monism would only corrupt other areas of his theology.

Other, more liberal reviewers, such as William Douglas Mackenzie and Lyman Abbott, also did not embrace ethical monism but viewed it as an indication that he was moving in their direction, that is to say, to the left. Their main criticisms were that they thought he was inconsistent in trying to maintain certain aspects of an older, more evangelical theology while affirming a view of God that was clearly outside the bounds of orthodoxy. In the end, neither conservatives nor liberals accepted Strong's ethical monism.

Although both of Strong's sons attended Rochester Theological Seminary, neither one appears to have embraced ethical monism. John, the younger of the two, eventually taught at the seminary, but he did not trumpet his father's characteristic doctrinal position. Charles rejected his father's theology altogether and became a skeptic.

Despite his desire for a wider influence and especially the establishment of a Baptist university in New York City, Strong remained at Rochester Theological Seminary for forty years. During his tenure, Strong added many new professors to the faculty, and several of these were theologically to his left. When he retired from the seminary in 1912, it was a far less conservative institution than he had inherited in 1872.

In the end, Strong's attempt to blend orthodoxy and modern thought fared no better than his attempt to blend orthodox and modernist faculty members at Rochester. At the seminary, the combination proved unstable as it tended to migrate away from orthodoxy. In Strong's theology, the combination resulted in logical contradictions that were detected by most of his peers. His attempt to bring together orthodox theology and modern thought in a concept he called ethical monism was both creative and ambitious, but it ultimately failed.

NOTES

Introduction

1. McGiffert, *Rise of Modern Religious Ideas*, 189. See also McGiffert, "Immanence," 168–69. Near the end of the nineteenth century another author wrote, "There is a very considerable hope abroad that we shall reach a higher conception of God by looking at Him as the immanent principle of all things. Some very harsh censures are passed at the same time on the contrary and older conception of the divine transcendence. The idea is gaining ground that we shall be brought a good deal on our way by discarding all language of the Creator as distinct and apart from the creature, and by cultivating a habit of religious speech in which, if they are not identified, they are at least brought very near together" (Tunis, "Doctrine of the Divine Immanence," 389). See also Hopkins, *Rise of the Social Gospel in American Protestantism*, 123–25, 320.

2. McConnell, *Diviner Immanence*, 9. About a decade earlier, William N. Clarke noted a tendency in contemporary literature away from materialism and toward immanence, that is, toward a "recognition of spirit as pervading and giving character to all" (*Circle of Theology*, 13).

3. Mackintosh, *Doctrine of the Person of Jesus Christ*, 431. Henry Burton Trimble similarly spoke about the "present emphasis of the doctrine of the divine immanence" and described it as "the most significant development in the thinking of the modern religious world" ("Christ in the Light of the Divine Immanence," 404).

4. E.g., Illingworth, *Divine Immanence*; Bowne, *Immanence of God*; McConnell, *Diviner Immanence*.

5. E.g., Machen, *Christianity and Liberalism*, 62–64.

6. To date a critical biography of Strong has not been written. The single most helpful source of information about Strong's life is his autobiography, which he began to write on his sixtieth birthday for the benefit of his children and grandchildren: Strong, *Autobiography of Augustus Hopkins Strong*. Two important monographs on Strong's thought are Henry, *Personal Idealism and Strong's Theology*; and Wacker, *Augustus H. Strong and the Dilemma of Historical Consciousness*. Shorter sketches include J. H. Strong, "Augustus Hopkins Strong"; Richardson, "Augustus Hopkins Strong"; Thornbury, "Augustus Hopkins Strong"; and Thornbury, "Legacy of Natural Theology," 120–74.

7. In 1872, the trustees of Rochester Theological Seminary asked Strong to return to his alma mater to teach theology. Strong recounted, "I was asked to accept the professorship of theology without the presidency. I declined, upon the grounds that I could not work easily unless I had affairs in my own hands. They thereupon elected me both professor and president, and I accepted the election before I returned to Cleveland"

(*Autobiography of Augustus Hopkins Strong*, 203). Strong served in this dual role from 1872 until his retirement in 1912.

One of Strong's sons summarized his impact on the seminary: "Dr. Strong returned to Rochester in 1872. He found the Seminary in debt, meagerly equipped, and not even paying the professors' salaries. Its students were ill-prepared. When he retired after forty years it was in many respects the foremost Baptist theological seminary in the world" (J. H. Strong, "Augustus Hopkins Strong," 238). William H. Brackney noted that Strong was "one of the most illustrious and heavily quoted Baptist theologians of his era. His wide scope of influence was due in part to the premier place in which he labored. Rochester Theological Seminary led student enrollment among the North American Baptist seminaries and boasted what was arguably the leading Baptist faculty at the end of the nineteenth century. Students arrived at Rochester from all corners of the United States and the British provinces to study theology, mostly with Strong" (*Genetic History of Baptist Thought*, 326).

8. Strong first published his theology notes in 1876 for the sake of his students: Strong, *Lectures on Theology*. These notes were later expanded into his *Systematic Theology*, which went through eight editions between its first appearance in 1886 and its final three-volume edition, which appeared in 1907–9. This work became a standard textbook in many North American seminaries throughout much of the twentieth century. Although its widespread use has tapered off, it is still required reading in a number of colleges and seminaries. As indication of Strong's influence on Baptist theology, Strong is the most frequently cited author in Henry Clarence Thiessen's *Introductory Lectures in Systematic Theology* (1949) and in the lesser-known *Systematic Theology* by R. V. Sarrels (1978).

9. In the preface to Strong's autobiography, its editor, Crerar Douglas, noted that "Strong's influence was as diverse as the interpretations of his controversial theology" (*Autobiography of Augustus Hopkins Strong*, 15).

10. Strong appears to have viewed himself much this way. Near the end of his life, he once described his theological position by stating, "My views are midway between two opposite extremes. Both sides fire into me, while I am only the more convinced that my middle ground is the only correct position" ("My Views of the Universe in General," 625). And in a posthumously published book, Strong sought to distinguish himself from both the fundamentalists and the higher critics before suggesting that the answer lay somewhere between the two groups (*What Shall I Believe?*, 62–63). Irwin Reist believed that Strong was "attempting to mediate between the old orthodoxy which was hardening into fundamentalism and the new liberalism which seemed to be losing the core of the Christian confession" ("Augustus Hopkins Strong and William Newton Clarke," 28). James Hastings once wrote that Strong "is conservative but not cramped, liberal but not loose" (review of *Christ in Creation and Ethical Monism*, 316).

11. Wacker, *Augustus H. Strong and the Dilemma of Historical Consciousness*, 8; see 7–8 for representatives of each of these views.

12. Wacker, *Augustus H. Strong and the Dilemma of Historical Consciousness*, 12.

13. Strong, "My Views of the Universe in General," 625.

14. Evans, *Kingdom Is Always but Coming*, 40. Strong's own assessment of Bushnell's view of the atonement can be found in Strong, *Systematic Theology* (1907), 733–40.

15. Minus, *Walter Rauschenbusch*, 44.

16. Evans, *Kingdom Is Always but Coming*, 40. Rauschenbusch graduated from the seminary in 1886.

17. Evans, *Kingdom Is Always but Coming*, 124. Even as Strong extended the job offer to Rauschenbusch, he was concerned about the younger man's liberal proclivities. Among the factors that troubled Strong was Rauschenbusch's view of the atonement: "The two men apparently exchanged their perspectives on the doctrine of the atonement, and Strong worried that Rauschenbusch did not give enough credence to the power of the cross to forgive sinners" (72). Rauschenbusch and Strong maintained a good relationship throughout their careers at Rochester, and a few years after Strong's retirement Rauschenbusch dedicated his *Theology for the Social Gospel* (1917) to Strong, "a theologian whose best beloved doctrine has been the mystic union with Christ."

18. Moore, "Academic Freedom," 66: Woelfkin was "the chief spokesman for Baptist liberals during the fundamentalist controversy," and Moehlman was "an unrepentant modernist to the day of his death" (66). Gregory Alan Thornbury has noted that, although Strong considered his own theology a defense of theological orthodoxy, his "appointments include some of the most noted theological liberals in Northern Baptist life in the early twentieth century" ("Legacy of Natural Theology," 175). Interestingly, in his autobiography Strong suggests that his tenure at Rochester was marked by orthodoxy while his hiring of liberal faculty members is silently passed over. His only mention of Rauschenbusch is as a friend of his eldest son, Charles, who incidentally abandoned the Christian faith (*Autobiography of Augustus Hopkins Strong*, 255–56, 260).

19. Carl F. H. Henry traced Strong's theological development through three different periods which he believed reflected Strong's "early, middle, and late convictions" (*Personal Idealism and Strong's Theology*, 15).

20. As late as January 1888, Strong argued directly against any type of monism (Strong, "Modern Idealism"). Wacker discusses possible explanations for this change in Strong's thinking, but he ultimately concedes that why Strong adopted ethical monism so quickly is unknown (*Augustus H. Strong and the Dilemma of Historical Consciousness*, 60–62).

21. Strong, *Systematic Theology* (1907), 105.

22. Strong, *Systematic Theology* (1907), vii.

Chapter 1

1. The bronze bust was sculpted by William Couper (1853–1942); a picture appears in Couper, *American Sculptor on the Grand Tour*, 82.

2. The address was delivered January 13, 1913, and published later that year in Strong, *One Hundred Chapel-Talks*, 3–33.

3. Strong, *One Hundred Chapel-Talks*, 4. Similarly, another writer listed three prerequisites to understanding Strong's system of theology; the first was understanding the historical background of Strong's life (Johnson, "Prerequisites to an Understanding," 333–36).

4. Strong, *Autobiography of Augustus Hopkins Strong*; A. Strong, *Autobiography of Alvah Strong*.

5. Either one or both men appear in the following sources: McIntosh, *History of Monroe County, New York*; McKelvey, *Rochester: The Water-Power City*; McKelvey, *Rochester: The Flower City*; McKelvey, *Rochester: The Quest for Quality*; McKelvey, *Rochester on the Genesee*; Parker, *Rochester*; Peck, *Semi-centennial History of the City of Rochester*; Peck, *History of Rochester*; and Ward, *Churches of Rochester*.

6. Emerson, *Conduct of Life*, 7; Strong, *Systematic Theology* (1907), 496. Strong cited Emerson's question in the context of his own theological discussion of the transmission of sin.

7. Sources provide conflicting information regarding the date of John Strong's emigration to New England. William Richard Cutter and Benjamin W. Dwight both state that Strong made the journey aboard the *Mary and John* in the spring of 1630. Although Augustus Strong seems to have followed their lead on this, Alvah Strong lists the date of his ancestor's emigration as "about 1639" (Cutter, *Genealogical and Personal Memoirs*, 1104; Dwight, *History of the Descendants of Elder John Strong*, 1:xxv–xxvi, 15; Strong, *Autobiography of Augustus Hopkins Strong*, 28, 371; A. Strong, *Autobiography of Alvah Strong*, 4). One might assume that Cutter and Dwight were correct and that Alvah Strong's "about 1639" was a general guess, but additional information further complicates the issue. Jeanne W. Strong has reproduced a manuscript page from a port book in London that appears to show John Strong sailed from England to the New World aboard the *Hopewell* in May 1635 (J. W. Strong, *Strong Men and Strong Women*, 3–4). One possible explanation for the 1630/35 discrepancy is that John Strong first sailed to New England in 1630, then returned to England, and sailed back to New England in 1635.

8. Strong, *Autobiography of Augustus Hopkins Strong*, 28. In this same context, Strong apologetically noted that his own offspring were only "the meager number of six." And he wrote concerning his children, "Let them read Professor Dwight's *History*, in two octavo volumes of eight hundred pages each, one of the most voluminous family records yet published in this country, and as they see what their progenitors have accomplished in the way of multiplication, let them go and do likewise" (28). Prior to his death, Elder John Strong had more than 160 descendants, including 18 children, 114 grandchildren, and 33 great grandchildren (Reynolds, *Genealogical and Family History of Southern New York*, 1071).

9. A. Strong, *Autobiography of Alvah Strong*, 16. Warren, Connecticut, was also the birthplace of Charles G. Finney (1792–1875), who had significant impact on several members of the Strong family, as described in this chapter.

10. A. Strong, *Autobiography of Alvah Strong*, 15.

11. A. Strong, *Autobiography of Alvah Strong*, 16, 21–23; McKelvey, *Rochester on the Genesee*, 24–27. The Erie Canal was completed in October 1825, but cities along its route, such as Rochester, began booming in the years leading up to its official opening. Canal construction provided jobs in an era when high immigration rates were producing high unemployment rates in much of the country, and the eight-hundred-foot aqueduct that carried canal boats over the Genesee River at Rochester was one of the canal's largest structures (Bernstein, *Wedding of the Waters*, 231–32; McKelvey, "Rochester and the Erie Canal"). Elsewhere, Blake McKelvey cites the population growth of Rochester as 512 percent during 1820–1830 (*Rochester: The Water-Power City*, 100).

12. A. Strong, *Autobiography of Alvah Strong*, 17. See also, Parker, *Rochester*, 392–93.

13. Strong, *Autobiography of Augustus Hopkins Strong*, 29.

14. Strong, *Autobiography of Augustus Hopkins Strong*, 32. Alvah similarly referred to the printing office as the "Poor Boy's College" (*Autobiography of Alvah Strong*, 56).

15. A. Strong, *Autobiography of Alvah Strong*, 30–31.

16. A. Strong, *Autobiography of Alvah Strong*, 32.

17. Strong, *Autobiography of Augustus Hopkins Strong*, 32–33; Strong, *Reminiscences of Early Rochester*, 10.

18. A. Strong, *Autobiography of Alvah Strong*, 32.

19. A. Strong, *Autobiography of Alvah Strong*, 35. Erastus Shepard purchased the *Anti-Masonic Inquirer* in fall 1831 and published it from November 1831 through December 1833. Alvah Strong became his partner in November 1832 (Follett, *History of the Press of Western New-York*, 47).

20. Strong, *Autobiography of Augustus Hopkins Strong*, 35.

21. The house has long since been torn down. According to public records, a moderate-size brick home was built on that site in 1875. When Augustus Strong was thirteen or fourteen, his family moved to "more comfortable quarters" on South Saint Paul Street, on the east side of the Genesee River (Strong, *Reminiscences of Early Rochester*, 4). Interestingly, the old house on Troup Street soon became the site of the famous "Rochester knockings," in which spirits of the deceased allegedly communicated with the daughters of John D. Fox. Strong's account of the Rochester knockings and his interaction with the Fox sisters appears in his *Autobiography of Augustus Hopkins Strong* (54–56) and in his *Reminiscences of Early Rochester* (4–6). Additional information about the Fox sisters and the Rochester knockings can be found in Berg, "Spirit Rappings a Fraud," 54–62; Derby, *Rochester Knockings!*; Dewey, *History of the Strange Sounds or Rappings*; Peck, *History of Rochester and Monroe County*, 1:76–77; Todd, *Hydesville*; Vanderhoof, *Historical Sketches of Western New York*, 208–32; and Weisberg, *Talking to the Dead*.

22. Strong, *Autobiography of Alvah Strong*, 42.

23. In his autobiography, Strong gave his age as three; in a paper he delivered in 1915, he stated that he was four (Strong, *Autobiography of Augustus Hopkins Strong*, 36–37; Strong, *Reminiscences of Early Rochester*, 4). Pharcellus Church (1801–86) was pastor of the First Baptist Church in Rochester from 1835 until 1848 (Ward, *Churches of Rochester*, 136). During his time at Rochester, Church published two books in which he argued for

greater cooperation among Protestant denominations: Church, *Philosophy of Benevolence*; Church, *Religious Dissentions*.

24. Strong, *Autobiography of Augustus Hopkins Strong*, 38–39.

25. Strong, *One Hundred Chapel-Talks*, 6.

26. Strong, *Autobiography of Augustus Hopkins Strong*, 36.

27. The *Anti-Masonic Inquirer* ceased publication at the end of 1833, merged with the *National Republican*, and was relaunched as the *Rochester Daily Democrat* in February 1834. Erastus Shepard and Alvah Strong published the paper until August 1836, when it became simply the *Rochester Democrat*. This paper was published by Erastus Shepard, Alvah Strong, and George Dawson until June 1840, when it once again assumed the title *Rochester Daily Democrat*. The paper was published by Erastus Shepard, Alvah Strong, and others until December 1857, when it merged with the *Rochester Daily American* to become the *Rochester Democrat and American*, published by "A. Strong & Co." until December 1860. With some additional editorial shuffling, it persisted under that name through March 1864, when Alvah Strong retired from the paper and it once again became known as the *Rochester Daily Democrat* (Follett, *History of the Press of Western New-York*, 47; French, *Gazetteer of the State of New York*, 396–97).

28. Strong, *Autobiography of Augustus Hopkins Strong*, 47.

29. Strong, *Autobiography of Augustus Hopkins Strong*, 56.

30. Chester Wright Heywood (1823–90) graduated from the University of Rochester with his A.B. in 1853 and his A.M. in 1856. He went on to teach at numerous academies in the decades that followed (*General Catalogue of the University of Rochester, 1850–1911*, 4).

31. Strong, *Reminiscences of Early Rochester*, 9.

32. A. Strong, *Autobiography of Alvah Strong*, 100.

33. Strong, *Autobiography of Augustus Hopkins Strong*, 51–54; quote at 54.

34. For reasons unknown, Alvah Strong incorrectly lists the date of Augustus's internship as 1850 (*Autobiography of Alvah Strong*, 68).

35. Strong, *Reminiscences of Early Rochester*, 9; Strong, *One Hundred Chapel-Talks*, 8. Strong's lifelong love of poetry is evident in two of his lesser-known works: Strong, *Great Poets and Their Theology*; and Strong, *American Poets and Their Theology*.

36. Strong, *Reminiscences of Early Rochester*, 9–10.

37. Strong, *Autobiography of Augustus Hopkins Strong*, 58.

38. For information about Alvah Strong's role in the founding of the University of Rochester, see A. Strong, *Autobiography of Alvah Strong*, 55–62; and Rosenberger, *Rochester*, 20, 47–48.

39. Strong, *Autobiography of Augustus Hopkins Strong*, 59. Ironically, Whittlesey himself was unable to attend Yale due to financial setbacks, and Strong headed to New Haven alone.

40. Strong, *One Hundred Chapel-Talks*, 9.

41. Strong, *Autobiography of Augustus Hopkins Strong*, 60. Strong was not alone in this tendency. As one Yale historian has noted, the recitation method and the older-style liberal arts curriculum were dying in the 1850s, and students were increasingly giving

their attention to clubs, athletics, and various other extracurricular activities (Kelley, *Yale*, 178–79).

42. Strong, *One Hundred Chapel-Talks*, 9–10; Strong, *Autobiography of Augustus Hopkins Strong*, 61.

43. Strong, *Autobiography of Augustus Hopkins Strong*, 61.

44. Strong, *Autobiography of Augustus Hopkins Strong*, 62–63. For an explanation of Yale professors' preference for the recitation method, see Porter, *American Colleges and the American Public*, 119–33. Noah Porter was professor of moral philosophy and metaphysics while Strong was a student during the 1850s, and he later served as president of Yale (1871–86).

45. Strong, *Autobiography of Augustus Hopkins Strong*, 64.

46. Strong, *Autobiography of Augustus Hopkins Strong*, 64; Kelley, *Yale*, 172.

47. Strong, *Autobiography of Augustus Hopkins Strong*, 64, 66 (p. 65 is a photograph).

48. Strong, *Autobiography of Augustus Hopkins Strong*, 66.

49. Strong, *Autobiography of Augustus Hopkins Strong*, 66.

50. Strong, *Autobiography of Augustus Hopkins Strong*, 67.

51. Strong, *Autobiography of Augustus Hopkins Strong*, 81.

52. The cousins were Jenny Farr (who was older than Strong) and Lillie Fowler (who was about his own age). Strong, *Autobiography of Augustus Hopkins Strong*, 81–82.

53. Strong, *One Hundred Chapel-Talks*, 10.

54. Strong, *Autobiography of Augustus Hopkins Strong*, 82.

55. Strong, *One Hundred Chapel-Talks*, 10.

56. Strong, *Autobiography of Augustus Hopkins Strong*, 82.

57. Less than a decade later Strong asked Smith about the encounter, and Smith could not recall their brief conversation (Strong, *Autobiography of Augustus Hopkins Strong*, 83; Strong, *One Hundred Chapel-Talks*, 11–12).

58. Strong, *Autobiography of Augustus Hopkins Strong*, 82.

59. The dates of Finney's three Rochester crusades were 1830–31, 1842, and 1856. For Finney's discussion of these crusades, see Finney, *Original Memoirs*, 234–52, 312–22, 396–401. Finney seemed to take a special liking to Rochester. In addition to its being the hometown of his second wife, Elizabeth, he once declared, "I never preached anywhere with more pleasure than in Rochester. They are a highly intelligent people and have ever manifested a candor, an earnestness, and an appreciation of the truth excelling anything I have seen on so large a scale in any other place" (400).

60. Strong, *Autobiography of Augustus Hopkins Strong*, 83–84. In February 1842, Finney held meetings in this church, during which some 350 persons professed conversion. This church changed names several times between its founding in 1836 and its dedication of a new building in 1858. Although Strong referred to it as "Bethel Church on South Washington Street," it was apparently named "Washington Street Church" in 1856 (Ward, *Churches of Rochester*, 39–47).

61. Strong, *Autobiography of Augustus Hopkins Strong*, 85–86.

62. Strong, *Autobiography of Augustus Hopkins Strong*, 86. Elsewhere, he called it a "purely Arminian or Pelagian conversion" (Strong, *What Shall I Believe?*, 86). For a

helpful discussion of New School Presbyterianism, see Marsden, *Evangelical Mind and the New School Presbyterian Experience*. Interestingly, Strong nowhere mentions that either Finney or Ellinwood ever talked about the death of Christ in relationship to salvation. In fact, near the end of his life, Strong wrote, "I had absolutely no sense that the change in me was in any way due to the influence of the Holy Spirit, or had been made possible by the work of Christ. Except for the fact that I had a sort of traditional and theoretical belief in these things, in the background of my consciousness, my conversion might have been a purely Unitarian or agnostic reliance upon the love and truth of God. This fact makes me tolerant of Unitarian Christianity, though I now recognize it as an infantile faith" (*What Shall I Believe?*, 88).

63. Strong, *Autobiography of Augustus Hopkins Strong*, 88; Strong, *One Hundred Chapel-Talks*, 14–15.

64. Strong, *Autobiography of Augustus Hopkins Strong*, 88.

65. Strong, *Autobiography of Augustus Hopkins Strong*, 90.

66. Of course, it is also possible that Strong, reflecting on these early days of his Christian experience, read his later theology back into the narrative.

67. Strong, *Autobiography of Augustus Hopkins Strong*, 92.

68. Strong, *Autobiography of Augustus Hopkins Strong*, 93.

69. Strong, *Autobiography of Augustus Hopkins Strong*, 93–94.

70. Strong, *Miscellanies*, 1:136.

71. May, *History of the University of Rochester*, 21.

72. *An Outline History of the University of Rochester*, 14.

73. May, *History of the University of Rochester*, 37.

74. A. Strong, *Autobiography of Alvah Strong*, 55.

75. Strong, *Autobiography of Augustus Hopkins Strong*, 101–2. Ezekiel Gilman Robinson was elected professor of theology at Rochester Theological Seminary in 1853 (the same year Strong headed to Yale), but also taught both theology and homiletics in the small school for many years. Robinson served as president of the seminary from 1860 to 1872, when he accepted the presidency of Brown University ("Death of the Rev. E. G. Robinson"). For Strong's assessment of Robinson as a theologian, see Strong, "Dr. Robinson as a Theologian."

76. Strong, *Autobiography of Augustus Hopkins Strong*, 102. While Strong was a student, the classes at Rochester were relatively small. His own class comprised just sixteen men.

77. Strong described Robinson as "a convert to the doctrine of relativity propounded by Kant" (Strong, *Autobiography of Augustus Hopkins Strong*, 102). For additional discussion of Kant's relationship to relativity, see Mitchell, "Kantian Relativity."

78. Strong, *Autobiography of Augustus Hopkins Strong*, 66, 102–3; quote at 102.

79. Strong, *Autobiography of Augustus Hopkins Strong*, 121.

80. Strong, *Philosophy and Religion*, 844–45.

81. Strong, *Autobiography of Augustus Hopkins Strong*, 122.

82. Strong, *Autobiography of Augustus Hopkins Strong*, 113–14.

83. Strong, *Autobiography of Augustus Hopkins Strong*, 115.

84. Strong, *Autobiography of Augustus Hopkins Strong*, 116–17.

85. At the time, the seminary curriculum was two years long. It was later lengthened to three years.

86. Strong, *Autobiography of Augustus Hopkins Strong*, 123–24.

87. Although he left early, seminary documents indicate that Strong was considered an 1859 graduate of the school (*Rochester Theological Seminary General Catalogue, 1850 to 1920*, 68).

88. On February 25, 1878, Strong delivered a lecture before the Robinson Rhetorical Society concerning his travels in Egypt and Palestine. The lecture was subsequently published in his *Philosophy and Religion*, 468–83.

89. Strong, *Philosophy and Religion*, 137.

90. Strong, *Autobiography of Augustus Hopkins Strong*, 134–36.

91. Strong, *Autobiography of Augustus Hopkins Strong*, 141–42.

92. Strong, *One Hundred Chapel-Talks*, 22.

93. Strong, *Autobiography of Augustus Hopkins Strong*, 143–44.

94. Chase, *History of Haverhill*, 660; Strong, *Autobiography of Augustus Hopkins Strong*, 144. Although not a very large or prestigious church, the First Baptist Church of Haverhill had a solid history. The church had been organized by Hezekiah Smith and twenty-three others in 1765, and almost immediately it began to grow: within three years it had more than one hundred members (Brush, *Heritage of Faith and Freedom*, 13–21; *Haverhill: Foundation Facts*, 5, 26; Chase, *History of Haverhill*, 586).

95. Strong, *Autobiography of Augustus Hopkins Strong*, 144.

96. Strong, *Autobiography of Augustus Hopkins Strong*, 145.

97. Strong, *Autobiography of Augustus Hopkins Strong*, 169–70.

98. Strong, *Autobiography of Augustus Hopkins Strong*, 148, 150.

99. Strong, *Autobiography of Augustus Hopkins Strong*, 150.

100. Strong's initial salary at the church was $1,200 a year. In 1860, the average manufacturing job in the United States paid about $300 a year, and in Haverhill many shoemakers made between $5 and $8 a week. Strong had expensive tastes—"I was originally intended for a millionaire"—so even this generous salary had to be supplemented by his father (Strong, *Autobiography of Augustus Hopkins Strong*, 173; Long, *Wages and Earnings in the United States*, 68; Blewett, *Men, Women, and Work*, 109–10).

101. Strong, *Autobiography of Augustus Hopkins Strong*, 170.

102. Strong, *Autobiography of Augustus Hopkins Strong*, 157, 158.

103. Strong, *Autobiography of Augustus Hopkins Strong*, 161–64.

104. During Strong's four years in Haverhill, ninety-six names were added to the church membership roll (Graves, *Historical Sketch of the Baptist Religious Society of Haverhill*, 18).

105. Strong, *Autobiography of Augustus Hopkins Strong*, 173.

106. Strong, *Autobiography of Augustus Hopkins Strong*, 176; Strong, *One Hundred Chapel-Talks*, 23–24.

107. The city of Cleveland had grown from just over 43,000 inhabitants in 1860 to around 65,000 in 1865 and would reach nearly 93,000 in 1870 (Robison, *History of Cleveland*, 98; Miller and Wheeler, *Cleveland*, 199).

108. Several of these lectures were later published in his *Philosophy and Religion*, 1–18, 19–30, 443–60.

109. Strong, *Autobiography of Augustus Hopkins Strong*, 180–82.

110. Strong, *Autobiography of Augustus Hopkins Strong*, 186.

111. *Memorial Volume of Denison University*, 196.

112. Strong, *Autobiography of Augustus Hopkins Strong*, 196. One of Strong's 1870 institute sermons was eventually published in his *Miscellanies*, 2:277–97.

113. Strong, *Autobiography of Augustus Hopkins Strong*, 197, 198.

114. The initial source of this error appears to be an entry in the *Dictionary of American Biography* (1937), which stated that Rockefeller was among Strong's parishioners in Cleveland (s.v. "Augustus Hopkins Strong," by William H. Allison). Carl F. H. Henry then repeated the error when he incorrectly called the First Baptist Church of Cleveland the "Rockefeller church" (*Personal Idealism and Strong's Theology*, 47). Several years later, an article in the *Encyclopedia of Southern Baptists* incorrectly stated that Rockefeller was a member of the First Baptist Church of Cleveland (*Encyclopedia of Southern Baptists*, s.v. "Augustus Hopkins Strong," by C. Penrose St. Amant). Following Henry and these two reference works, the error has been repeated by many others (Moore, "Rise of Religious Liberalism," 33; Hesselgrave, "Relationship between A. H. Strong and Walter Rauschenbusch," 26; Bowman, *Cambridge Dictionary of American Biography*, 707; *Evangelical Dictionary of Theology*, 2nd ed., s.v. "Augustus Hopkins Strong," by W. R. Estep, Jr.; Randall Balmer, *Encyclopedia of Evangelicalism*, 557; *Biographical Dictionary of Evangelicals*, s.v. "Augustus Hopkins Strong," by R. G. Robins; Evans, *Kingdom Is Always but Coming*, 33; Olson, *Westminster Handbook to Evangelical Theology*, 134).

115. Young John D. Rockefeller moved with his parents to Cleveland in 1853. He joined the church the following year at age fifteen and remained a member there until his death in 1937. Originally a mission church started by the First Baptist Church of Cleveland, it was founded in 1851 as the Erie Street Baptist Church. In 1869, the church moved into a new building on Euclid Avenue and changed its name to the Second Baptist Church of Cleveland. Then in the late 1870s, the church changed its name again, to the Euclid Avenue Baptist Church. The Rockefellers themselves lived on Euclid Avenue, which during much of the late nineteenth century was widely considered one of the most affluent neighborhoods in America (*Historical Sketches*, 31–36; Chernow, *Titan*, 51–54; Goulder, *John D. Rockefeller*, 85–86, Cigliano, *Showplace of America*, 106).

116. Strong, *Autobiography of Augustus Hopkins Strong*, 237–38.

117. The pastor of Euclid Avenue Baptist Church and therefore Rockefeller's pastor at this time was Samuel W. Duncan (*Historical Sketches: Seventy-Five Years of the Euclid Avenue Baptist Church, Cleveland, Ohio, 1851–1926*, 34–36). In addition to the statement by Strong and the history of Euclid Avenue Baptist Church just cited, numerous other sources indicate that Rockefeller was a longtime member at the Euclid Avenue Baptist Church, which was often called the "Rockefeller church" (Cathcart, *Baptist*

Encyclopedia, s.v. "John D. Rockefeller," 1007; Smith, *History of the Baptists in the Western States*, 119; Brown, *Study of John D. Rockefeller*, 54, 61, 108, 131; "Big Institutional Church"; *History of Cleveland and Its Environs*, 2:2; Rose, *Cleveland*, 937; Goulder, *John D. Rockefeller*, 85–86; Chernow, *Titan*, 51–52). Strangely, William H. Brackney refers to Euclid Avenue Baptist Church as Rockefeller's home church but then later states that Strong was Rockefeller's former pastor (*Congregation and Campus*, 112, 218, 265). Similarly, although a *Dictionary of American Biography* entry on Strong appears to have been the source of the confusion about Rockefeller's church membership, the entry on Rockefeller which appeared in a supplement volume published twenty years later correctly identifies Rockefeller's church membership as in the Erie Street/Euclid Avenue Baptist Church (*Dictionary of American Biography*, suppl. vol. 2, s.v. "John Davison Rockefeller," by Allan Nevins).

118. Strong, *Autobiography of Augustus Hopkins Strong*, 202–5.

119. Strong eventually received six honorary degrees: D.D., Brown University (1870); D.D., Yale University (1890); LL.D., Bucknell University (1891); LL.D., Alfred University (1894); D.D., Princeton University (1896); and Litt.D., University of Rochester (1912). Some questions remain about the dates of several of these degrees. Documents produced by both Princeton and Yale list the degree from Alfred University as being awarded in 1904 (instead of 1894). A catalog produced by Brown University shows the degree from Bucknell University as being awarded in 1892 (instead of 1891, though a later catalogue has the earlier date). Even Strong's own autobiography lists the degree from Yale as having been awarded in 1892 (instead of 1890). Nonetheless, the list at the beginning of this note appears to include the correct dates: it agrees with two catalogs produced by the Rochester Theological Seminary, with a catalog published in 1917 by the Psi Upsilon Fraternity, and (except for the anomalies mentioned) with Strong's autobiography and catalogs published by Brown, Princeton, Rochester, and Yale (*General Catalogue of Princeton University*, 445; *Catalogue of the Officers and Graduates of Yale University*, 142; *Historical Catalogue of Brown University, 1764–1894*; *Historical Catalogue of Brown University, 1764–1914*, 656; Strong, *Autobiography of Augustus Hopkins Strong*, 320–21; *Rochester Theological Seminary General Catalogue, 1850 to 1910*, 4; *Rochester Theological Seminary General Catalogue, 1850 to 1920*, 31; Wertheimer, *Twelfth General Catalogue of the Psi Upsilon Fraternity*, 87; *General Catalogue of the University of Rochester, 1850–1928*, 394).

120. Strong, *Autobiography of Augustus Hopkins Strong*, 203.

121. Robinson, *Ezekiel Gilman Robinson*, 107; Strong, *Autobiography of Augustus Hopkins Strong*, 203.

122. Robinson, *Ezekiel Gilman Robinson*, 97–99, 102–6.

123. Strong, "Dr. Robinson as a Theologian," 166.

124. Strong, *Autobiography of Augustus Hopkins Strong*, 182–84, 203.

125. Strong, *Autobiography of Augustus Hopkins Strong*, 206–18.

126. Robinson's notes were expanded and published just a few months after his death in 1894 (Robinson, *Christian Theology*). Strong also admitted, "I not only wished to be independent, but I had also begun to suspect that Dr. Robinson was wrong in some important points" (Strong, *Autobiography of Augustus Hopkins Strong*, 219).

127. This evaluation was first published as a part of Robinson's autobiography (*Ezekiel Gilman Robinson*, 163–208) and was later republished in Strong's *Miscellanies*, 2:58–109.

128. Strong, *Autobiography of Augustus Hopkins Strong*, 220. Representative works by these writers that were later cited by Strong include Dorner, *Geschichte der protestantischen Theologie* (English transl.: Dorner, *History of Protestant Theology*—Strong apparently read this work by Dorner in both languages; see his *Systematic Theology* [1907], 5, 13); Philippi, *Kirchliche Glaubenslehre*; and Thomasius, *Christi Person und Werk*. English translations and discussions of Dorner and Thomasius can be found in Welch, *God and Incarnation*.

Chapter 2

1. By 1792, Kant had published his three great critiques: *Critique of Pure Reason* (1781), *Critique of Practical Reason* (1788), and *Critique of Judgment* (1790). The publisher of the first edition of Fichte's work accidentally omitted the author's preface and the original title page signed by Fichte (Fichte, *Attempt at a Critique of All Revelation*, 3). In this work, Fichte argued that any divine revelation must be consistent with standards of morality derived from practical reason.

2. Fichte, *Science of Knowledge*, 4.

3. Fichte, *Comparison between Prof. Schid's System and the* Wissenschaftslehre, 325; Hegel, *Difference between Fichte's and Schelling's System*, xxxiv. As Tom Rockmore has pointed out, Fichte's view of the thing-in-itself was neither stable nor wholly consistent ("Fichte, German Idealism, and the Thing in Itself"). For a nuanced discussion of Fichte's understanding of "thing-in-itself," see Beiser, *German Idealism*, 269–72.

4. Copleston, *History of Philosophy*, 7:44.

5. For discussion of the Fichte atheism controversy, see Estes and Bowman, *Fichte and the Atheism Dispute*; and Gerrish, *Thinking with the Church*, 65–80.

6. Fichte, "On the Foundation of Our Belief," 26. This essay, first published (in German) in the *Philosophisches Journal*, vol. 8 (1798), sparked the controversy over Fichte's alleged atheism.

7. Talbot, "Fichte's Conception of God," 50.

8. Copleston, *History of Philosophy*, 7:92–93. Some have argued that pantheism is ultimately equivalent to atheism (Owen, *Concepts of Deity*, 70, 74).

9. This address was later published in Strong, *Philosophy and Religion*, 21. Although Strong did not cite the exact source of this statement by Fichte, he was apparently quoting from Fichte's *Vocation of Man* (102), which was first published in 1800 and had been translated into English in 1846.

10. Strong, *Lectures on Theology*, 103. Strong followed up this quote from Fichte with additional quotes from Hegel and D. F. Strauss. This string of quotes also appeared in the first edition of his *Systematic Theology* (1886, 200–201). Interestingly, when William G. T. Shedd, then professor of systematic theology at Union Theological Seminary in

New York City, published his *Dogmatic Theology* just a couple years later (1888), he used these same three quotations in a similar discussion of creation (1:469).

11. Strong, *Systematic Theology* (1886), 3.

12. Strong, *Systematic Theology* (1886), 21.

13. Strong, *Systematic Theology* (1886), 234–35.

14. In a paper on "Christian Miracles" read before the Baptist Pastors' Conference of the State of New York in October 1878, Strong interacted with Fichte's thought at a level beyond that of casual quotation. This essay was published in the *Baptist Review* (April 1879) and was later reprinted in Strong, *Philosophy and Religion*, 129–47, esp. 134–35. In an article titled "Modern Idealism" published in *Bibliotheca Sacra* in January 1888, Strong compared the philosophies of Kant, Fichte, Schelling, and Hegel. Once again, he demonstrated a thorough grasp of Fichte's philosophical position. This article was reprinted in Strong, *Philosophy and Religion*, 58–74, esp. 60–61.

15. Pinkard, *Hegel*, 21. Hölderlin would later become a widely published German poet associated with the Romantic movement. Hegel is discussed below.

16. Pinkard, *German Philosophy*, 172.

17. Schelling's thought is often divided into about five periods, which are given different names in the literature (Dunham, Grant, and Watson, *Idealism*, 129).

18. Bowie, *Schelling and Modern European Philosophy*, 57–59.

19. Schelling, *Philosophy of Art*, 14.

20. Strong, *Philosophy and Religion*, 8. This address was delivered before the alumni of Rochester Theological Seminary at their annual meeting on May 20, 1868. It was later printed in Strong, *Philosophy and Religion*, 1–18.

21. Strong, *Systematic Theology* (1886), 189.

22. Strong, *Philosophy and Religion*, 60.

23. See, e.g., Strong, *Systematic Theology* (1907), 101, 252, 490; Schelling is named along with Fichte and Hegel (43).

24. See also Beiser, *German Idealism*, 577–84.

25. Copleston, *History of Philosophy*, 7:159.

26. Singer, *Hegel*, preface.

27. Strong, *Lectures on Theology*, 8, 84, 103.

28. Strong, *Systematic Theology* (1886), 12. This statement had also appeared in his *Lectures on Theology*, 8.

29. Strong, *Systematic Theology* (1886), 85, 269.

30. Strong, *Systematic Theology* (1907), 27, 42, 344–34.

31. According to Strong, Hegel described God as "the absolute Idea, the unity of Life and Cognition, the Universal that thinks itself and thinkingly recognizes itself in an Actuality, from which, as its Immediacy, it no less distinguishes itself again" (Strong, *Systematic Theology* [1907], 345). This quote also appeared earlier in Strong, *Systematic Theology* (1886), 167.

32. Strong, *Systematic Theology* (1907), 97.

33. Strong, *Philosophy and Religion*, 61.

34. Strong, *Philosophy and Religion*, 60–61.

35. Horstmann, "Early Philosophy of Fichte and Schelling," 117.

36. Lotze, *Outlines of a Philosophy of Religion*, 55–69; Copleston, *History of Philosophy*, 7:380.

37. Copleston, *History of Philosophy*, 7:380.

38. Strong, *Systematic Theology* (1907), 104.

39. Strong, *Christ in Creation and Ethical Monism*, 163; Strong, *Systematic Theology* (1907), 123.

40. Strong, *Systematic Theology* (1886), 57, 260.

41. See, e.g., Strong, *Systematic Theology* (1907), 12, 38, 89, 96, 254, 273, 279, 282, 385, 388, 416, 474.

42. Strong, *Systematic Theology* (1907), 96. The terms *materialism* and *idealism* are usually considered conceptually incompatible. However, Strong used the compound phrase *materialistic idealism* a number of times, and in fact, in his *Systematic Theology* (1907) he used it as a section heading in his chapter on the existence of God. Strong explained the concept this way: "The idealism of the present day is mainly a materialistic idealism. It defines matter and mind alike in terms of sensation, and regards both as opposite sides or successive manifestations of one underlying and unknowable force" (95). Then after a bit more explanation, he concluded that "Materialistic Idealism, in truth, is but a half-way house between Materialism and Pantheism, in which no permanent lodging is to be found by the logical intelligence" (96).

43. Strong, *Systematic Theology* (1907), 99, 100.

44. Lotze, *Microcosmus*, 1:446; Strong, *Systematic Theology* (1907), 254.

45. Strong, *Systematic Theology* (1907), 273; Lotze, *Outlines of a Philosophy of Religion*, 139. After discussing Lotze's view on this subject, Strong replied, "In spite of these utterances of Lotze . . . we must maintain that, as truth of being logically precedes truth of knowing, and as a loving nature precedes loving emotions, so purity of substance precedes purity of will" (*Systematic Theology* [1907], 273).

46. Strong, *Systematic Theology* (1907), 282; Lotze, *Metaphysic in Three Books*, 2:183. In this context Strong pointed out that Lotze's statement also appears in Illingworth, *Divine Immanence*, 135.

47. Strong, *Systematic Theology* (1907), 282. Strong's view of divine omnipresence seems to overlook the fact that God's wisdom and glory fill all being, wherever it is, even if he alone exists. Creation does not establish God's presence or serve as an expansion of his presence.

48. Strong, *Systematic Theology* (1907), 372.

49. Bowne, *Kant and Spencer*, 8. See also, Burrow, *Personalism*, 28.

50. Copleston, *History of Philosophy*, 8:291–92. According to Francis McConnell, in 1905, shortly before embarking on a tour around the world, Bowne announced to his friends that he had at last decided to call his system *personalism* (McConnell, *Borden Parker Bowne*, 131). As revealed in a letter written by Bowne less than a year before his death, the attempt to assign a single label to his philosophy was and is a slippery

task: "It is hard to classify me with accuracy. I am a theistic idealist, a personalist, a transcendental empiricist, an idealistic realist, a realistic idealist; but all these phrases need to be interpreted. They cannot be made out well from the dictionary" (quoted in McConnell, *Borden Parker Bowne*, 280).

51. McConnell, *Borden Parker Bowne*, 131.

52. Dorrien, *Making of American Liberal Theology: Imagining Progressive Religion*, 391–92.

53. Bowne, *Philosophy of Herbert Spencer*; Bowne, *Metaphysics*.

54. Strong, *Systematic Theology* (1886), 55. Also see Bowne, *Metaphysics*, 97–100, 129, 163–64.

55. Strong, *Systematic Theology* (1907), 99 (emphasis added).

56. Strong, *Systematic Theology* (1893), 55; Strong, *Systematic Theology* (1896), 55.

57. Kuklick, *Josiah Royce*, 7.

58. Clendenning, *Life and Thought of Josiah Royce*, 21–22.

59. Clendenning, *Life and Thought of Josiah Royce*, 64. In February 1876, Royce wrote, "I have a strong desire to hear *Lotze* at Göttingen, a professor who seems generally acknowledged as the first in constructive philosophy now living in Germany" (Clendenning, *Letters of Josiah Royce*, 49). While in Göttingen, Royce took two courses from Lotze, one on metaphysics and the other on practical philosophy (17). Royce later acknowledged his debt to Lotze in a speech he delivered in December 1915, just a few months before his death (Royce, *Hope of the Great Community*, 128). Years earlier, when George Santayana (a close friend of the Strong family) had approached Royce about writing his doctoral dissertation on the philosophy of Arthur Schopenhauer, Royce had instead proposed that Santayana write on Lotze (Santayana, *Lotze's System of Philosophy*, 62).

60. Buranelli, *Josiah Royce*, 63.

61. *Johns Hopkins University Celebration*, 112.

62. Although this lectureship was a short-term position, Royce was anxious to head east and get away from California, which he deemed an intellectual wasteland. For example, in January 1879 he wrote to William James, "There is no philosophy in California. From Siskiyou to Ft. Yuma, and from the Golden Gate to the summit of the Sierras there could not be found brains enough [to] accomplish the formation of a single respectable idea that was not a manifest plagiarism. Hence the atmosphere for the study of metaphysics is bad. And I wish I were out of it" (Clendenning, *Letters of Josiah Royce*, 66; also see 19–20 and 59).

63. Van Til, *Christianity and Idealism*, 45; Royce, *California from the Conquest in 1846 to the Second Vigilance Committee*; Royce, *Feud of Oakfield Creek*.

64. Royce, *Religious Aspect of Philosophy*, v.

65. Strong, *Systematic Theology* (1886), 55.

66. Strong, *Systematic Theology* (1907), 99.

67. Buranelli, *Josiah Royce*, 128.

68. Strong, *Systematic Theology* (1907), 55.

69. Buckham, "Monism, Pluralism, and Personalism," 480.

Chapter 3

1. A number of writers both before and after Strong have used *ethical monism* in a sense quite different from what Strong meant by the term. See, e.g., Schmid, *Theories of Darwin*, 384; Seth, *Study of Ethical Principles*, 191; Fuller, "Ethical Monism and the Problem of Evil"; Laing, *Study in Moral Problems*, 125; Schweitzer, *Civilization and Ethics*, 54, 60, 90; Van Til, *Christianity and Barthianism*, 246–51; Gay, "Ethical Pluralism"; King, "Hume and Ethical Monism"; Thomas, *Introduction to Ethics*, 8–9; Skillen, "Pluralism as a Matter of Principle," 258–59; and Bonotti, "Pluralism and Moderation," 57, 62–72. Most often writers have distinguished ethical monism from ethical pluralism and have viewed the former as a kind of moral absolutism.

2. The geographical migration of *Bibliotheca Sacra* is briefly traced in Hannah, "History of *Bibliotheca Sacra*." Founded at Union Theological Seminary in 1843, *Bibliotheca Sacra* has been published successively at Andover Theological Seminary (1844–1883), Oberlin College (1884–1921), Xenia Theological Seminary (1922–1933), and Dallas Theological Seminary (1934–present).

3. Strong, "Modern Idealism," 84.

4. Strong, "Modern Idealism," 98.

5. Strong, "Modern Idealism," 100, 103.

6. Strong, "Modern Exaggerations of Divine Immanence," 278. This article was reprinted from the *Examiner* (Baptist), New York, December 4 and 11, 1890.

7. Strong, *Systematic Theology* (1886), 55.

8. Strong, *Systematic Theology* (1886), 56.

9. Strong, *Systematic Theology* (1896), 56 (emphasis added).

10. Strong, *Autobiography of Augustus Hopkins Strong*, 251.

11. Strong, *Autobiography of Augustus Hopkins Strong*, 251.

12. Strong later wrote, "My theological gains at Rochester have been mainly in the understanding of these two factors [Christ's deity and atonement] and their mutual relations" (Strong, *Autobiography of Augustus Hopkins Strong*, 251–52).

13. Strong, *Autobiography of Augustus Hopkins Strong*, 252. Ezekiel Robinson (1815–1894) was Strong's theology professor at Rochester during the late 1850s and early 1860s. Robinson's discussion of the doctrine of justification appears in Robinson, *Christian Theology*, 297–307.

14. Strong, *Autobiography of Augustus Hopkins Strong*, 252.

15. Strong, *Autobiography of Augustus Hopkins Strong*, 252–53. Strong's rather unusual view of the atonement and Christ's relationship to the human race is discussed at length in chapter 4.

16. Strong, *Autobiography of Augustus Hopkins Strong*, 253–54. The body of Strong's autobiography lists only ten theological lessons, and ethical monism appears as the apex of his theological development. However, in 1908 Strong described two additional theological lessons he had learned during his long academic career, included in a section of "later additions" at the end of his autobiography. Lesson 11 had to do with the recognition of "an evolutionary process in divine revelation." Strong acknowledged the validity

of higher criticism and stated that inerrancy need not be claimed "in matters not essential to . . . moral and religious teaching." Lesson 12 involved Strong's "new conviction of a present God and Savior": "Of late I have been impressed as never before that God is *here* and *now*. . . . The soul even here and now, possessing in Christ the present God, possesses all things in him. The Lord is our inheritance, and even in this life we sit with him upon his throne, wield his power, and are made rulers of the world" (Strong, *Autobiography of Augustus Hopkins Strong*, 345–46). Both additional lessons in some way fleshed out his ethical monism.

17. Strong, *Autobiography of Augustus Hopkins Strong*, 254.

18. Hovey, *Studies in Ethics and Religion*.

19. Augustus Hopkins Strong to Alvah Hovey, 7 February 1892 (Alvah Hovey Papers, Divinity Library, Yale Divinity School), cited in Shrader, "Thoughtful Christianity," 263–64.

20. The second article is a reprint of the first. Both Carl Henry and Grant Wacker list the wrong date for the *Examiner* article: Henry states it was published "early in 1894," and Wacker lists 6 October 1894 (Henry, *Personal Idealism and Strong's Theology*, 102; Wacker, *Augustus H. Strong and the Dilemma of Historical Consciousness*, 59n1). Neither author mentions the reprinting of the article in the November 1892 issue of the *Magazine of Christian Literature*, and neither author lists either printing of the 1892 "Christ in Creation" article in his bibliography. These omissions, combined with the confusion about when the "Christ in Creation" article was first published, are no doubt factors that led Henry to declare that "the year 1894 marks a turning-point in Strong's theology" (*Personal Idealism and Strong's Theology*, 95).

21. Hartog, "Ethical Monism in the Writings of A. H. Strong," 93–95.

22. Strong, "Christ in Creation," *Magazine of Christian Literature*, 166–67.

23. Strong, "Christ in Creation," *Magazine of Christian Literature*, 167–68.

24. Strong, "Christ in Creation," *Magazine of Christian Literature*, 168–70.

25. Hartog, "Ethical Monism in the Writings of A. H. Strong," 95.

26. Strong, *Autobiography of Augustus Hopkins Strong*, 254.

27. These three articles originally appeared in successive issues of the *Examiner* (1, 8, 15 November 1894). A few years later these articles, along with Strong's earlier "Christ in Creation" article and another three-part series of articles titled "Ethical Monism Once More" (*Examiner* [17, 24, 31 October 1895]) were reprinted in a pamphlet published by the *Examiner* titled *Ethical Monism in Two Series of Three Articles Each and Christ in Creation with a Review by Elias H. Johnson*. A few years after that, all seven articles in the pamphlet were reprinted in Strong, *Christ in Creation and Ethical Monism*, 1–86; for ease of reference, citations are taken from this book. Interestingly, the "Christ in Creation" article was included in the pamphlet on ethical monism, as stated on the title page, "at the request of Dr. Strong, as having a vital bearing upon the subsequent discussion of 'Ethical Monism.'" This seems to confirm that Strong had embraced the essential elements of ethical monism when the "Christ and Creation" article was first published in the fall of 1892.

28. Goodspeed, *History of the University of Chicago*, 212–13, 230, 486.

29. Strong, *Christ in Creation and Ethical Monism*, 16–17.

30. Strong, *Christ in Creation and Ethical Monism*, 19.

31. Elsewhere Strong reaffirmed that Browning was a monist, though not a pantheist. Strong was somewhat more critical of Browning's theological speculations (Strong, *Great Poets and Their Theology*, 393, 422, 441–42). Numerous other authors have noted that Browning was not a pantheist, but their need to make this point suggests that he came fairly close to embracing pantheism (Berdoe, *Browning and the Christian Faith*, 3; Roberts, *That One Face*, 94; Raymond, "'Jeweled Bow,'" 118; Gupta, *Robert Browning*, 181).

32. Strong, *Christ in Creation and Ethical Monism*, 20. Here Strong is citing Dorner, *History of the Development of the Doctrine*, 101, 231.

33. Strong, *Christ in Creation and Ethical Monism*, 20.

34. Strong, *Christ in Creation and Ethical Monism*, 20–21.

35. Strong, *Christ in Creation and Ethical Monism*, 21–22.

36. Strong, *Christ in Creation and Ethical Monism*, 22.

37. Strong, *Christ in Creation and Ethical Monism*, 23–24.

38. Strong, *Christ in Creation and Ethical Monism*, 25.

39. Strong, *Christ in Creation and Ethical Monism*, 27.

40. Strong, *Christ in Creation and Ethical Monism*, 29–30.

41. Strong, *Christ in Creation and Ethical Monism*, 30.

42. Strong, *Christ in Creation and Ethical Monism*, 33.

43. Strong, *Systematic Theology* (1907), 304–52. This point is briefly noted in Henry, *Personal Idealism and Strong's Theology*, 206–8.

44. Strong, *Christ in Creation and Ethical Monism*, 45.

45. Strong, *Christ in Creation and Ethical Monism*, 50.

46. E.g., Bunnin and Yu, *Blackwell Dictionary of Western Philosophy*, s.v. "Dualism" and "Monism"; Craig, *Shorter Routledge Encyclopedia of Philosophy*, s.v. "Monism," by Edward Craig.

47. Strong, *Christ in Creation and Ethical Monism*, 53.

48. Strong, *Christ in Creation and Ethical Monism*, 53–54.

49. Strong, *Christ in Creation and Ethical Monism*, 60–61.

50. Strong, *Christ in Creation and Ethical Monism*, 63–64.

51. Strong, *Christ in Creation and Ethical Monism*, 65.

52. Strong, *Christ in Creation and Ethical Monism*, 73.

53. Strong, *Christ in Creation and Ethical Monism*, 74.

54. Strong, *Christ in Creation and Ethical Monism*, 76.

55. Elsewhere, Strong declared, "The universe is full of [God's] life and is the constant expression of his mind and will" (Strong, *Christ in Creation and Ethical Monism*, 187). In a discussion of Ralph Waldo Emerson's theology, Strong pointed out that any denial of God's personality would also necessarily involve a denial of his will. He further noted that such a denial would inevitably make God identical with nature and "coterminous with nature," rather than above nature and expressing his will through nature. Although Strong certainly emphasized the immanence of God in the world, he was careful to

affirm God's transcendence as well, lest he fall into the ditch of unqualified pantheism (Strong, *American Poets and Their Theology*, 64).

56. Strong, *Christ in Creation and Ethical Monism*, 76.

57. Strong, *Christ in Creation and Ethical Monism*, 78.

58. Strong, *Christ in Creation and Ethical Monism*, 78.

59. Strong, *Christ in Creation and Ethical Monism*, 79–80.

60. Strong, *Christ in Creation and Ethical Monism*, 79, 81.

61. Strong, *Christ in Creation and Ethical Monism*, 79, 83.

62. Strong, *Christ in Creation and Ethical Monism*, 84.

63. Strong's view of the atonement is discussed in chapter 4.

64. Strong, *Christ in Creation and Ethical Monism*, 85.

65. "Editorial Notes," 130–31.

66. Hovey, "Dr. Strong's Ethical Monism [First Article]"; Hovey, "Dr. Strong's Ethical Monism: Second Article"; Hovey, "Dr. Strong's Ethical Monism: Third Article."

67. Malone, *Dictionary of American Biography*, s.v. "Hovey, Alvah," by William H. Allison. For a brief discussion of Hovey's career at Newton, see Bendroth, *School of the Church*, 35–39, 97–99. William Brackney rightly identifies Strong and Hovey as two of the great landmarks in Baptist theological education (*Congregation and Campus*, 278).

68. Hovey, "Dr. Strong's Ethical Monism [First Article]," 10.

69. Hovey, "Dr. Strong's Ethical Monism [First Article]," 10.

70. For discussion of the concept of divine simplicity, see the classic works Augustine, *De Trinitate* 5–7; Anselm, *Monologion* 17; Thomas Aquinas, *Summa Theologica* I, Q. 3; and *Belgic Confession* art. 1. See also Holmes, "'Something Much Too Plain to Say'"; Bavinck, *Reformed Dogmatics*, 2:173–77; and Muller, *Post-Reformation Reformed Dogmatics*, 3:38–44, 53–58, 70–76, 217–23, and esp. 271–84.

71. Hovey, "Dr. Strong's Ethical Monism [First Article]," 10–11.

72. Hovey, "Dr. Strong's Ethical Monism: Second Article," 10.

73. Hovey, "Dr. Strong's Ethical Monism: Second Article," 10.

74. Hovey, "Dr. Strong's Ethical Monism: Third Article," 11.

75. Hovey, "Dr. Strong's Ethical Monism: Third Article," 11.

76. Strong, *Christ in Creation and Ethical Monism*, 188–90, 202.

77. Behrends, "Ethical Monism."

78. By the time he wrote the article, Behrends was no longer pastoring in Cleveland and was in fact no longer a Baptist but, rather, a Congregationalist minister living in Brooklyn, New York. Nevertheless, he remained a lifelong admirer of Strong (Behrends, *In Memoriam*, 12, 16; *Congregational Year-Book*, 15).

79. Behrends, "Ethical Monism," 357.

80. Behrends, "Ethical Monism," 360–361.

81. Behrends, "Ethical Monism," 369.

82. Behrends, "Ethical Monism," 370.

83. Strong, *Systematic Theology* (1896), "preface to the fifth edition" (on an unnumbered page appearing between pp. x and xi).

84. "Erroneous Explanations of the Facts" is the third chapter in part 2 ("The Existence of God") of the fifth edition of Strong's *Systematic Theology* (1896). On the other three pages, 203, 205, and 413, Strong briefly discussed ethical monism's relationship to other doctrines.

85. Strong, *Systematic Theology* (1896), 51.

86. The final edition of Strong's *Systematic Theology* was published in three volumes. Vols. 1 and 2 first appeared in 1907, and vol. 3 appeared in the spring of 1909.

87. Strong, *Systematic Theology* (1907), 105.

88. Shortly after retiring from Rochester, Strong decided to visit a number of the seminary's alumni who were serving overseas as missionaries in China, Japan, and especially India. In his book that followed, *A Tour of the Missions*, Strong did not directly discuss the topic of ethical monism, but interestingly, he concluded that the missionary who has experienced union with Christ and maintains a proper understanding of God's transcendence as well as his immanence "is the only type of missionary that is fitted to meet the pantheistic religionists of the Orient. [Such religionists] believe in the immanence of God, but they deny his transcendence. All things are deified, because God dwells in all; but there is no personality in man, and so, no ethical responsibility or sin" (241). Having witnessed firsthand the worship of various eastern pantheists, Strong believed that they failed to recognize the transcendence of God and therefore held a form of monism that was not ultimately ethical in nature. Strong, of course, believed his ethical monism was significantly different from that type of pantheistic understanding of the world.

89. Strong, *Systematic Theology* (1907), 105. In the translation Strong cited, these texts read, "Whither shall I go from thy spirit? Or whither shall I flee from thy presence?" (Ps 139:7); "Am I a God at hand, saith Jehovah, and not a God afar off? . . . Do not I fill heaven and earth?" (Jer 23:23–24); and "He is not far from each one of us: for in him we live, and move, and have our being" (Acts 17:27–28).

90. Strong, *Systematic Theology* (1907), 105. These "transcendence" texts state, "The heaven and the heaven of heavens cannot contain thee" (1 Kgs 8:27); "That hath his seat on high" (Ps 113:5); and "The high and lofty One inhabiteth eternity" (Isa 57:15).

91. Strong, *Systematic Theology* (1907), 105–6. As was his general practice, Strong cited Augustine and Anselm without indicating the exact source of the quotations. The quotes from Augustine appear in his *Confessions* 1.1–2, and the quotes from Anselm come from his *Proslogion* 3, 18.

92. Helpful discussions of this section of Strong's *Systematic Theology* appear in Hartog, "Ethical Monism in the Writings of A. H. Strong," 22–31; and Houghton, "Examination and Evaluation," 210–16.

93. Strong, *Systematic Theology* (1907), 106.

94. Strong, *Systematic Theology* (1907), 106.

95. Strong, *Systematic Theology* (1907), 107.

96. E.g., Ralph Waldo Emerson (1803–1882) and Alfred Tennyson (1809–1892). Strong's life-long interest in poetry and its intersection with theology is reflected in two of his lesser-known books: *Great Poets and Their Theology* and *American Poets and Their Theology*.

97. Strong, *Systematic Theology* (1907), 108.
98. Strong, *Systematic Theology* (1907), 108.
99. Strong, *Systematic Theology* (1907), 109.
100. Strong, *Systematic Theology* (1907), 109 (emphasis added).
101. Strong, *Systematic Theology* (1907), 109.
102. Strong, *Systematic Theology* (1907), 109.
103. Strong, *Systematic Theology* (1907), vii.

Chapter 4

1. Writing about Strong's theology in 1897, Benjamin Breckinridge Warfield rightly observed that ethical monism "must eat deeper into the system or again recede from it" (review of *Systematic Theology*, 358).
2. Strong, *Systematic Theology* (1907), 109. Similarly, in the preface to the final edition of his *Systematic Theology*, Strong wrote, "My philosophical and critical point of view meantime has also somewhat changed [since the 1886 ed.]. While I hold to the old doctrines, I interpret them differently and expound them more clearly, because I seem to myself to have reached a fundamental truth which throws new light upon them all" (vii).
3. Strong, *Lectures on Theology*, 50, 51–53.
4. Strong, *Lectures on Theology*, 51.
5. Strong, *Lectures on Theology*, 52.
6. Strong, *Lectures on Theology*, 52–53.
7. Strong, *Lectures on Theology*, 53.
8. Houghton, "Examination and Evaluation," 51–52.
9. Strong, *Lectures on Theology*, 54.
10. Strong, *Lectures on Theology*, 55–59.
11. Strong, *Systematic Theology* (1902), 104a. Rather than repaginating the remainder of the book, this new volume included two new pages (104a and 104b) inserted between pp. 104 and 105.
12. Strong, *Systematic Theology* (1902), 104a. As early as 1899, Strong had expressed similar sentiments on the doctrine of inspiration. In a speech delivered that year, Strong declared, "No particular theory of inspiration is essential to Christianity, for Christianity existed in full vigor when no New Testament book had been composed" (Strong, *Christ in Creation and Ethical Monism*, 204).
13. Strong, *Lectures on Theology*, 55.
14. Strong, *Christ in Creation and Ethical Monism*, 203.
15. Strong, *Systematic Theology* (1902), 104a.
16. Strong, *Systematic Theology* (1907), 196.
17. Compare this to the definition in Strong's *Lectures on Theology*, 50, which remained unchanged through the seventh edition of *Systematic Theology* (1902), 95. Grant Wacker correctly noted that Strong's new definition of inspiration differed from his older definition in three significant ways: the newer definition (1) depicted Scripture as the record of

revelation rather than as revelation itself; (2) described that revelation as "progressive"; and (3) omitted the word *infallible* and instead merely described Scripture as *sufficient* (Wacker, *Augustus H. Strong and the Dilemma of Historical Consciousness*, 67).

18. Strong, *Lectures on Theology*, 54.

19. E.g., Strong, *Systematic Theology* (1902), 103.

20. Strong, *Systematic Theology* (1907), 216.

21. Strong, *Systematic Theology* (1907), 228. Based on quotations Strong cited nearby, he was apparently following the lead of Robert Verrell Foster, who similarly claimed that "an error is that which misleads; but there is no inexactness in the Bible that *in any serious or important sense* whatever can mislead any one" (Foster, *Systematic Theology*, 144, emphasis added). Foster's book cited Strong at least twice (38, 418).

22. Warfield, *Westminster Assembly and Its Work*, esp. 155–333; Warfield, *Inspiration and Authority of the Bible*; Feinberg, "Meaning of Inerrancy"; Bush and Nettles, *Baptists and the Bible*.

23. Strong, *Systematic Theology* (1907), 207, 215.

24. Strong, *Systematic Theology* (1907), 228. At the end of this quotation, Strong is quoting William Sanday (*Inspiration: Eight Lectures on the Early History and Origin of the Doctrine of Biblical Inspiration*, 3rd ed. [London: Longmans, 1896], 400).

25. Strong was thinking here especially of 1 and 2 Kings and 1 and 2 Chronicles.

26. Strong, *Lectures on Theology*, 50.

27. Strong, *Systematic Theology* (1907), 196.

28. Houghton, "Examination and Evaluation," 68.

29. Strong, *Autobiography of Augustus Hopkins Strong*, 345–46.

30. Brown, review of *Systematic Theology*. Earlier editions had been a one-volume work, but Strong added so much new material to the final edition that it was released in three volumes. Brown's review covered only volume 1.

31. Brown, review of *Systematic Theology*, 151, 154.

32. Brown, review of *Systematic Theology*, 151, 153–155.

33. Strong, *Lectures on Theology*, 99.

34. Strong, *Systematic Theology* (1907), 393.

35. Strong, *Lectures on Theology*, 99; "Dr. Augustus Strong on Authority in Religion."

36. Strong, *Lectures on Theology*, 99–100.

37. Strong, *Lectures on Theology*, 121–22.

38. Strong, *Christ in Creation and Ethical Monism*, 169. The final edition of Strong's *Systematic Theology* contains what appear to be contradictory statements on this point. On the one hand, the text describes "the whole process of man's creation as equally the work of nature and the work of God"; it asserts that humans were created from "existing material in the shape of animal forms"; and it states that man "has a brute ancestry." On the other hand, it also asserts, "Since the soul, then, is an immediate creation of God, and the forming of man's body is mentioned by the Scripture writer in direct connection with this creation of the spirit, man's body was in this sense an immediate creation also" (Strong, *Systematic Theology* [1907], 466, 469, 470). The tension that exists between these quotes can be traced to the fact that the statement affirming the immediate

creation of man's body and soul had been present in the text since 1876, but the statements that affirm man's brute ancestry, depict humans as coming from animal forms, and describe the creation of humanity as "equally the work of nature and the work of God" each appeared for the first time in either the 1902 or the 1907 edition. Strong never managed to work out all of the tensions that existed between his earlier and later views and never fully purged from his theology text some of the earlier statements that, at least by the early 1900s, no longer reflected his true beliefs.

39. Strong, *Systematic Theology* (1907), 465.

40. This address was later published in Strong, *Philosophy and Religion*, 39–57.

41. Strong, *Philosophy and Religion*, 45. Herbert Spencer was a polymath and a thoroughgoing evolutionist who attempted to reconcile a vague notion of religion with the concept of biological evolution. See, e.g., Spencer, *Factors of Organic Evolution*; Spencer, *First Principles*.

42. Thornbury, "Legacy of Natural Theology," 158.

43. Strong, *Christ in Creation and Ethical Monism*, 71.

44. Strong, *Systematic Theology* (1907), 466; Strong, *Christ in Creation and Ethical Monism*, 193.

45. Strong, *Christ in Creation and Ethical Monism*, 72.

46. Strong, *Christ in Creation and Ethical Monism*, 11. In 1916, Arthur Cushman McGiffert identified the doctrine of divine immanence as one of the key ideas to flow out of the teaching of evolution over the previous fifty years ("Progress of Theological Thought").

47. Strong, *Christ in Creation and Ethical Monism*, 20.

48. Strong, *Lectures on Theology*, 33.

49. Strong, *Philosophy and Religion*, 132.

50. Houghton, "Examination and Evaluation," 83.

51. Strong, "Miracles as Attesting Divine Revelation."

52. E.g., Brown, review of *Systematic Theology*, 152; Hartog, "Ethical Monism in the Writings of A. H. Strong," 88.

53. Strong, *Systematic Theology* (1907), 117. This preferable definition also appears in Strong, "Miracle at Cana," 69.

54. Strong, *Systematic Theology* (1907), 118–19. These same reasons also appear in Strong, "Miracle at Cana," 69.

55. As McGiffert observed in 1916, "The modern doctrine of divine immanence . . . so widely current in these days, has served to bridge the old chasm between nature and the supernatural and to make them completely one" ("Progress of Theological Thought," 323). Strong was not willing to go quite as far as McGiffert, but his ethical monism did significantly shrink the "old chasm" between the universe and the immanent Christ.

56. Strong, "Miracle at Cana," 68.

57. Brown, review of *Systematic Theology*, 152.

58. In the conclusion to his dissertation on Strong, Carl Henry noted the "unsystematic integration" of Strong's later views into his earlier, more conservative theology. Such an integration took place "without a thorough revision of the earlier system, but

rather by way of absorption, modification, and limited revision" (*Personal Idealism and Strong's Theology*, 228).

59. Strong, *Miscellanies*, 2:110–28.

60. Strong, "Modern Exaggerations of Divine Immanence," 278.

61. Strong, *Lectures on Theology*, 122; Strong, *Systematic Theology* (1907), 476.

62. Strong, *Systematic Theology* (1907), 476.

63. Strong, *Lectures on Theology*, 140, 144; Strong, *Systematic Theology* (1907), 549, 567.

64. Strong, *Systematic Theology* (1886), 308; cf. Strong, *Systematic Theology* (1907), 593.

65. Strong, *Lectures on Theology*, 151–56, 158; Strong, *Systematic Theology* (1907), 597–612, 619, 622. See also Crisp, "Federalism vs Realism."

66. Strong, *Lectures on Theology*, 158. Cf. Strong, *Systematic Theology* (1907), 619.

67. Strong, *Lectures on Theology*, 158–60; Strong, *Systematic Theology* (1907), 624, 625.

68. Houghton, "Examination and Evaluation," 57.

69. Strong, *Our Denominational Outlook*, 16.

70. Strong, *Christ in Creation and Ethical Monism*, 78.

71. Strong, *Lectures on Theology*, 194.

72. Strong, *Lectures on Theology*, 194–95.

73. Strong, *Philosophy and Religion*, 213; Strong, *Christ in Creation and Ethical Monism*, 78; Strong, *What Shall I Believe?*, 93. As the latter quote suggests, Strong held to a universal atonement. See, e.g., Strong, *Lectures on Theology*, 196; and Strong, *Systematic Theology* (1907), 771–73.

74. Strong, *What Shall I Believe?*, 93. For further discussion of imputation in the theology of Shedd and Strong, see Crisp, "Federalism vs Realism."

75. Strong, *Systematic Theology* (1907), 715.

76. Strong, *Systematic Theology* (1907), 715. In Strong's view, the guilt Christ bore "was not only an imputed, but also an imparted guilt" (759).

77. Strong, *Philosophy and Religion*, 214.

78. Strong, *Systematic Theology* (1907), 715, quote at 758. See also Strong, *Christ in Creation and Ethical Monism*, 34.

79. Strong, *Christ in Creation and Ethical Monism*, 173; Strong, *Systematic Theology* (1907), 762, 715. In an ordination sermon Strong preached in 1902, he very forcefully argued for divine passibility stemming from Christ's connection to humanity, which began at creation (*Miscellanies*, 2:340–58). In other words, Strong affirmed that Christ had been suffering on account of sin from the time of the Fall due to his connection to the human race. However, a few years later in the final edition of his *Systematic Theology*, Strong appeared to equivocate a bit on this point. On the one hand, he stated that "God is passible, or capable of suffering." On the other hand, he also stated that "the God-man, although in his divine nature impassible, was capable, through his union with humanity, of absolutely infinite suffering" (Strong, *Systematic Theology* [1907], 266, 697). This reference to Christ's "union with humanity" could refer to his connection to the race that Strong thought began at creation, but in context, it appears to refer to Christ's incarnation. If in this last quote Strong meant to say that Christ became passible when

he became incarnate, then this would appear to be another section of Strong's theology text that was never completely updated to reflect his ethical monism.

Chapter 5

1. The final edition of Strong's *Systematic Theology* was originally printed in three volumes, which were released between 1907 and 1909. This same edition has since been reprinted numerous times in a single volume.

2. Smith, "Quarter-Century of Theological Thinking," 578.

3. Review of *Systematic Theology* (1886 ed.), 941.

4. Review of *Systematic Theology* (1889 ed.), 147.

5. Girardeau, review of *Systematic Theology*.

6. Warfield, review of *Systematic Theology*, 357–58.

7. Warfield, review of *Christ in Creation and Ethical Monism*, 325–26.

8. Hodge, review of *Systematic Theology* (vols. 1 and 2), 336, 341.

9. Hodge, review of *Systematic Theology* (vol. 3), 335.

10. Hodge, review of *What Shall I Believe?*, 681

11. Valentine, review of *Christ in Creation and Ethical Monism*, 279, 282, 283.

12. Mackenzie, review of *Christ in Creation and Ethical Monism*, 648, 650.

13. In his biography of Rockefeller, Ron Chernow mistakenly described Strong as a proponent of the social gospel. Admittedly, Rauschenbusch dedicated his book *Theology for the Social Gospel* to Strong, his beloved mentor, but Strong was not, and never would have considered himself, a supporter of the social gospel. In fact, in the foreword to that same book, Rauschenbusch himself described Strong as "an eminent representative of the older theology" which stood in contrast to his own position (Chernow, *Titan*, 302; Rauschenbusch, *Theology for the Social Gospel*).

14. Abbott, *Theology of an Evolutionist*; Abbott, *Personality of God*; Abbott, *Letters to Unknown Friends*, 16–22.

15. Abbott, review of *Christ in Creation and Ethical Monism*, 130.

16. Brown, *Christian Theology in Outline*, 169, 198.

17. Brown, review of *Systematic Theology*, 151–52.

18. Augustus Hopkins Strong to Edgar Young Mullins, 9 September 1905, Edgar Young Mullins papers. Strong's comments were in reference to Mullins's discussion of pantheism in Mullins, *Why Is Christianity True?*, 20–32, esp. 26.

19. Augustus Hopkins Strong to Edgar Young Mullins, 16 April 1912 and 26 April 1912, Edgar Young Mullins papers.

20. Strong, *Autobiography of Augustus Hopkins Strong*, 255.

21. Christian, "Theology of Augustus Hopkins Strong," 402.

22. Strong, *Autobiography of Augustus Hopkins Strong*, 348–50.

23. Wacker, *Augustus H. Strong and the Dilemma of Historical Consciousness*, 84.

24. Strong, *Autobiography of Augustus Hopkins Strong*, 271.

25. *Rochester Theological Seminary General Catalogue, 1850 to 1920*, 193.

26. Strong, *Autobiography of Augustus Hopkins Strong*, 351–52, 204.

27. Strong, *Autobiography of Augustus Hopkins Strong*, 260.

28. William James to Mrs. James, 13 May 1905, in James, *Letters of William James*, 2:229.

29. Santayana, *Persons and Places*, 249.

30. Strong, *Autobiography of Augustus Hopkins Strong*, 260–61.

31. Strong, *Autobiography of Augustus Hopkins Strong*, 261.

32. Concerning the tendency of American academics to study abroad, Gary Dorrien has written, "Approximately ten thousand Americans matriculated in German universities between 1830 and 1930, half of them at the University of Berlin. . . . The traffic of Americans to Germany reached its peak . . . in the 1890s, when approximately 2,000 Americans studied in German universities, more than 1,300 of them at Berlin" (*Making of American Liberal Theology: Imagining Progressive Religion*, 404).

33. At this point, according to Strong, Charles "sold his Hebrew Bible and his theological books, as if to burn his ships and to put the ministry of Christ forever behind him" (*Autobiography of Augustus Hopkins Strong*, 262).

34. Dorrien, *Making of American Liberal Theology: Imagining Progressive Religion*, 262. According to Ron Chernow, Charles's teaching position at Columbia was initially secured by his father-in-law, who gave the university a $100,000 endowment with the understanding that Charles would be offered a chair (Chernow, *Titan*, 411).

35. Strong, *Autobiography of Augustus Hopkins Strong*, 262, 351. For an interesting discussion of this reversal and Strong's efforts to win his son back to the faith, see Straub, "'Letters to a Skeptic.'"

36. Strong, "Christ in Creation," *Examiner*; Strong, "Christ in Creation," *Magazine of Christian Literature*—the second article is a reprint of the first.

37. E.g., C. A. Strong, *Creed for Sceptics*. See also the discussion in Houghton, "Examination and Evaluation," 224–30.

38. Chernow, *Titan*, 302. In 1888, Strong dedicated one of his books to Rockefeller, describing Rockefeller as "the friend and helper of every good cause, through whose liberality the author is enabled to put these essays into print" (*Philosophy and Religion*, v).

39. Strong, *Autobiography of Augustus Hopkins Strong*, 248.

40. Chernow, *Titan*, 303.

41. Wacker, *Augustus H. Strong and the Dilemma of Historical Consciousness*, 61.

42. Brackney, *Congregation and Campus*.

43. Storr, *Harper's University*, 11.

44. Pierce, *History of Chicago*, 20, 94.

45. Chernow, *Titan*, 305–6.

46. Strong, *Autobiography of Augustus Hopkins Strong*, 249.

47. Chernow, *Titan*, 306.

48. Miller, *Piety and Profession*, 229.

49. Rockefeller would eventually give more than $26 million to the University of Chicago, but his donations were spread out over a number of years, and much of that money

was given after the introduction of the automobile brought his oil business massive prof-
its that he could not have anticipated in the 1880s (Miller, *Piety and Profession*, 229).

50. In addition to appealing to Rockefeller privately, Strong also presented his case to
a larger audience, and he was still doing so as late as 1889. That year, at his own expense
Strong had a pamphlet printed that argued for the need to establish a Baptist university
in New York (Strong, *Church and the University*).

51. William Rainey Harper to John D. Rockefeller, Sr., 11 January 1887, cited in Chernow, *Titan*, 307; Strong, *Autobiography of Augustus Hopkins Strong*, 250. Interestingly,
Strong himself had actually introduced Harper to Rockefeller and had suggested Harper
as one of the key men who could help establish a university in New York (Strong, *Autobiography of Augustus Hopkins Strong*, 249–50). Strong later expressed his opinion that
Harper had betrayed him by trying to persuade Rockefeller to establish the university in
Chicago rather than New York (250). Strong continued lobbying for a Baptist university
in New York until at least the fall of 1890 (Chernow, *Titan*, 313).

52. E.g., Howard Osgood (1831–1911), one of Strong's early hires, was a conservative Old Testament scholar who taught at Rochester from 1875 to 1900. On the other
end of the spectrum, both in timing and in ideology, was Conrad Henry Moehlman
(1879–1961), one of the most liberal professors Strong added to the faculty. He originally taught Old Testament history, next served as professor of English Bible and then
New Testament history, and finally succeeded Walter Rauschenbusch as professor of
church history.

53. Moore, "Rise of Religious Liberalism."

54. Moore, "Rise of Religious Liberalism," 43–45, 168.

55. Strong later wrote, "I felt that my son John was the man who ought to take my
place. But, at the time, to advocate John's claims seemed to me to savor of nepotism, and
I therefore studiously abstained from mentioning his name. I think I could then have
secured his election, but I made it a point of honor to be silent. I let the opportunity
slip by, and I mourned over the result" (*Autobiography of Augustus Hopkins Strong*, 356).

56. Strong, *Autobiography of Augustus Hopkins Strong*, 357.

57. Strong, *Autobiography of Augustus Hopkins Strong*, 357. See also Brackney, *Genetic
History of Baptist Thought*, 338.

58. *Rochester Theological Seminary General Catalogue, 1850 to 1920*, 39.

59. Between September 1911 and April 1912 Barbour organized the Men and Religion Forward Movement, which held mass meetings and smaller seminars in more than
a thousand cities and communities. Barbour later edited a history of this movement:
Making Religion Efficient.

60. Moore, "Rise of Religious Liberalism," 227–37.

61. A. H. Strong to C. A. Barbour, 13 January 1915, quoted in Straub, *Making of a
Battle Royal*, 253.

62. Strong, *Autobiography of Augustus Hopkins Strong*, 357.

63. Moore, "Rise of Religious Liberalism," 234.

64. Riley, "Modernism in Baptist Schools"; Kelly, *Theological Education in America*,
81; Tyson, *School of Prophets*, 95.

65. "Curriculum Preamble," in *Colgate Rochester Crozer Course Catalogue*, 8.

66. Interestingly, after his death both conservatives and liberals looked back on Strong and claimed him as one of their own. As Grant Wacker noted, "Strong's appeal to persons on both sides of the fence was essentially a matter of theological identity. Both groups had ample reason to believe that in his heart of hearts he was one of them" (*Augustus H. Strong and the Dilemma of Historical Consciousness*, 129).

BIBLIOGRAPHY

Books

Abbott, Lyman. *Letters to Unknown Friends*. Garden City, NY: Doubleday, Page &
Co., 1913.
———. *The Personality of God*. New York: Thomas Y. Crowell & Co., 1905.
———. *The Theology of an Evolutionist*. Boston: Houghton, Mifflin, & Co., 1897.
Allen, Alexander V. G. *The Continuity of Christian Thought: A Study of Modern
Theology in the Light of Its History*. Boston: Houghton, Mifflin, & Co., 1884.
Ameriks, Karl, ed. *The Cambridge Companion to German Idealism*. Cambridge:
Cambridge University Press, 2000.
An Outline History of the University of Rochester. Rochester, NY: Ezra R. Andrews, 1886.
Averill, Lloyd J. *American Theology in the Liberal Tradition*. Philadelphia: Westminster
Press, 1967.
Balmer, Randall. *Encyclopedia of Evangelicalism*. Louisville, KY: Westminster John
Knox, 2002.
Barbour, Clarence Augustus, ed. *Making Religion Efficient*. New York: Association
Press, 1912.
Bavinck, Herman. *Reformed Dogmatics*. Edited by John Bolt. Translated by John
Vriend. 4 vols. Grand Rapids, MI: Baker, 2003–8.
Beale, David O. *In Pursuit of Purity: American Fundamentalism Since 1850*. Greenville,
SC: Unusual Publications, 1986.
Beatty, Jack. *Age of Betrayal: The Triumph of Money in America, 1865–1900*. New York:
Knopf, 2007.
Beckley, Harlan. *Passion for Justice: Retrieving the Legacies of Walter Rauschenbusch,
John A. Ryan, and Reinhold Niebuhr*. Louisville, KY: Westminster John Knox, 1992.
Behrends, A. J. F. *In Memoriam, Harriet E. Hatch, Wife of A. J. F. Behrends*. Providence,
RI: Printed for private distribution, 1882.
Beiser, Frederick C. *The Fate of Reason: German Philosophy from Kant to Fichte*.
Cambridge, MA: Harvard University Press, 1987.
———. *German Idealism: The Struggle against Subjectivism, 1781–1801*. Cambridge,
MA: Harvard University Press, 2002.
———. *Hegel*. New York: Routledge, 2005.
Bendroth, Margaret Lamberts. *A School of the Church: Andover Newton across Two
Centuries*. Grand Rapids, MI: Eerdmans, 2008.
Berdoe, Edward. *Browning and the Christian Faith*. New York: Macmillan &
Co., 1896.

Bernstein, Peter L. *Wedding of the Waters: The Erie Canal and the Making of a Great Nation*. New York: W. W. Norton, 2005.

Blewett, Mary H. *Men, Women, and Work: Class, Gender, and Protest in the New England Shoe Industry, 1780–1910*. Urbana: University of Illinois Press, 1990.

Bodein, Vernon Parker. *The Social Gospel of Walter Rauschenbusch and Its Relation to Religious Education*. New Haven, CT: Yale University Press, 1944.

Bowie, Andrew. *Schelling and Modern European Philosophy: An Introduction*. New York: Routledge, 1993.

Bowman, John S. *The Cambridge Dictionary of American Biography*. New York: Cambridge University Press, 1995.

Bowne, Borden P. *The Immanence of God*. Boston: Houghton, Mifflin, & Co., 1905.

———. *Introduction to Psychological Theory*. New York: Harper & Bros., 1886.

———. *Kant and Spencer: A Critical Exposition*. Boston: Houghton Mifflin Co., 1912.

———. *Metaphysics: A Study in First Principles*. London: Sampson Low, Marston, Searle, & Rivington, 1882.

———. *Personalism*. Boston: Houghton Mifflin Co., 1908.

———. *The Philosophy of Herbert Spencer*. New York: Nelson & Phillips, 1876.

———. *Studies in Christianity*. Boston: Houghton Mifflin Co., 1909.

———. *Theism*. New York: American Book Co., 1902.

———. *Theory of Thought and Knowledge*. New York: Harper & Bros., 1897.

Brackney, William H. *Baptists in North America: An Historical Perspective*. Malden, MA: Blackwell, 2006.

———. *Congregation and Campus: North American Baptists in Higher Education*. Macon, GA: Mercer University Press, 2008.

———. *A Genetic History of Baptist Thought: With Special Reference to Baptists in Britain and North America*. Macon, GA: Mercer University Press, 2004.

Brands, H. W. *The Reckless Decade: America in the 1890s*. New York: St. Martin's Press, 1995.

Brown, Marcus M. *A Study of John D. Rockefeller: The Wealthiest Man in the World*. Cleveland, OH: N.p., 1905.

Brown, William Adams. *Christian Theology in Outline*. New York: Charles Scribner's Sons, 1906.

Brush, John Woolman. *Heritage of Faith and Freedom: A Short History of the First Baptist Church, Haverhill, Massachusetts*. Groveland, MA: Boyd-James Press, 1964.

Bunnin, Nicholas, and Jiyuan Yu, *The Blackwell Dictionary of Western Philosophy*. Malden, MA: Blackwell, 2004.

Buranelli, Vincent. *Josiah Royce*. New York: Twayne, 1964.

Burrow, Rufus, Jr. *Personalism: A Critical Introduction*. St. Louis: Chalice Press, 1999.

Burtchaell, James Tunstead. *The Dying of the Light: The Disengagement of Colleges and Universities from Their Christian Churches*. Grand Rapids, MI: Eerdmans, 1998.

Bush, L. Russ, and Tom J. Nettles. *Baptists and the Bible*. Rev. ed. Nashville, TN: Broadman, 1999.

Buswell, James Oliver. *A Systematic Theology of the Christian Religion.* 2 vols. in 1. Grand Rapids, MI: Zondervan, 1962.

Butler, Jon, Grant Wacker, and Randall Balmer. *Religion in American Life: A Short History.* New York: Oxford University Press, 2003.

Calkins, Mary Whiton. *The Persistent Problems of Philosophy: An Introduction to Metaphysics through the Study of Modern Systems.* 2nd ed. New York: Macmillan, 1910.

Campbell, R. J. *The New Theology.* New York: Macmillan, 1907.

Carter, Paul A. *The Spiritual Crisis of the Gilded Age.* DeKalb: Northern Illinois University Press, 1971.

Case, Jay Riley. *An Unpredictable Gospel: American Evangelicals and World Christianity, 1812–1920.* New York: Oxford University Press, 2012.

Cashman, Sean Dennis. *America in the Gilded Age: From the Death of Lincoln to the Rise of Theodore Roosevelt.* 3rd ed. New York: New York University Press, 1993.

Catalogue of the Officers and Graduates of Yale University in New Haven, Connecticut, 1701–1915. New Haven, CT: Published by the University, 1916.

Cathcart, William, ed. *The Baptist Encyclopedia.* Philadelphia: Louis H. Everts, 1881.

Cauthen, Kenneth. *The Impact of American Religious Liberalism.* New York: Harper & Row, 1962.

Chase, George Wingate. *The History of Haverhill, Massachusetts, from Its First Settlement in 1640, to the Year 1860.* Haverhill, MA: George Wingate Chase, 1861.

Chernow, Ron. *Titan: The Life of John D. Rockefeller, Sr.* New York: Random House, 1998.

Chesebrough, David B. *Charles G. Finney: Revivalistic Rhetoric.* Westport, CT: Greenwood Press, 2002.

Christiano, Kevin J. *Religious Diversity and Social Change: American Cities, 1890–1906.* Cambridge: Cambridge University Press, 1987.

Church, Pharcellus. *The Philosophy of Benevolence.* New York: Leavitt, Lord & Co., 1836.

———. *Religious Dissentions: Their Cause and Cure.* New York: Gould & Newman, 1838.

Cigliano, Jan. *Showplace of America: Cleveland's Euclid Avenue, 1850–1910.* Kent, OH: Kent State University Press, 1991.

Clarke, William N. *The Circle of Theology: An Introduction to Theological Study.* Cambridge: University Press, 1897.

———. *Outline of Christian Theology.* Edinburgh: T. & T. Clark, 1909.

Clayton, Philip, and Arthur Peacocke, eds. *In Whom We Move and Live and Have Our Being: Panentheistic Reflections on God's Presence in a Scientific World.* Grand Rapids, MI: Eerdmans, 2004.

Clendenning, John, ed. *The Letters of Josiah Royce.* Chicago: University of Chicago Press, 1970.

———. *The Life and Thought of Josiah Royce.* Rev. and exp. ed. Nashville, TN: Vanderbilt University Press, 1999.

Cole, Stewart G. *The History of Fundamentalism*. New York: Richard R. Smith, Inc., 1931.

Colgate Rochester Crozer Course Catalogue, 2020–21. Rochester, NY: Colgate Rochester Crozer Divinity School.

The Congregational Year-Book, 1901. Portland, OR: National Council of the Congregational Churches of the United States, [1901].

Cooper, John W. *Panentheism: The Other God of the Philosophers: From Plato to the Present*. Grand Rapids, MI: Baker, 2006.

Copleston, Frederick. *A History of Philosophy*. 9 vols. Mahwah, NJ: Paulist Press, 1946–74.

Craig, Edward, ed. *The Shorter Routledge Encyclopedia of Philosophy*. London: Routledge, 2005.

Cory, Daniel. *Santayana: The Later Years: A Portrait with Letters*. New York: George Braziller, 1963.

Couper, Greta Elena. *An American Sculptor on the Grand Tour: The Life and Works of William Couper (1853–1942)*. Los Angeles, CA: TreCavalli Press, 1988.

Crawford, Thomas J. *The Doctrine of Holy Scripture Respecting the Atonement*. 4th ed. Grand Rapids, MI: Baker, 1954.

Croce, Paul Jerome. *Science and Religion in the Era of William James*. Vol. 1, *Eclipse of Certainty, 1820–1880*. Chapel Hill: University of North Carolina Press, 1995.

Cross, George. *Christian Salvation: A Modern Interpretation*. Chicago: University of Chicago Press, 1925.

———. *What Is Christianity? A Study of Rival Interpretations*. Chicago: University of Chicago, 1918.

Cross, Whitney R. *The Burned-Over District: The Social and Intellectual History of Enthusiastic Religion in Western New York, 1800–1850*. Ithaca, NY: Cornell University Press, 1950.

Cutter, William Richard, ed. *Genealogical and Personal Memoirs Relating to the Families of the State of Massachusetts*. Vol. 2. New York: Lewis Historical Publishing, 1910.

Davis, Lawrence B. *Immigrants, Baptists, and the Protestant Mind in America*. Urbana: University of Illinois Press, 1973.

Denney, James. *Studies in Theology: Lectures Delivered in Chicago Theological Seminary*. 2nd ed. London: Hodder and Stoughton, 1895.

Derby, George H. *Rochester Knockings! Discovery and Explanation of the Source of the Phenomena Generally Known as the Rochester Knockings*. Buffalo, NY: George H. Derby & Co., 1851.

Dewey, D. M. *History of the Strange Sounds or Rappings, Heard in Rochester and Western New-York*. Rochester, NY: D. M. Dewey, 1850.

Dollar, George W. *A History of Fundamentalism in America*. Greenville, SC: Bob Jones University Press, 1973.

Dorner, Isaak August. *Geschichte der protestantischen Theologie besonders in Deutschland*. Munich: J. G. Cotta, 1867.

———. *History of Protestant Theology Particularly in Germany*. Translated by George Robson and Sophia Taylor. 2 vols. Edinburgh: T. & T. Clark, 1871.

———. *History of the Development of the Doctrine of the Person of Christ*. 2nd div., vol. 3. Edinburgh: T. & T. Clark, 1863.

Dorrien, Gary. *The Making of American Liberal Theology: Idealism, Realism, and Modernity, 1900–1950*. Louisville, KY: Westminster John Knox, 2003.

———. *The Making of American Liberal Theology: Imagining Progressive Religion, 1805–1900*. Louisville, KY: Westminster John Knox, 2001.

Drummond, Henry. *The Lowell Lectures on the Ascent of Man*. 10th ed. New York: James Pott & Co., 1900.

Dudley, Will. *Understanding German Idealism*. Stocksfield, UK: Acumen, 2007.

Dunham, Jeremy, Iain Hamilton Grant, and Sean Watson. *Idealism: The History of a Philosophy*. Montreal: McGill-Queen's University Press, 2011.

Dwight, Benjamin W. *The History of the Descendants of Elder John Strong, of Northampton, Mass*. 2 vols. Albany, NY: Joel Munsell, 1871.

Edwards, Rebecca. *New Spirits: Americans in the Gilded Age, 1865–1905*. New York: Oxford University Press, 2006.

Elwell, Walter A., ed. *Evangelical Dictionary of Theology*. Grand Rapids, MI: Baker, 2001.

Emerson, R. W. *The Conduct of Life*. Boston: Ticknor & Fields, 1860.

Encyclopedia of Southern Baptists. 2 vols. Nashville, TN: Broadman, 1958.

Estes, Yolanda, and Curtis Bowman, eds. *J. G. Fichte and the Atheism Dispute (1798–1800)*. Farnham, UK: Ashgate, 2010.

Eucken, Rudolph. *The Fundamental Concepts of Modern Philosophic Thought, Critically and Historically Considered*. Translated by M. Stewart Phelps. New York: D. Appleton & Co., 1880.

Evans, Christopher Hodge. *The Kingdom Is Always but Coming: A Life of Walter Rauschenbusch*. Grand Rapids, MI: Eerdmans, 2004.

———. *Liberalism without Illusions: Renewing an American Christian Tradition*. Waco, TX: Baylor University Press, 2010.

Fichte, Johann Gottlieb. *Attempt at a Critique of All Revelation*. Edited by Allen Wood. Translated by Garrett Green. Cambridge: Cambridge University Press, 2010.

———. *A Comparison between Prof. Schid's System and the* Wissenschaftslehre. In *Fichte: Early Philosophical Writings*. Translated and edited by Daniel Breazeale, 316–35. Ithaca, NY: Cornell University Press, 1988.

———. *The Science of Knowledge*. Edited and translated by Peter Heath and John Lochs. Cambridge: Cambridge University Press, 1982.

———. *The Vocation of Man*. 2nd ed. Translated by William Smith. Chicago: Open Court Publishing, 1910.

Fifty-First Annual Catalogue of the Officers and Students of the Rochester Theological Seminary, 1900–1901. Rochester, NY: E. R. Andrews, 1901.

Finney, Charles G. *Charles G. Finney: An Autobiography*. Old Tappan, NJ: Revell, 1908.
———. *The Original Memoirs of Charles G. Finney*. Edited by Garth M. Rosell and Richard A. G. Dupuis. Grand Rapids, MI: Zondervan, 2002.
Fisher, George W. *Early History of Rochester, 1810 to 1827, with Comparisons of Its Growth and Progress to 1860*. Rochester, NY: George W. Fisher, 1860.
Flanagan, Maureen. *America Reformed: Progressives and Progressivisms, 1890s–1920s*. New York: Oxford University Press, 2006.
Follett, Frederick. *History of the Press of Western New-York*. Rochester, NY: Jerome & Brother, 1847.
Foster, Robert Verrell. *Systematic Theology*. Nashville, TN: Cumberland Presbyterian Publishing House, 1898.
French, J. H., ed. *The Gazetteer of the State of New York*. Syracuse, NY: R. Pearsall Smith, 1860.
Gamble, Richard M. *The War for Righteousness: Progressive Christianity, the Great War, and the Rise of the Messianic Nation*. Wilmington, DE: ISI Books, 2003.
Garraty, John A. *The New Commonwealth, 1877–1890*. New York: Harper & Row, 1968.
Garrett, James Leo. *Baptist Theology: A Four-Century Study*. Macon, GA: Mercer University Press, 2009.
General Catalogue of Princeton University, 1746–1906. Princeton, NJ: Published by the university, 1908.
General Catalogue of the Rochester Theological Seminary, Rochester, N. Y., Embracing the First Twenty-Six Years of Its History. 1876. Rochester, NY: E. R. Andrews, 1876.
General Catalogue of the Rochester Theological Seminary, Rochester, N. Y., Embracing the First Thirty-Eight Years of Its History. 1889. Rochester, NY: E. R. Andrews, 1889.
General Catalogue of the University of Rochester, 1850–1911. Rochester, NY: University of Rochester, 1911.
General Catalogue of the University of Rochester, 1850–1928. Rochester, NY: University of Rochester, 1928.
Gerrish, B. A. *Thinking with the Church: Essays in Historical Theology*. Grand Rapids, MI: Eerdmans, 2010.
Ginger, Ray. *The Age of Excess: The United States from 1877 to 1914*. 2nd ed. New York: Macmillan, 1975.
Gladden, Washington. *Social Salvation*. 1902. Repr., Eugene, OR: Wipf & Stock, 2004.
Goodspeed, Thomas Wakefield. *A History of the University of Chicago*. Chicago: University of Chicago Press, 1972.
Gore, Charles. *The New Theology and the Old Religion*. London: John Murray, 1908.
Gould, Lewis L. *America in the Progressive Era, 1890–1914*. London: Longman, 2001.
Goulder, Grace. *John D. Rockefeller: The Cleveland Years*. Cleveland, OH: Western Reserve Historical Society, 1972.
Gragg, Alan. *George Burman Foster: Religious Humanist*. Danville, VA: Association of Baptist Professors of Religion, 1978.

Graves, Henry C. *Historical Sketch of the Baptist Religious Society of Haverhill, Massa-chusetts, and of the Church Edifices Built under Its Direction, with an Account of the Dedication Services, November 22d, 1883.* Haverhill, MA: James A. Hale, 1886.

Grenz, Stanley J., and Roger E. Olson. *Twentieth-Century Theology: God and the World in a Transitional Age.* Downers Grove, IL: InterVarsity Press, 1992.

Gupta, Arti. *Robert Browning: A Reassessment in the Light of Hindu Vision.* New Delhi, India: Sarup & Sons, 2002.

Hambrick-Stowe, Charles E. *Charles G. Finney and the Spirit of American Evangelical-ism.* Grand Rapids, MI: Eerdmans, 1996.

Handy, Robert T., ed. *The Social Gospel in America, 1870–1920.* New York: Oxford University Press, 1966.

Hardiman, Keith J. *Charles Grandison Finney, 1792–1875: Revivalist and Reformer.* Grand Rapids, MI: Baker, 1990.

Harnack, Adolf, and Wilhelm Herrmann. *Essays on the Social Gospel.* Translated by G. M. Craik. Edited by Maurice A. Canney. London: Williams & Norgate, 1907.

Hart, D. G. *The University Gets Religion: Religious Studies in American Higher Education.* Baltimore: Johns Hopkins University Press, 1999.

Haverhill: Foundation Facts concerning Its Settlement, Growth, Industries, and Societies. Haverhill, MA: Bridgeman & Gay, 1879.

Hays, Samuel P. *American Political History as Social Analysis: Essays by Samuel P. Hays.* Knoxville: University of Tennessee Press, 1980.

Hegel, G. W. F. *The Difference between Fichte's and Schelling's System of Philosophy.* Translated by H. S. Harris and Walter Cref. Albany: State University of New York Press, 1977.

———. *Lectures on the Philosophy of Religion: One-Volume Edition: The Lectures of 1827.* Edited by Peter C. Hodgson. Translated by R. F. Brown, P. C. Hodgson, and J. M. Stewart. Oxford: Clarendon Press, 2006.

———. *The Phenomenology of Spirit.* Translated by A. V. Miller. Delhi: Shri Jainendra Press, 1998.

Heim, Karl. *God Transcendent: Foundation for a Christian Metaphysic.* Translated by Edgar Primrose Dickie. New York: Charles Scribner's Sons, 1936.

Henrich, Dieter. *Between Kant and Hegel: Lectures on German Idealism.* Edited by David S. Pacini. Cambridge, MA: Harvard University Press, 2003.

Henry, Carl F. H. *Personal Idealism and Strong's Theology.* Wheaton, IL: Van Kampen Press, 1951.

Hewitt, Nancy A. *Women's Activism and Social Change: Rochester, New York, 1822–1872.* Lanham, MD: Lexington Books, 2001.

Historical Catalogue of Brown University, Providence, Rhode Island, 1764–1894. Providence, RI: P. S. Remington & Co., 1895.

Historical Catalogue of Brown University, 1764–1914. Providence, RI: Published by the university, 1914.

Historical Sketches: Seventy-Five Years of the Euclid Avenue Baptist Church, Cleveland, Ohio, 1851–1926. N.p.: Historical Committee, 1927.

A History of Cleveland and Its Environs: The Heart of New Connecticut. Vol. 2. Chicago: Lewis Publishing Co., 1918.

Holifield, E. Brooks. *Theology in America: Christian Thought from the Age of the Puritans to the Civil War.* New Haven, CT: Yale University Press, 2003.

Hopkins, Charles Howard. *The Rise of the Social Gospel in American Protestantism, 1865–1915.* New Haven, CT: Yale University Press, 1940.

Hovey, Alvah. *Studies in Ethics and Religion.* Boston: Silver, Burdett, & Co., 1892.

Hovey, George R. *Alvah Hovey: His Life and Letters.* Philadelphia: Judson Press, 1928.

Howe, Daniel Walker. *What Hath God Wrought: The Transformation of America, 1815–1848.* New York: Oxford University Press, 2007.

Hudson, Winthrop S. *Baptists in Transition: Individualism and Christian Responsibility.* Valley Forge, PA: Judson Press, 1979.

Hutchison, William R., ed. *American Protestant Thought: The Liberal Era.* New York: Harper & Row, 1968.

———. *Errand to the World: American Protestant Thought and Foreign Missions.* Chicago: Chicago University Press, 1987.

———. *The Modernist Impulse in American Protestantism.* New York: Oxford University Press, 1976.

Illingworth, J. R. *Divine Immanence: An Essay on the Spiritual Significance of Matter.* New York: Macmillan, 1898.

Ironside, H. A. *The Teaching of the So-Called Plymouth Brethren: Is It Scriptural? Reply to an Attack in Dr. Strong's "Systematic Theology."* New York: Loizeaux Brothers, n.d.

James, William. *The Letters of William James.* Edited by Henry James. 2 vols. Boston: Atlantic Monthly Press, 1920.

Johns Hopkins University Celebration of the Twenty-Fifth Anniversary of the Founding of the University. Baltimore: Johns Hopkins Press, 1902.

Kelley, Brooks Mather. *Yale: A History.* New Haven, CT: Yale University Press, 1974.

Kelly, Robert L. *Theological Education in America: A Study of One Hundred Sixty-One Theological Schools in the United States and Canada.* New York: George H. Doran Co., 1924.

Knudson, Albert Cornelius. *The Philosophy of Personalism.* Boston: Boston University Press, 1949.

Krapohl, Robert H., and Charles H. Lippy. *The Evangelicals: A Historical, Thematic, and Biographical Guide.* Westport, CT: Greenwood Press, 1999.

Kuklick, Bruce. *A History of Philosophy in America, 1720–2000.* Oxford: Oxford University Press, 2001.

———. *Josiah Royce: An Intellectual Biography.* Indianapolis: Bobbs-Merrill, 1972.

Ladd, George Trumbull. *Introduction to Philosophy: An Inquiry after a Rational System of Scientific Principles in Their Relation to Ultimate Reality.* New York: Charles Scribner's Sons, 1903.

Laing, B. M. *A Study in Moral Problems*. London: George Allen & Unwin, 1922.

Larsen, Timothy, ed. *Biographical Dictionary of Evangelicals*. Downers Grove, IL: InterVarsity Press, 2003.

Latourette, Kenneth Scott. *A History of the Expansion of Christianity*. Vol. 4, *The Great Century in Europe and the United States of America, a.d. 1800–a.d. 1914*. New York: Harper & Brothers, 1941.

Lears, T. J. Jackson. *No Place of Grace: Antimodernism and the Transformation of American Culture, 1880–1920*. Chicago: University of Chicago Press, 1994.

Leonard, Bill J. *Baptists in America*. New York: Columbia University Press, 2005.

Livingston, James C. *Modern Christian Thought*. Vol. 1, *The Enlightenment and the Nineteenth Century*. 2nd ed. Minneapolis: Fortress, 2006.

Livingston, James C., and Francis Schüssler Fiorenza. *Modern Christian Thought*. Vol. 2, *The Twentieth Century*. 2nd ed. With Sarah Coakley and James H. Evans Jr. Minneapolis: Fortress, 2006.

Long, Clarence D. *Wages and Earnings in the United States, 1860–1890*. New York: Arno Press, 1975.

Lotze, Hermann. *Metaphysic in Three Books Ontology, Cosmology, and Psychology*. 2nd ed. Edited by Bernard Bosanquet. 2 vols. Oxford: Clarendon Press, 1887.

———. *Microcosmus: An Essay Concerning Man and His Relation to the World*. 3rd ed. Translated by Elizabeth Hamilton and E. E. Constance Jones. 2 vols. Edinburgh: T. & T. Clark, 1888.

———. *Outlines of Metaphysic: Dictated Portions of the Lectures of Hermann Lotze*. Translated and edited by George T. Ladd. Boston: Ginn, Heath, & Co., 1884.

———. *Outlines of the Philosophy of Religion: Dictated Portions of the Lectures of Hermann Lotze*. Edited by George T. Ladd. Boston: Ginn & Co., 1886.

Lucas, Christopher J. *American Higher Education: A History*. New York: St. Martin's Griffin, 1994.

Machen, J. Gresham. *Christianity and Liberalism*. 1923. Repr., Grand Rapids, MI: Eerdmans, 2001.

Macintosh, Douglas Clyde. *The Problem of Knowledge*. New York: Macmillan, 1915.

———. *Theology as an Empirical Science*. 1919. Repr., New York: Arno Press, 1980.

Mackintosh, Hugh Ross. *The Christian Apprehension of God*. London: Student Christian Movement, 1929.

———. *The Doctrine of the Person of Jesus Christ*. New York: Charles Scribner's Sons, 1914.

Malone, Dumas, ed. *Dictionary of American Biography*. Vol. 5. New York: Charles Scribner's Sons, 1961.

Marsden, George M. *The Evangelical Mind and the New School Presbyterian Experience: A Case Study of Thought and Theology in Nineteenth-Century America*. New Haven, CT: Yale University Press, 1970.

———. *Fundamentalism and American Culture*. 2nd ed. New York: Oxford University Press, 2006.

———. *The Soul of the American University: From Protestant Establishment to Established Nonbelief.* New York: Oxford University Press, 1994.

The Materials of Religious Education Being the Principal Papers Presented at, and the Proceedings of the Fourth General Convention of the Religious Education Association, Rochester, New York, February 5–7, 1907. Chicago: Executive Office of the Association, 1907.

May, Arthur J. *A History of the University of Rochester, 1850–1962.* Edited and abridged by Lawrence Eliot Klein. Rochester, NY: University of Rochester Press, 1977.

McBeth, H. Leon. *The Baptist Heritage.* Nashville, TN: Broadman, 1987.

McConnell, Francis J. *Borden Parker Bowne: His Life and His Philosophy.* New York: Abingdon, 1929.

———. *The Diviner Immanence.* New York: Methodist Book Concern, 1906.

McCune, Rolland. *A Systematic Theology of Biblical Christianity.* 3 vols. Allen Park, MI; Detroit Baptist Theological Seminary, 2008–10.

McDannell, Colleen. *The Christian Home in Victorian America, 1840–1900.* Bloomington: Indiana University Press, 1986.

McGerr, Michael. *A Fierce Discontent: The Rise and Fall of the Progressive Movement in America, 1870–1920.* New York: Oxford University Press, 2003.

McGiffert, Arthur Cushman. *The Rise of Modern Religious Ideas.* New York: Macmillan, 1922.

McIntosh, W. H. *History of Monroe County, New York: With Illustrations Descriptive of Its Scenery, Palatial Residences, Public Buildings, Fine Blocks, and Important Manufactories.* Philadelphia: Everts, Ensign & Everts, 1877.

McKelvey, Blake. *Rochester on the Genesee: The Growth of a City.* 2nd ed. Syracuse, NY: Syracuse University Press, 1993.

———. *Rochester: The Flower City, 1855–1890.* Cambridge, MA: Harvard University Press, 1949.

———. *Rochester: The Quest for Quality, 1890–1925.* Cambridge, MA: Harvard University Press, 1956.

———. *Rochester: The Water-Power City, 1812–1854.* Cambridge, MA: Harvard University Press, 1945.

McKelvey, Blake, and Ruth Rosenberg-Naparsteck. *Rochester: A Panoramic History.* Sun Valley, CA: American Historical Press, 2001.

Memorial Volume of Denison University, 1831–1906. Granville, OH: Published by the university, 1907.

Merrill, William Pierson. *Liberal Christianity.* New York: Macmillan, 1925.

Miller, Carol Poh, and Robert A. Wheeler. *Cleveland: A Concise History, 1796–1996.* 2nd ed. Bloomington: Indiana University Press, 1997.

Miller, Glenn T. *Piety and Profession: American Protestant Theological Education, 1870–1970.* Grand Rapids, MI: Eerdmans, 2007.

Miller, Perry. *The Life of the Mind in America from the Revolution to the Civil War.* New York: Harcourt, Brace & World, 1965.

Minus, Paul M. *Walter Rauschenbusch: American Reformer.* New York: Macmillan, 1988.

Mulford, Elisha. *The Nation: The Foundations of Civil Order and Political Life in the United States.* Boston: Houghton, Mifflin, & Co., 1887.

———. *The Republic of God: An Institute of Theology.* Boston: Houghton, Mifflin, & Co., 1881.

Muller, Richard A. *Post-Reformation Reformed Dogmatics.* 2nd ed. 4 vols. Grand Rapids, MI: Baker, 2003.

Mullins, Edgar Young. *The Christian Religion in Its Doctrinal Expression.* Philadelphia: Roger Williams Press, 1917.

———. *Why Is Christianity True? Christian Evidences.* Philadelphia: Judson Press, 1905.

Murphy, Nancey. *Beyond Liberalism and Fundamentalism: How Modern and Postmodern Philosophy Set the Theological Agenda.* Harrisburg, PA: Trinity Press International, 2007.

Nettles, Tom. *The Baptists: Key People Involved in Forming a Baptist Identity.* Vol. 3, *The Modern Era.* Geanies House, UK: Christian Focus, 2007.

———. *By His Grace and for His Glory: A Historical, Theological and Practical Study of the Doctrines of Grace in Baptist Life.* Rev. and exp. ed. Cape Coral, FL: Founders Press, 2006.

Newman, Albert Henry, ed. *A Century of Baptist Achievement.* Philadelphia: American Baptist Publication Society, 1901.

Nixon, Justin Wroe, and Winthrop Still Hudson, eds. *Christian Leadership in a World Society: Essays in Honor of Conrad Henry Moehlman.* Rochester, NY: Colgate-Rochester Divinity School, 1945.

Olson, Roger E. *The Westminster Handbook to Evangelical Theology.* Louisville, KY: Westminster John Knox, 2004.

O'Reilly, Henry. *Settlement in the West: Sketches of Rochester with Incidental Notices of Western New-York.* Rochester, NY: W. Alling, 1838.

Ostrander, Rick. *The Life of Prayer in a World of Science: Protestants, Prayer, and American Culture, 1870–1930.* New York: Oxford University Press, 2000.

Owen, H. P. *Concepts of Deity.* New York: Herder and Herder, 1971.

Parker, Jenny Marsh. *Rochester: A Story Historical.* Rochester, NY: Scrantom, Wetmore & Co., 1884.

Peck, William F. *History of Rochester and Monroe County, New York, From the Earliest of Historic Times to the Beginning of 1907.* 2 vols. New York: Pioneer Publishing, 1908.

———. *Semi-centennial History of the City of Rochester with Illustrations and Biographical Sketches of Some of Its Prominent Men and Pioneers.* Syracuse, NY: D. Mason & Co., 1884.

Perciaccante, Marianne. *Calling Down Fire: Charles Grandison Finney and Revivalism in Jefferson County, New York, 1800–1840.* Albany, NY: State University of New York Press, 2003.

Pfaefflin, Hermann. *A One-Hundred-Year History of the German Community in Rochester, New York (1815–1915)*. Exp. ed. Translated by Rudolf Wallenburg and H. J. Swinney. Rochester, NY: Federation of German-American Societies, 2007.

Philippi, Friedrich Adolf. *Kirchliche Glaubenslehre*. 7 vols. in 10. Stuttgart: S. G. Liesching, 1864–82.

Pierce, Bessie Louise. *A History of Chicago*. Vol. 3, *The Rise of a Modern City, 1871–1893*. Chicago: University of Chicago Press, 1957.

Pinkard, Terry. *German Philosophy 1760–1860: The Legacy of Idealism*. Cambridge: Cambridge University Press, 2002.

———. *Hegel: A Biography*. Cambridge: Cambridge University Press, 2000.

Porter, Noah. *The American Colleges and the American Public*. New Haven, CT: Charles C. Chatfield & Co., 1870.

———. *The Human Intellect with an Introduction upon Psychology and the Soul*. 4th ed. New York: Charles Scribner & Co., 1872.

Rauschenbusch, Walter. *Christianity and the Social Crisis*. New York: Hodder & Stoughton, 1907.

———. *Christianizing the Social Order*. New York: Macmillan, 1914.

———. *A Theology for the Social Gospel*. New York: Macmillan, 1917.

Reeves, Thomas C. *The Empty Church: The Suicide of Liberal Christianity*. New York: Free Press, 1996.

Reynolds, Cuyler, comp. *Genealogical and Family History of Southern New York and the Hudson River Valley*. Vol. 3. New York: Lewis Historical Publishing, 1914.

Roberts, Richard. *That One Face: Studies of the Place of Jesus in the Minds of Poets and Prophets*. New York: Association Press, 1919.

Robinson, Ezekiel Gilman. *Christian Theology*. Rochester, NY: E. R. Andrews, 1894.

———. *Ezekiel Gilman Robinson: An Autobiography with a Supplement by H. L. Wayland and Critical Estimates*. Edited by E. H. Johnson. Boston: Silver, Burdett & Co., 1896.

Robison, W. Scott., ed. *The History of Cleveland: Its Settlement, Rise and Progress*. Cleveland, OH: Robison & Cockett, 1887.

Rochester Theological Seminary General Catalogue, 1850 to 1900, Together with the Historical Discourse Delivered as a Part of the Semi-Centennial Exercises May the Ninth 1900, by President Augustus H. Strong. Rochester, NY: E. R. Andrews, 1900.

Rochester Theological Seminary General Catalogue, 1850 to 1910. Rochester, NY: E. R. Andrews, 1910.

Rochester Theological Seminary General Catalogue, 1850 to 1920. Rochester, NY: E. R. Andrews, 1920.

Rose, William Ganson. *Cleveland: The Making of a City*. 1950. Repr., Kent, OH: Kent State University Press, 1990.

Rosenberger, Jesse Leonard. *Rochester and Colgate: Historical Backgrounds of the Two Universities*. Chicago: University of Chicago Press, 1925.

———. *Rochester: The Making of a University*. Rochester, NY: University of Rochester Press, 1927.

Royce, Josiah. *California from the Conquest in 1846 to the Second Vigilance Committee in San Francisco*. Boston: Houghton, Mifflin, & Co., 1886.

———. *The Feud of Oakfield Creek: A Novel of California Life*. Boston: Houghton, Mifflin, & Co., 1887.

———. *The Hope of the Great Community*. New York: Macmillan, 1916.

———. *Lectures on Modern Idealism*. New Haven, CT: Yale University Press, 1919.

———. *The Religious Aspect of Philosophy*. Boston: Houghton, Mifflin, & Co., 1885.

Royce, Josiah, Joseph Le Conte, G. H. Howison, and Sidney Edward Mezes. *The Conception of God*. New York: Macmillan, 1897.

Rudolph, Frederick. *The American College and University: A History*. New York: Vintage Books, 1962.

Russell, Bertrand. *The History of Western Philosophy*. New York: Simon & Schuster, 1972.

Ryan, W. Carson. *Studies in Early Graduate Education: The Johns Hopkins, Clark University, the University of Chicago*. New York: Carnegie Foundation, 1939.

Santayana, George. *Lotze's System of Philosophy*. Edited by Paul Grimley Kuntz. Bloomington: Indiana University Press, 1971.

———. *Persons and Places: The Background of My Life*. New York: Scribner's Sons, 1944.

Sarrels, R. V. *Systematic Theology*. Azle, TX: Harmony Hill, 1978.

Schelling, F. W. J. *The Philosophy of Art*. Edited and translated by Douglas W. Stott. Minneapolis: University of Minnesota Press, 1989.

Schlereth, Thomas J. *Victorian America: Transformations in Everyday Life, 1876–1915*. New York: HarperCollins, 1991.

Schmid, Rudolf. *The Theories of Darwin and Their Relation to Philosophy, Religion, and Morality*. Translated by G. A. Zimmermann. Chicago: Jansen, McClurg, & Co., 1883.

Schweitzer, Albert. *Civilization and Ethics*. 3rd ed. London: Adam & Charles Black, 1946.

Seth, James. *A Study of Ethical Principles*. Edinburgh: William Blackwood & Sons, 1894.

Sharpe, Dores Robinson. *Walter Rauschenbusch*. New York: Macmillan, 1942.

Shedd, William G. T. *Dogmatic Theology*. 2nd ed. 3 vols. Nashville, TN: Thomas Nelson, 1980.

Singer, Peter. *Hegel: A Very Short Introduction*. Oxford: Oxford University Press, 2001.

Smith, Justin A. *A History of the Baptists in the Western States East of the Mississippi*. Philadelphia: American Baptist Publication Society, 1896.

Smith, Ted A. *The New Measures: A Theological History of Democratic Practice*. Cambridge: Cambridge University Press, 2007.

Smucker, Donovan E. *The Origins of Walter Rauschenbusch's Social Ethics*. Montreal: McGill-Queen's University Press, 1994.

Snow, Dale E. *Schelling and the End of Idealism*. Albany, NY: State University of New York Press, 1996.

Spencer, Herbert. *The Factors of Organic Evolution*. New York: D. Appleton and Co., 1887.

———. *First Principles*. New York: D. Appleton and Co., 1909.

Steeples, Douglas, and David O. Whitten. *Democracy in Desperation: The Depression of 1893*. Westport, CT: Greenwood Press, 1998.

Storr, Richard J. *Harper's University: The Beginnings*. Chicago: University of Chicago Press, 1966.

Straub, Jeffrey Paul. *The Making of a Battle Royal: The Rise of Liberalism in the Northern Baptist Convention, 1870–1920*. Eugene, OR: Pickwick, 2018.

Strong, Alvah. *Autobiography of Alvah Strong*. N.p.: privately printed, n.d.

Strong, Augustus Hopkins. *American Poets and Their Theology*. Philadelphia: Griffith & Rowland, 1916.

———. *Autobiography of Augustus Hopkins Strong*. Edited by Crerar Douglas. Valley Forge, PA: Judson Press, 1981.

———. *Christ in Creation and Ethical Monism*. Philadelphia: Roger Williams Press, 1899.

———. *The Church and the University: A Sermon Preached before the Ohio Baptist Education Society at Its Annual Meeting in Cleveland, Ohio, October 23, 1888,—to Which Is Appended a Detailed Argument and Plan for the Establishment of a University in the City of New York, under the Control of Baptists*. Rochester, NY: E. R. Andrews, 1889.

———. *Ethical Monism in Two Series of Three Articles Each and Christ in Creation with a Review by Elias H. Johnson*. New York: Examiner, 1896.

———. *The Great Poets and Their Theology*. Philadelphia: American Baptist Publication Society, 1897.

———. *Henry A. Ward: Reminiscence and Appreciation, with an Appreciation of Doctor Strong*. Rochester, NY: Rochester Historical Society, 1922.

———. *Lectures on Theology*. Rochester, NY: E. R. Andrews, 1876.

———. *Miscellanies*. 2 vols. Philadelphia: Griffith & Rowland, 1912.

———. *One Hundred Chapel-Talks to Theological Students together with Two Autobiographical Addresses*. Philadelphia: Griffith & Rowland, 1913.

———. *Our Denominational Outlook*. N.p., 1904.

———. *Outlines of Systematic Theology Designed for the Use of Theological Students*. Philadelphia: American Baptist Publication Society, 1908.

———. *Philosophy and Religion: A Series of Addresses, Essays and Sermons Designed to Set Forth Great Truths in Popular Form*. New York: A. C. Armstrong & Son, 1888.

———. *Popular Lectures on the Books of the New Testament*. Philadelphia: Griffith & Rowland, 1914.

———. *Reminiscences of Early Rochester: A Paper Read before the Rochester Historical Society, December 27, 1915*. Rochester, NY: Rochester Historical Society, 1916.

———. *Systematic Theology: A Compendium and Commonplace-Book Designed for the Use of Theological Students*. Rochester, NY: Press of E. R. Andrews, 1886.

————. *Systematic Theology: A Compendium and Commonplace-Book Designed for the Use of Theological Students.* 2nd ed. rev. and enl. New York: A. C. Armstrong and Son, 1889.

————. *Systematic Theology: A Compendium and Commonplace-Book Designed for the Use of Theological Students.* 4th ed. rev. and enl. New York: A. C. Armstrong and Son, 1893.

————. *Systematic Theology: A Compendium and Commonplace-Book Designed for the Use of Theological Students.* 5th ed. rev. and enl. New York: A. C. Armstrong and Son, 1896.

————. *Systematic Theology: A Compendium and Commonplace-Book Designed for the Use of Theological Students.* 6th ed. rev. and enl. New York: A. C. Armstrong and Son, 1899.

————. *Systematic Theology: A Compendium and Commonplace-Book Designed for the Use of Theological Students.* 7th ed. rev. and enl. New York: A. C. Armstrong and Son, 1902.

————. *Systematic Theology: A Compendium Designed for the Use of Theological Students.* 3 vols. in 1. Valley Forge, PA: Judson Press, 1907.

————. *A Tour of the Missions: Observations and Conclusions.* Philadelphia: Griffith & Rowland, 1918.

————. *Union with Christ: A Chapter of Systematic Theology.* Philadelphia: American Baptist Publication Society, 1913.

————. *What Shall I Believe? A Primer of Christian Theology.* New York: Revell, 1922.

Strong, Charles Augustus. *A Creed for Sceptics.* London: Macmillan, 1936.

————. *The Origin of Consciousness: An Attempt to Conceive the Mind as a Product of Evolution.* London: Macmillan, 1918.

————. *A Theory of Knowledge.* London: Constable and Co., 1923.

————. *Why the Mind Has a Body.* New York: Macmillan, 1903.

————. *The Wisdom of the Beasts.* Boston: Houghton Mifflin Co., 1922.

Strong, Jeanne Waters. *Strong Men and Strong Women: Some Ancestors and Descendants of John Strong of Chard, England.* Los Altos Hills, CA: Jeanne Waters Strong, 1988.

Stuart, Nancy Rubin. *The Reluctant Spiritualist: The Life of Maggie Fox.* Orlando, FL: Harcourt, 2005.

Sturt, Henry, ed. *Personal Idealism: Philosophical Essays by Eight Members of the University of Oxford.* London: Macmillan, 1902.

Temple, William. *Nature, Man and God, Being the Gifford Lectures Delivered in the University of Glasgow in the Academical Years 1932–1933 and 1933–1934.* London: Macmillan, 1934.

Thelin, John R. *A History of American Higher Education.* Baltimore: Johns Hopkins University Press, 2004.

Thiessen, Henry Clarence. *Introductory Lectures in Systematic Theology.* Grand Rapids, MI: Eerdmans, 1949.

Thomas, Geoffrey. *An Introduction to Ethics: Five Central Problems of Moral Judgement.* Indianapolis, IN: Hackett Publishing, 1993.

Thomasius, Gottfried. *Christi Person und Werk*. 4 vols. Erlangen: Theodor Bläsing, 1853–61.

Todd, Thomas Olman. *Hydesville: The Story of the Rochester Knockings Which Proclaimed the Advent of Modern Spiritualism*. Sunderland, UK: Keystone Press, 1905.

Torbet, Robert G. *A History of the Baptists*. Rev. ed. Valley Forge, PA: Judson Press, 1963.

Tyson, John R. *School of Prophets: A Bicentennial History of Colgate Rochester Crozer Divinity School*. Valley Forge, PA: Judson Press, 2019.

Urann, C. A. *Centennial History of Cleveland*. Cleveland, OH: n.p., 1896.

Vanderhoof, E. W. *Historical Sketches of Western New York*. Buffalo, NY: Matthews-Northrup Works, 1907.

Van Til, Cornelius. *Christianity and Barthianism*. Phillipsburg, NJ: Presbyterian & Reformed, 1962.

———, *Christianity and Idealism*. Philadelphia: Presbyterian & Reformed, 1955.

Vedder, Henry C. *A History of the Baptists in the Middle States*. Philadelphia: American Baptist Publication Society, 1898.

———. *A Short History of Baptist Missions*. Philadelphia: Judson Press, 1927.

———. *A Short History of the Baptists*. New and illus. ed. Philadelphia: American Baptist Publication Society, 1907.

Wacker, Grant. *Augustus H. Strong and the Dilemma of Historical Consciousness*. Waco, TX: Baylor University Press, 2018.

Walker, W. L. *Christian Theism and a Spiritual Monism: God, Freedom, and Immortality in View of Monistic Evolution*. Edinburgh: T. & T. Clark, 1906.

Ward, F. DeW. *Churches of Rochester: Ecclesiastical History of Rochester, N.Y.* Rochester, NY: Erastus Darrow, 1871.

Warfield, Benjamin Breckinridge. *The Inspiration and Authority of the Bible*. Edited by Samuel G. Craig. Phillipsburg, NJ: Presbyterian & Reformed, 1948.

———. *The Works of Benjamin B. Warfield*. Vol. 6, *The Westminster Assembly and Its Work*. New York: Oxford University Press, 1932.

Weisberg, Barbara. *Talking to the Dead: Kate and Maggie Fox and the Rise of Spiritualism*. New York: HarperCollins, 2004.

Welch, Claude. *Protestant Thought in the Nineteenth Century*. Vol. 1, *1799–1870*. New Haven, CT: Yale University Press, 1972.

———. *Protestant Thought in the Nineteenth Century*. Vol. 2, *1870–1914*. New Haven, CT: Yale University Press, 1985.

———, ed. and trans. *God and Incarnation in Mid-Nineteenth Century German Theology*. New York: Oxford University Press, 1965.

Welch, Lewis Sheldon, and Walter Camp. *Yale: Her Campus, Class-Rooms, and Athletics*. 2nd ed. Boston: L. C. Page & Co., 1900.

Wertheimer, Leo Weldon, ed. *Twelfth General Catalogue of the Psi Upsilon Fraternity*. N.p.: Executive Council of the Psi Upsilon Fraternity, 1917.

Wiley, H. Orton, and Paul T. Culbertson. *Introduction to Christian Theology*. Kansas City, MO: Beacon Hill, 1969.

Wilson, John E. *Introduction to Modern Theology: Trajectories in German Tradition.* Louisville, KY: Westminster John Knox, 2007.

Wind, James P. *The Bible and the University: The Messianic Vision of William Rainey Harper.* Atlanta: Scholars Press, 1987.

Woelfkin, Cornelius. *Chambers of the Soul.* Boston: United Society of Christian Endeavor, 1901.

———. *Religion: Thirteen Sermons.* Edited by Robert A. Ashworth. Garden City, NY: Doubleday, Doran & Co., 1928.

Young, Warren Cameron. *Commit What You Have Heard: A History of Northern Baptist Theological Seminary, 1913–1988.* Wheaton, IL: Harold Shaw, 1988.

Articles

Abbott, Lyman. Review of *Christ in Creation and Ethical Monism*, by Augustus Hopkins Strong. *Outlook* 64 (13 January 1900): 129–30.

Anderson, Willis A. Review of *Systematic Theology* (1886 ed.), by Augustus Hopkins Strong. *Andover Review* 8 (July–December 1887): 96–99.

Ash, Martha Montague. "The Social and Domestic Scene in Rochester, 1840–1860." *Rochester History* 18 (April 1956): 1–20.

Barbour, Clarence A. "President-Emeritus Augustus Hopkins Strong." *Watchman-Examiner*, 29 December 1921, 1649–50.

Bass, Dorothy C. "Ministry on the Margin: Protestants and Education." In *Between the Times: The Travail of the Protestant Establishment in America, 1900–1960*, ed. William R. Hutchison, 48–71. New York: Cambridge University Press, 1989.

Beckwith, Clarence Augustine. Review of *Systematic Theology* (vol. 2, 1907 ed.), by Augustus Hopkins Strong. *American Journal of Theology* 12 (July 1908): 502–5.

Behrends, A. J. F. "Ethical Monism." *Methodist Review* 77 (May–June 1895): 357–70.

Berg, Joseph F. "Spirit Rappings a Fraud." *Protestant Quarterly Review* 10 (January 1853): 39–68.

"Big Institutional Church: Rockefeller's Pastor Will Build Greatest in World in Cleveland." *New York Times*, 5 September 1907, 6.

Brown, William Adams. Review of *Systematic Theology* (vol. 1, 1907 ed.), by Augustus Hopkins Strong. *American Journal of Theology* 12 (January 1908): 150–55.

Buckham, John Wright. "Monism, Pluralism, and Personalism." *Harvard Theological Review* 1 (October 1908): 477–91.

Burton, Ernest D. "Recent Tendencies in the Northern Baptist Churches." *American Journal of Theology* 24 (July 1920): 321–38.

Chapin, David. "The Fox Sisters and the Performance of Mystery." *New York History* (April 2000): 157–88.

Christian, Timothy K. "The Experimental Theology of Augustus Hopkins Strong after a Century." *Southwestern Journal of Theology* 50 (Spring 2008): 183–206.

Crisp, Oliver D. "Federalism vs Realism: Charles Hodge, Augustus Strong and William Shedd on the Imputation of Sin." *International Journal of Systematic Theology* 8 (January 2006): 55–71.

Cross, George. "Christianity and Christology." *Journal of Religion* 4 (November 1924): 600–610.

"Death of the Rev. E. G. Robinson." *New York Times*, 14 June 1894, 1.

Douglas, Crerar. "The Cost of Mediation: Augustus Hopkins [Strong] and P. T. Forsyth." *Congregational Journal* 3 (January 1978): 28–35.

———. "The Hermeneutics of Augustus Hopkins Strong: God and Shakespeare in Rochester." *Foundations* 21 (January–March 1978): 71–76.

"Dr. Augustus Strong on Authority in Religion." *The Outlook*, May 25, 1901.

Eckler, A. Ross. "A Measure of the Severity of Depressions, 1873–1932." *Review of Economic Statistics* 15 (May 1933): 75–81.

"Editorial Notes," *McMaster University Monthly* 4 (December 1894): 129–31.

Ellis, Walter E. Review of *Autobiography of Augustus Hopkins Strong*, ed. Crerar Douglas. *Theodolite* 7 (1986): 51–52.

Feinberg, Paul D. "The Meaning of Inerrancy." In *Inerrancy*, ed. Norman L. Geisler, 267–304. Grand Rapids, MI: Zondervan, 1980.

Fichte, Johann Gottlieb. "On the Foundation of Our Belief in a Divine Government of the Universe." 1798. Repr. in *Nineteenth-Century Philosophy*, ed. Patrick Gardiner, 19–26. New York: Free Press, 1969.

Fisk, Daniel T. "The Necessity of the Atonement." *Bibliotheca Sacra and Biblical Repository* 18 (April 1861): 284–324.

Fuller, B. A. G. "Ethical Monism and the Problem of Evil." *Harvard Theological Review* 1 (April 1908): 207–22.

Garrett, James Leo. "Representative Modern Baptist Understandings of Biblical Inspiration." *Review and Expositor* 71 (Spring 1974): 179–95.

Gay, Robert. "Ethical Pluralism: A Reply to Dancy." *Mind* 94 (1985): 250–62.

Girardeau, J. L. Review of *Systematic Theology* (1889 ed.), by Augustus Hopkins Strong. *The Presbyterian Quarterly* 4 (January 1890): 122–24.

Hannah, John D. "The History of *Bibliotheca Sacra*." *Bibliotheca Sacra* 531 (July–September 1976): 229–42.

Hastings, James. Review of *Christ in Creation and Ethical Monism*, by Augustus Hopkins Strong. *Expository Times* 11 (April 1900): 315–16.

———. Review of *Outlines of Systematic Theology*, by Augustus Hopkins Strong. *Expository Times* 20 (November 1908): 84.

———. Review of *Systematic Theology* (vol. 1, 1907 ed.), by Augustus Hopkins Strong. *Expository Times* 19 (October 1907): 29–30.

———. Review of *Systematic Theology* (vol. 2, 1907 ed.), by Augustus Hopkins Strong. *Expository Times* 19 (April 1908): 317–18.

———. Review of *Systematic Theology* (vol. 3, 1909 ed.), by Augustus Hopkins Strong. *Expository Times* 20 (July 1909): 466.

Hinson, E. Glenn. "Baptists and the Social Gospel and the Turn toward Social Justice: 1898–1917." In *Turning Points in Baptist History: A Festschrift in Honor of Harry Leon McBeth*, ed. Michael E. Williams Sr. and Walter B. Shurden, 235–48. Macon, GA: Mercer University Press, 2008.

Hodge, Caspar Wistar, Jr. Review of *Systematic Theology* (vols. 1 and 2, 1907 ed.), by Augustus Hopkins Strong. *Princeton Theological Review* 6 (April 1908): 335–41.

———. Review of *Systematic Theology* (vol. 3, 1909 ed.), by Augustus Hopkins Strong. *Princeton Theological Review* 8 (April 1910): 333–35.

———. Review of *What Shall I Believe? A Primer of Christian Theology*, by Augustus Hopkins Strong. *Princeton Theological Review* 20 (October 1922): 681–82.

Holmes, Stephen R. "'Something Much Too Plain to Say' Towards a Defence of the Doctrine of Divine Simplicity." *Neue Zeitschrift für systematische Theologie und Religionsphilosophie* 43 (2001): 137–54.

Horosz, William. "The Liberal Commitment to Divine Immanence." In *Religion and Human Purpose: A Cross Disciplinary Approach*, ed. William Horosz and Tad Clements, 197–231. Dordrecht: Martinus Nijhoff, 1987.

Horstmann, Rolf-Peter. "The Early Philosophy of Fichte and Schelling." In *The Cambridge Companion to German Idealism*, ed. Karl Ameriks, 117–40. Cambridge: Cambridge University Press, 2000.

Hovey, Alvah. "Dr. Strong's Ethical Monism [First Article]." *Watchman*, 13 December 1894, 10–11.

———. "Dr. Strong's Ethical Monism: Second Article." *Watchman*, 20 December 1894, 10–11.

———. "Dr. Strong's Ethical Monism: Third Article." *Watchman*, 27 December 1894, 11–12.

Hovey, Alvah, Augustus H. Strong, William N. Clarke, and John A. Broadus. "Reforms in Theological Education." *Baptist Quarterly Review* 7 (1885): 407–42.

Iverach, James. Review of *Christ in Creation and Ethical Monism*, by Augustus Hopkins Strong. *The Critical Review of Theological and Philosophical Literature* 10 (1900): 387–90.

Jeffries, Elizabeth. "The Strong Family of Rochester, New York." *Epitaph* 27 (Summer 2007): 1–3.

Johnson, John W. "Prerequisites to an Understanding of the System of Theology of Augustus Hopkins Strong." *Review and Expositor* 19 (1922): 333–41.

King, James. "Hume and Ethical Monism." *History of Philosophy Quarterly* 5 (April 1988): 157–71.

Langford, S. Fraser. "The Gospel of Augustus H. Strong and Walter Rauschenbusch." *The Chronicle* 14 (January 1951): 3–18.

Loewen, Howard J. "Augustus H. Strong: Baptist Theologian for the Mennonite Brethren." In *Mennonites and Baptists: A Continuing Conversation*, ed. Paul Toews, 193–210. Winnipeg, MB: Kindred Press, 1993.

162 Bibliography

Mackenzie, W. Douglas. Review of *Christ in Creation and Ethical Monism*, by Augustus Hopkins Strong. *American Journal of Theology* 4 (July 1900): 648–50.

McGiffert, Arthur Cushman. "Immanence." In *Encyclopedia of Religion and Ethics*. Edited by James Hastings. Vol. 7. New York: Charles Scribner's Sons, 1915.

———. "The Progress of Theological Thought During the Past Fifty Years." *American Journal of Theology* 20 (July 1916): 321–32.

McKelvey, Blake. "Rochester and the Erie Canal." *Rochester History* 11 (July 1949): 1–24.

———. "The Population of Rochester." *Rochester History* 12 (October 1950): 1–24.

———. "Touring Backwards: A Visit to Rochester in 1818, and Again in 1838." *Rochester History* 2 (January 1940): 1–24.

———. "Walter Rauschenbusch's Rochester." *Rochester History* 14 (October 1952): 1–27.

"Memorial Number, Dr. Cornelius Woelfkin." *Rochester Theological Seminary Bulletin* (May 1928): 221–304.

Mitchell, E. T. "Kantian Relativity." *The Monist* 37 (April 1927): 207–25.

Moehlman, Conrad Henry. "The Story of the Curriculum of the Rochester Theological Seminary." *Rochester Theological Seminary Bulletin* (November 1926): 265–84.

Moore, LeRoy, Jr. "Academic Freedom: A Chapter in the History of the Colgate Rochester Divinity School." *Foundations* 10 (January–March 1967): 64–79.

Moxom, Philip S. Response to Augustus Hopkins Strong's "Divine Immanence in Recent Theology." In *Ninth Annual Session of the Ninth Baptist Congress for the Discussion of Current Questions, Held in the Calvary Baptist Church, New Haven, Conn., November 11th, 12th, and 13th, 1890*, 181–87. New York: Baptist Congress Publishing, 1890.

Newman, Albert Henry. "Strong's Systematic Theology." *Baptist Review and Expositor* 2 (January 1905): 41–66.

Patton, F. L. Review of *Systematic Theology* (1886 ed.), by Augustus Hopkins Strong. *Presbyterian Review* 8 (April 1887): 365–67.

Perkins, Dexter. "Rochester One Hundred Years Ago." *Rochester History* 1 (July 1939): 1–24.

Pugh, Willard J. "A 'Curious Working of Cross Purposes' in the Founding of the University of Chicago." In *The American College in the Nineteenth Century*, ed. Roger Geiger, 242–63. Nashville, TN: Vanderbilt University Press, 2000.

Raymond, William O. "'The Jeweled Bow': A Study in Browning's Imagery and Humanism." In *Robert Browning: A Collection of Critical Essays*, ed. Philip Drew, 110–30. London: Methuen & Co., 1966.

Reist, Irwin. "Augustus Hopkins Strong and William Newton Clarke." *Foundations* 13 (January–March 1970): 26–39.

Review of *Systematic Theology* (1886 ed.), by Augustus Hopkins Strong. *Methodist Review* 68 (November 1886): 939–41.

Review of *Systematic Theology* (1889 ed.), by Augustus Hopkins Strong. *Methodist Review* 72 (January 1890): 146–47.

Richardson, Kurt A. "Augustus Hopkins Strong." In *Baptist Theologians*, ed. Timothy
     George and David S. Dockery, 289–306. Nashville, TN: Broadman, 1990.
Riley, W. B. "Modernism in Baptist Schools." In *Baptist Fundamentals Being Addresses
     Delivered at the Pre-Convention Conference at Buffalo, June 21 and 22, 1920*, 167–87.
     Philadelphia: Judson Press, 1920.
Rockmore, Tom. "Fichte, German Idealism, and the Thing in Itself." In *Fichte,
     German Idealism, and Early Romanticism*, ed. Daniel Breazeale and Tom
     Rockmore, 9–20. Amsterdam: Rodopi, 2010.
Savage, Doris M. "The Rochester Theological Seminary in the Old United States
     Hotel." *Rochester History* 31 (July 1969): 1–23.
Skillen, James W. "Pluralism as a Matter of Principle." In *The Many and the One:
     Religious and Secular Perspectives on Ethical Pluralism in the Modern World*, ed.
     Richard Madsen and Tracy B. Strong, 257–68. Princeton, NJ: Princeton University
     Press, 2003.
Smith, Gary S. "Calvinists and Evolution, 1870–1920." *Journal of Presbyterian History*
     61 (Fall 1983): 335–52.
Smith, Gerald Birney. "The Field of Systematic Theology Today." *Biblical World* 32
     (August 1908): 113–23.
———. "A Quarter-Century of Theological Thinking in America." *Journal of Religion*
     5 (November 1925): 576–94.
Stewart, J. W. A. "Notes and Impressions." In *Centennial Celebration, First Baptist
     Church, 1818–1918, Rochester, N.Y.*, 35–37. Rochester, NY: First Baptist Church, 1918.
Straub, Jeff. "'Letters to a Skeptic': The Final Correspondence of Augustus Hopkins
     Strong to His Son Charles Augustus Strong." Paper presented at the annual meeting
     of the Evangelical Theological Society, Atlanta, GA, 18 November 2010.
Strong, Augustus Hopkins. "Address at the Dedication of Rockefeller Hall." Delivered
     May, 19, 1880. Rochester, NY: Press of E. R. Andrews, 1880.
———. "Christ in Creation." *The Examiner* (6 October 1892): front page.
———. "Christ in Creation." *Magazine of Christian Literature* 7 (November 1892):
     166–71.
———. "Divine Immanence in Recent Theology." In *Ninth Annual Session of the
     Ninth Baptist Congress for the Discussion of Current Questions, Held in the Calvary
     Baptist Church, New Haven, Conn., November 11th, 12th, and 13th, 1890*, 167–81.
     New York: Baptist Congress Publishing, 1890.
———. "Dr. Robinson as a Theologian." In *Ezekiel Gilman Robinson: An Autobiography with a Supplement by H. L. Wayland and Critical Estimates*, ed. E. H. Johnson,
     163–208. Boston: Silver, Burdett & Co., 1896.
———. "Ethical Monism [Part 1]." *The Examiner*, 1 November 1894.
———. "Ethical Monism [Part 2]." *The Examiner*, 8 November 1894.
———. "Ethical Monism [Part 3]." *The Examiner*, 15 November 1894.
———. "Ethical Monism Once More [Part 1]." *The Examiner*, 17 October 1895.
———. "Ethical Monism Once More [Part 2]." *The Examiner*, 24 October 1895.

———. "Ethical Monism Once More [Part 3]." *The Examiner*, 31 October 1895.

———. "The Fall and the Redemption of Man in the Light of Evolution." In *Christ in Creation and Ethical Monism*, 163–80. Philadelphia: Roger Williams Press, 1899.

———. "Historical Sketch." In *Centennial Celebration, First Baptist Church, 1818–1918, Rochester, N.Y.*, 3–30. Rochester, NY: First Baptist Church, 1918.

———. "Introductory Note." In *Control in Evolution*, by George F. Wilkin, xi–xiii. New York: A. C. Armstrong and Son, 1903.

———. "The Miracle at Cana: With an Attempt at a Philosophy of Miracles." In *Addresses on the Gospel of St. John*, 63–70. Providence, RI: St. John Conference Committee, 1906.

———. "Miracles as Attesting Divine Revelation." *Baptist Review* 1 (1879): 274–304.

———. "Modern Exaggerations of Divine Immanence." *Magazine of Christian Literature* 3 (January 1891): 276–83.

———. "Modern Idealism." *Bibliotheca Sacra* 45 (January 1888): 84–109.

———. "Modified Calvinism: Or, Remainders of Freedom in Man." *Baptist Quarterly Review* 5 (1883): 219–43.

———. "My Views of the Universe in General." *The Baptist*, 29 May 1920, 625–26.

———. "The New Theology." *Baptist Quarterly Review* 10 (January 1888): 1–29.

———. Response to Papers and Addresses on "The Relative Authority of Scripture and Reason." In *Tenth Annual Session of the Baptist Congress for the Discussion of Current Questions Held in the First Baptist Church, Philadelphia, PA, May 19th, 20th, and 21st, 1892*, 200–202. New York: Baptist Congress Publishing, 1892.

———. "The Will in Theology, Number Two." *Baptist Review* 3 (1881): 30–47.

Strong, John H. "Augustus Hopkins Strong." In *Publications of the Rochester Historical Society*, vol. 1, 235–41. Rochester, NY: Rochester Historical Society, 1922.

Talbot, Ellen Bliss. "Fichte's Conception of God." *The Monist* 23 (1913): 42–58.

Thilly, Frank. "Can Christianity Ally Itself with Monistic Ethics?" *American Journal of Theology* 12 (1908): 547–64.

Thomas, Jesse B. "Dr. Strong's Last Work." *The Watchman* 81 (1900): 11.

Thornbury, Gregory Alan. "Augustus Hopkins Strong." In *Theologians of the Baptist Tradition*, ed. Timothy George and David S. Dockery, 139–62. Nashville, TN: Broadman, 2001.

Trimble, Henry Burton. "Christ in the Light of the Divine Immanence." *Methodist Quarterly Review* 75 (July 1926): 404–11.

Truesdale, Dorothy S. "The Younger Generation: Their Opinions, Pastimes and Enterprises, 1830–1850." *Rochester History* 1 (April 1939): 1–24.

Tunis, John. "The Doctrine of the Divine Immanence." *Andover Review* 14 (October 1890): 389–404.

Valentine, Milton. Review of *Christ in Creation and Ethical Monism*, by Augustus Hopkins Strong. *Lutheran Quarterly* 30 (April 1900): 279–84.

Vedder, Henry C. "Fifty Years of Baptist History." *Bibliotheca Sacra* 57 (October 1900): 660–79.

Wacker, Grant. "The Dilemmas of Historical Consciousness: The Case of Augustus H. Strong." In *In the Great Tradition: In Honor of Winthrop S. Hudson: Essays on Pluralism, Voluntarism, and Revivalism,* ed. Joseph D. Ban and Paul R. Dekar, 223–36. Valley Forge, PA: Judson Press, 1982.

———. "A Plural World: The Protestant Awakening to World Religions." In *Between the Times: The Travail of the Protestant Establishment in America, 1900–1960,* ed. William R. Hutchison, 253–77. Cambridge: Cambridge University Press, 1989.

———. Review of *Autobiography of Augustus Hopkins Strong,* ed. Crerar Douglas. *Christian Century* 18 May 1983, 502–3.

Warfield, Benjamin Breckinridge. Review of *Christ in Creation and Ethical Monism,* by Augustus Hopkins Strong. *Presbyterian and Reformed Review* 12 (April 1901): 325–26.

———. Review of *Systematic Theology* (5th ed., 1896), by Augustus Hopkins Strong. *Presbyterian and Reformed Review* 8 (April 1897): 356–58.

Wilkins, Brandon. "Augustus Hopkins Strong and His Journey toward Ethical Monism." *Reformed Baptist Theological Review* 4 (July 2007): 127–42.

Williams, Edwin. "Sketch of Rochester, Monroe County, New York." *Fisher's National Magazine* 3 (November 1846): 568–79.

Wood, Nathan. "Movements of Baptist Theological Thought during the Nineteenth Century." In *A Century of Baptist Achievement,* ed. A. H. Newman, 428–38. Philadelphia: American Baptist Publication Society, 1901.

Wright, George Frederick. Review of *Systematic Theology* (vol. 1, 1907 ed.), by Augustus Hopkins Strong. *Bibliotheca Sacra* 64 (October 1907): 773–76.

———. Review of *Systematic Theology* (vol. 2, 1907 ed.), by Augustus Hopkins Strong. *Bibliotheca Sacra* 65 (1908): 591.

———. "Strong's Systematic Theology." *Bibliotheca Sacra* 44 (April 1887): 306–34.

Youtz, Herbert Alden. Review of *Systematic Theology* (vol. 3, 1909 ed.), by Augustus Hopkins Strong. *American Journal of Theology* 13 (1909): 468–70.

Dissertations and Theses

Bonotti, Matteo. "Pluralism and Moderation in an Inclusive Political Realm: A Normative Defense of Religious Political Parties." Ph.D. diss., University of Edinburgh, 2009.

Christian, Timothy Keith. "The Theology of Augustus Hopkins Strong: The Role of His Key Concepts and the Influence of Modernism as Reflected in the Eighth Edition of His Systematic Theology." D.Th. diss., University of South Africa, 2007.

Hartog, John, III. "Ethical Monism in the Writings of A. H. Strong." Th.M. thesis, Grace Theological Seminary, 1990.

Hesselgrave, D. Dennis. "The Relationship between A. H. Strong and Walter Rauschenbusch at Colgate Rochester Divinity School." M.A. thesis, Trinity Evangelical Divinity School, 1970.

Houghton, Myron James. "An Examination and Evaluation of A. H. Strong's Doctrine of Holy Scripture." Th.D. diss., Concordia Seminary, 1986.

Massey, John David. "Solidarity in Sin: An Analysis of the Corporate Conceptions of Sin in the Theologies of Augustus Hopkins Strong and Walter Rauschenbusch." Ph.D. diss., Southwestern Baptist Theological Seminary, 2000.

Moore, James Herbert. "A Critique of the Position of Ethical Monism on the Atonement as Set Forth by Augustus Hopkins Strong." B.D. thesis, Gordon Divinity School, 1951.

Moore, LeRoy, Jr. "The Rise of Religious Liberalism at the Rochester Theological Seminary, 1872–1928." Ph.D. diss., Claremont Graduate School, 1966.

Nelson, Roland Tenus. "Fundamentalism and the Northern Baptist Convention." Ph.D. diss., University of Chicago, 1964.

Shrader, Matthew C. "Thoughtful Christianity: Alvah Hovey and the Problem of Authority within the Context of Nineteenth-Century Northern Baptists." Ph.D. diss., Trinity Evangelical Divinity School, 2019.

Straub, Jeffrey Paul. "The Making of a Battle Royal: The Rise of Religious Liberalism in Northern Baptist Life, 1870–1920." Ph.D. diss., Southern Baptist Theological Seminary, 2004.

Thornbury, Gregory Alan. "The Legacy of Natural Theology in the Northern Baptist Theological Tradition, 1827–1918." Ph.D. diss., Southern Baptist Theological Seminary, 2001.

Van Pelt, Peter S. "An Examination of the Concept of the Atonement in Selected Northern Baptist Theologians: William Newton Clarke, Augustus Hopkins Strong, and Shailer Mathews." Th.D. diss., Mid-America Baptist Theological Seminary, 1994.

West, William Beryl. "Theistic Evolution in the Writings of A. H. Strong and Bernard Ramm." Ph.D. diss., Southwestern Baptist Theological Seminary, 1962.

Archival Material

John Albert Broadus Papers, James Petigru Boyce Library, Southern Baptist Theological Seminary, Louisville, KY.

Edgar Young Mullins Papers, James Petigru Boyce Library, Southern Baptist Theological Seminary, Louisville, KY.

Archibald T. Robertson Papers, James Petigru Boyce Library, Southern Baptist Theological Seminary, Louisville, KY.

William H. Whitsitt Papers, James Petigru Boyce Library, Southern Baptist Theological Seminary, Louisville, KY.

Printed in the United States
by Baker & Taylor Publisher Services